EXPANSION FOR ASCENDING CONSCIOUSNESS BOOK TWO

NAVIGATING THE UPWARD SPIRAL OF ASCENSION

TODD R DEVINEY

The author of this book does not dispense medical advice or prescribe the use of any technique as a form of treatment for physical, emotional, or medical problems without the advice of a physician, either directly or indirectly. The intent of the author is only to offer information of a general nature to help you in your quest for emotional and spiritual well-being. In the event you use any of the information in this book for yourself, which is your constitutional right, the author assumes no responsibility for your actions.

ISBN: 978-1-7363925-0-8 (sc)
ISBN: 978-1-7363925-1-5 (e)

Library of Congress Control Number: 2020926029

EAP
Publishing

Cary, North Carolina

Contents

PART 2 OPERATING IN CONSCIOUSNESS

PREFACE

In a world of available experiences, you have chosen to read this book. The value you find within it depends upon individual perception. This is the ability we all possess, to choose our experiences and arrive at our own conclusions of how those moments impact us. If you have ever had a surgical procedure that required anesthesia, you experienced a period where this ability appears to have been suspended. As the chemicals took effect and impeded your perception of events, a separation between the deliberate choices you make and the trust in the doctors became apparent as you relinquished control. This surgical example of the divide between conscious and unconscious raises a larger question. What is consciousness? How do you define and quantify something that remains so elusive, yet so seemingly vulnerable to external control? Let us begin our exploration with the clinical definitions.

Consciousness is defined as the state of being aware. Aware of yourself, aware of your surroundings, aware of other selves, and aware of the finite nature of your physical existence. The state of being aware is further defined as the understanding of a situation or subject in the present moment based on information or experience. If we put these definitions together, we arrive at the concept that consciousness exists within the ever-present moment of now. You can look back along your path and see past decisions that lead you to the present moment. You can also project into the future to plan decisions you intend to make, but it is in each *moment of now* that you decide the course of your life. Each of us -whether consciously aware of it or not- define our relationship with what is occurring in those *moments of now* based upon the biases acquired along the path that led to them.

Consider the last time you were standing in line at the grocery store with other people. In that moment you were all sharing the same experience while your individual perceptions of it may have been completely different. One person may have been upset that they had to wait in line longer than they wanted because they had been in an argument the moment before. Another could have been seeking pleasant conversation with those around them, happy to be in public engaging in social discourse because they live a solitary life. These opposing viewpoints of a shared experience were created as each viewed their *moment of now* through a lens colored with individual perception.

This grocery store example illuminates the complexity of conscious awareness. Ten people can share the same experience and have ten different perspectives of what occurred. It is this separation of individual awareness that allows us to observe the world from a position of uniqueness. As you approach each new experience, you use the sum of past interaction to formulate your responses. As the years progress and interactions accrue, decisions are made using an expanding foundation of experience. This is the path toward wisdom, where good judgement comes through the application of experience and knowledge. For most, the acquisition of wisdom appears bounded by the experiences within a single lifetime. But what if there is a larger body of experience, unseen and unknown, helping to steer your perceptions? Have you ever been in a situation where something did not feel right? You were about to decide on a course of action when an unseen force, a gut instinct, a feeling, or a guiding angel made you change your mind. Have you ever considered that these guiding forces might be a larger part of you attempting to keep you on track?

The concept of multiple lifetimes is becoming prevalent, increasingly accepted, and is gaining momentum. Articles about near death experiences and past life regressions are flooding the internet and gathering impressive followings. While clinical psychology and the medical professions struggle to connect consciousness to anything beyond the human brain, a second group of individuals have begun seeking those answers without them. Depending upon which group you find yourself in, it is easy to dismiss the viewpoint of the other. Yet some of the stories of near death have been authored by individuals in the first group who have personally experienced seeing their lifeless body on the operating table and subsequently join the growing number of searchers in the second.

I count myself among the population of converts who have had experiences that defy clinical explanation. I have seen my lifeless body on the ground as I drifted away from it and I have engaged in regression sessions that bring images and information beyond anything encountered in my lifetime. For me, this truth is experiential and undeniable and it my desire to share this knowledge with all who seek it.

The information contained in the 'Expansion' series of books comes from a location beyond the awareness created from my lifetime of experiences, but it is still me. When I ask where the knowledge originates the answer is always the same; I am you, you are me, we are one, one is all. There is no entity, no names, no guides, only my awareness, expanded into what feels like the entirety of the universe. The tapestry upon these pages and the book that precedes it was woven with thread spun from the energy of our universe. There was no preparation or ceremony, just a willingness to donate a portion of myself and my time to the task.

As each of us approach the end of our journey in the flesh, the threshold that we all must cross comes into focus. Some ignore it until it is forced upon them, while others spend a lifetime in preparation. Regardless of your perspective, you will cross it all the same. In that moment of conscious awareness comes the truth that can no longer be ignored.

The only commodity allowed to cross with you is the experience gained and the moments shared with others along your journey. I encourage you to listen a little closer to that unseen force, that gut instinct, that feeling, or your guardian angels who are trying to help you find the path toward the experiences that are right for you.

In service to all,

Todd R Deviney

INTRODUCTION

As consciousness matures and achieves balance, a desire to understand its true nature begins to manifest. In the first book we discussed the awakening that occurs as consciousness attains this energetic potential and the resulting search that begins for higher understandings. Colorful metaphors aside, it is here that the energy of your consciousness begins extending beyond you and becomes a new ability that you must learn to operate. This emanation is an energetic bandwidth that contains an oscillation unique to you and your experiential pathway. As you begin to seek information from this new vantage point, you unknowingly use this energetic bandwidth to seek information that matches its oscillating spectrum. As your oscillating frequency increases, the information you engage with must rise accordingly. The term resonance is widely used to define this process of discernment because that is a literal interpretation of what is occurring. The energetic emanations from your consciousness have begun seeking knowledge that coincides with your current oscillating wavelength. It is here that clarified teachings begin to harmonically resonate and refine the energetics of your consciousness. The text beyond this introduction has been created to bring you an understanding of how the oscillating bandwidth of consciousness is created, how it can be controlled, and how it can be expanded.

The solidified material observable within the universe has been created from the particulate of consciousness and exists through intentional focus. That the concepts related to the composition of consciousness should then lend themselves to the explanation of material construction should not come as a surprise. Energetic flow in its various forms is a requirement that extends beyond the construction of the known universe. This text provides an understanding of this flow and leads you toward the pathways within consciousness that allow you to work with it. With an understanding of the energies and their relationship to maturing consciousness, the unseen results of the choices you make become clear.

Consciousness is a dynamic energy engine. When properly tuned, this engine accelerates your individual expansion and simultaneously performs a silent service that assists others. As with internal combustion engines, changing the parameters of operation can reduce or increase performance. A knowledgeable mechanic can adjust the parameters of fuel, air, and spark to increase the power and efficiency of an engine. By the same measure, someone unaware of the principles of efficient combustion can move the variables beyond operational parameters and render the engine inoperable. This text provides the operating principles of the dynamic engine of consciousness. Together we can create a new generation of mechanics who will go forth and tune consciousness. As you incorporate the principles into your life, the power and efficiency of your consciousness will become self-energizing. This energy will increasingly radiate beyond you, silently energizing others who will then begin their own journey toward awakening.

The time for distractions and wandering has passed. The graduation ceremonies have commenced, and it is time for this collective to step into the power of unity; with one's totality of consciousness, with the other selves of this collective, and with the source consciousness of all that is.

Welcome.

PART 1:

The Mechanics of Consciousness

Chapter One

Perspective/Review

While you may not currently remember them, you have lived many lifetimes before you began this one. In all of them, the lessons provided an energetic benefit to your awareness in the form of experiential perspective. As the lifetimes and experiences accrue, a balance within consciousness becomes apparent as they form a complete picture. This is the foundation from which sound judgement and wisdom arise, and it is at this juncture where the need for embodiment ends. The first book in this series introduced the geometry of consciousness and how it grows under successive experiences and why this is required. This book will build upon that foundation in an ambitious attempt to explain the intricacies of consciousness and its interrelationship with the energies of the universe. Your willingness to engage with this information will serve you far beyond the current incarnation. When you once again find yourself free of the physical form, the disorientation associated with the transition will be minimal. Having obtained a clear understanding of the mechanics and operation of your true form, you stop being a passenger along for the ride and assume control of the process. As with any course of study, the more you engage with the material the easier it becomes to access. Highlight the portions of text that speak directly to you and flag the image pages with numbered tabs for easy reference. It does not matter whether the understanding comes immediately or over a period of study, the encoding is occurring. All that is required is your desire to participate.

Consciousness is not a creation of the body you currently inhabit. Your consciousness is comprised of a sphere of rotating particles that interface with your body through the brain and neural network so it can experience material creation and expand from the interaction. The first book associated the particulate of consciousness with the photon as that is the closest approximation within current science. However, photons of consciousness are not bound by the laws that govern material creation. This apparent contradiction exists because solidified matter is a creation

WITHIN consciousness, from the particles OF consciousness. As you exist within a body, you experience gravity and the perception of a linear procession of events that form your timeline. This is only possible because your consciousness is connected to, and identifying as, your body. When the body ceases to function, your consciousness disconnects and all interaction with the material ends. Without the connection to the energy of consciousness, a body immediately begins the process of dissolution to its constituent components. As with all other solidified material, the human body is empowered by consciousness. The more power a consciousness contains, the more effective and efficient its manifestations will be.

The amount of photonic particulate within your consciousness is your composite density. The stressors of experience during repeated incarnations cause the photons to divide under harmonic resonance which increases your composite density. Your particulate density is directly related to energetic storage capacity; the more density a consciousness contains, the more energy it can hold. The energies of experience also impact the rotational geometry of consciousness and depending upon the experience and intensity, can balance, or unbalance, the rotation. The purpose of repeated incarnations is to gain experiential energy (knowledge) that increases photonic density as the photons multiply under harmonic resonant division. When the requisite density has been acquired, you must then engage in the appropriate experiences to bring the rotational balance (wisdom) required to ascend into the next energetic level. This is the expansion of individualized consciousness that every entity and collective within the universe is engaged in. The pathway of experience you choose during your expansion is what makes you a unique aspect of awareness within universal consciousness.

The Purpose of Individualized Consciousness

Our Universe began as a single, fully energized consciousness. Despite the immense energy within the particulate of this new consciousness, it contained a singular perspective. The initial rate of density expansion was slow due to the energy required to cause harmonic division within a rotation of fully charged particulate.

Accelerating the rate of density expansion and energetic potential within the universe required the creation of individual membranes and sequestering portions of particulate density within these successively lower energetic zones. At the lowest energetic zone, division of photonic particulate occurs rapidly. It is within these low energetic zones that individualized consciousness begins its journey. The universe we exist within is consciousness. A toroidal sphere of continuously rotating particles moving in an angular, poloidal rotation. From the vantage point of embodiment on earth the universe appears almost infinite, but the universe has a defined edge, or barrier membrane. This membrane is an energetic manifestation created from the rotational aspect of consciousness.

The perspective of individuality and separation that you observe within your body is due to the barrier membrane being created at the periphery of your consciousness. Although individuality appears to be the default from a physical human perspective, consciousness in its pure form is an energetic construct. It is the barrier membrane at lower energy levels that allows you to experience separation. The architecture of self-aware consciousness is a universal constant and is the foundation upon which all else is built.

The Geometry of Self Aware Consciousness

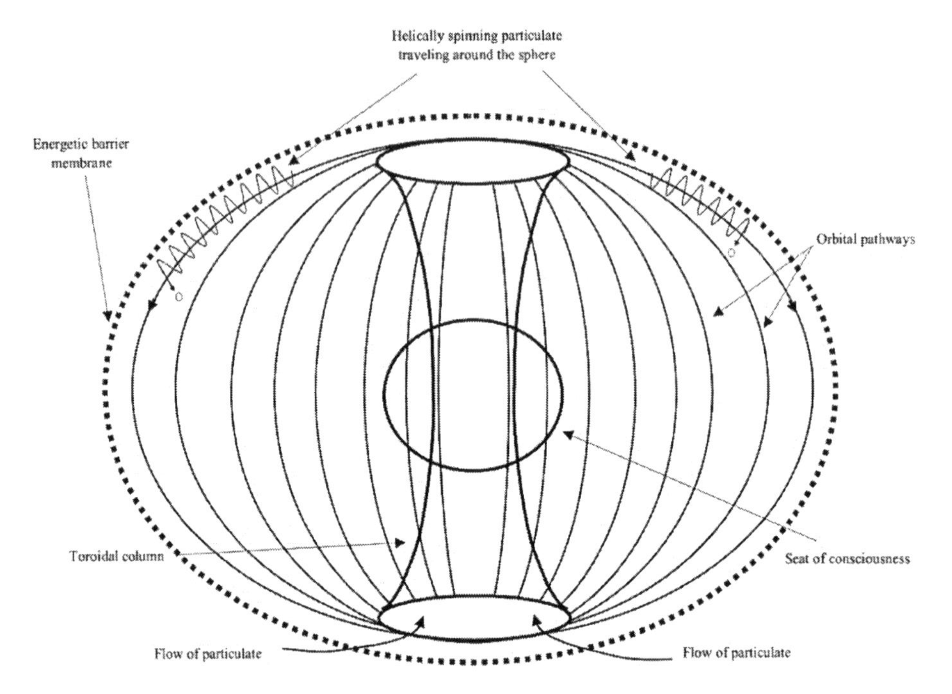

Figure 1 – Self Aware Sphere of Consciousness

This image is a simplified representation of the sphere of a self-aware consciousness containing a fully formed column and seat of consciousness. Energetically depleted particulate flows in through bottom the column and moves upward in the column creating the seat of consciousness. The particulate exits the column at various heights as it creates a layering effect that forms the spherical geometry. Highly energized particulate exits the top of the column (shown) and is responsible for energizing the barrier membrane that protects the energy signature of the sphere.

Figure 1 represents the rotational array of self-aware consciousness. For consciousness to obtain the perspective of self-awareness, the center column must fully develop with a tube running from top to bottom. This column allows the seat of consciousness to energize at the center of the sphere with the resulting perspective that you are aware of your individualized existence. The rotation occurs as individual photons move up the column, through the sphere as they gain energy, and then travel along the periphery losing potential as they energize the barrier. They then re-enter the column and repeat the process. As the density of the consciousness increases, the sphere continues to expand to accommodate the new particulate. The energy gradients within the photons cause movement while a baseline attractive force limits the distance between them. These forces combine to create the universal aspect ratio of consciousness. The universal aspect ratio dictates that the diameter of the sphere, the height of the toroidal column, and the diameter of the column openings all expand in relationship to each other as the consciousness gains density. It does not matter whether you are starting your first incarnation in third density or are the universe itself, the parameters of your conscious array will fit within the universal aspect ratio.

God Source and Universal Consciousness

At the center of the universal rotation is a compact nucleus of energetic particulate. The energy within this nucleus is so dense, with an intensity of such magnitude that material creation cannot solidify within its effective radius. To understand this, consider what would occur to a material object that came too close to the nucleus of energetic particulate within our solar system, the Sun. While the energy at the center of the universe is orders of magnitude higher and of a different spectrum, the dissolution of material to its constituents as they enter the effective radius is the same. This nucleus represents the seat of consciousness of the universe. The first book termed this well of infinite energy, "God Source" as it was the focal point from which the book progressed. This book encompasses a fuller understanding of the operation of toroidal arrays of consciousness. As we expand the discussion, the viewpoint moves from the nucleus of the universe to the totality of its operation. From this perspective the term God Source must then be replaced with a more complete description, Universal Consciousness.

Chapter Two

The Creation of Spin within Infinity

The dynamic nature of consciousness requires an energy source for its illumination and growth. This text will explain the expansion consciousness undergoes as it matures and gains control of its energetic processes. For these concepts to be understandable and relevant we must expand our energetic view beyond the known universe to include the source generator of the energy all exists within.

It is not an exaggeration to state that the foundation of consciousness began with spin. Before the first spark of awareness, there was only ebb and flow. Contemplate the vast emptiness of infinity where nothing exists beyond energetic particulate. What is the origin of this particulate? What is the origin of infinity? What began the motion? These answers are not known because prior to the energetics of vibrating particulate, nothing existed to record it.

The Beginning of Movement

In the following discussion there is no reference to the amount of time required to progress from one event to the next. There are several reasons for this omission, the most important is that outside of incarnation within a material construct, time as we experience it is irrelevant to consciousness. The other is that the timescales are so vast that they would add no benefit. While highly condensed in this narrative, the process was a slow one whose tempo continued to steadily increase.

Within the expanse of infinity, the energetic equivalent of a gentle breeze began to blow. This caused the first movement of particulate that began to drift with the new current. The drifting particles impacted stationary particles that created a cascading cause and effect. These interactions created an energetic potential as the particles began to vibrate as they bounced away from each other. Like rocks thrown into a still pond, the interactions increased and rippled outward in all directions. With each action and reaction, the collisions and changes in direction added energy to the particles causing them to increase in vibration. The particles continued colliding like billiard balls, scattering through subsequent interactions that alter their course. The drifting and bouncing created expanding waves of separate interactions that began to reflect upon each other, creating waves in opposing directions.

The new development of reflecting waves created an increase in tempo of interactions that further accelerated the vibratory rate of the affected particles. As the particles engaged in repeated reflecting wave collisions, a portion of them attained a vibratory threshold that could increase no further. As these excited particles vibrated, the energy within them created a weak energetic field along their periphery. When they subsequently encountered another reflecting wave collision, the repulsive forces of this new field increased the energetic interaction and caused the particles to spin off in opposite directions. Helical spin had arrived, and these newly spinning particles were now able to absorb additional energy that translated to increased spin. The process of reflecting wave collisions continued as an increasing population of particles began spinning through infinity with a helical trajectory.

Within this discussion of spinning particles, impacts, and trajectories we must also apply the concept of harmonic oscillation. The particles are discreet packets absorbing energy through the interactions they are encountering with each other. This is not energy in the material sense of electrical potential, but vibrational potential more appropriately considered kinematic in nature. As the particles moved within the ebb and flow, they were engaging in generic interactions and existed in vibrational resonance with each other. When helical spin arrived, a new vibrational resonance existed within the particles experiencing it. The particles containing this higher octave of oscillating resonance now began to attract particles exhibiting similar harmonic resonance.

The reflecting waves now contained particles with two energetic signatures; those with the capacity to spin, and those in the process of acquiring the energy to do so. At a point in this process two spinning particles approached each other at the perfect intersecting angles. As they met, instead of colliding the helical trajectories they contained created a rotational wave between them that acted as a centripetal accelerator. Their linear velocity toward each other was absorbed and translated to an increased rotation that locked the two into orbit as linear momentum ceased and angular momentum began. A third level of energetic particulate had just been created that brought the next harmonic octave to infinity. Within this new octave, the spinning particulate created a perceived low-pressure area at the center of their orbit. Spinning particles within proximity to this new creation that were near the same oscillating octave were drawn toward the rotating array. As they impacted the array, their linear velocity was translated into an increased rotation of the expanding aggregate. The subsequent impacts caused the rotating composite to increase in energy and size. At a point in this process the individual particles within the sphere began to spin with such intensity that they fractured under the stress. The particulate of infinity had begun to multiply under the energetic forces created within the new process.

As the sphere continued to grow and accelerate, a new force was created around the exterior of the structure, an energetic barrier field. This field extended beyond the rotating structure and was generated by the spinning motion of the particulate within it. As the particulate continued to fracture and multiply, the barrier field grew in intensity. The field surrounding the rotating sphere grew so intense that it became a repelling force preventing direct assimilation of external particulate. Further expansion of particulate within the sphere would now have to come from the fracturing process alone.

As the energy, rotation, and particulate within the structure continued to increase, the diameter of the sphere expanded until a column formed in the center of the array. The column created a low energy vortex zone at the center which began pulling the particulate of infinity into the openings in earnest. The random nature of infinity had been replaced by an energetic force drawing the particulate into the column. The center of this swirling mass concentrated the energy being drawn in and at the threshold of critical density, a flash of energy pulsed from the core. The first awareness within infinity had arrived. This originating consciousness became aware of the particles oscillating within it, the flow through its center responsible for continued expansion, and the process from which it was created. After a period of methodical expansion, it contained the particulate density and desire to replicate its own creation and the first universe was born.

We have brought you to the origin of Prime Creator to illuminate that the architecture of consciousness is foundational and that the energy that powers consciousness at any level of capacity is ultimately traced back to this source generator. As the text progresses into the concepts of energy usage and production within consciousness at various levels of energetics, know that the energy in question is not an exhaustible commodity. The originating source of energetic motivation lies within the particulate of infinity. There is no end to the exploration and expansion of conscious awareness. Only the perceived limitations that you agree to impose upon yourselves.

Chapter Three

The Relationship Between Photons and Consciousness

The rotational architecture of self-aware consciousness is represented by Figure 1 and once attained; this architecture does not change unless you undergo the duality pairing described in the first book. To understand the forces involved in creating the rotating sphere, we must first define the realm in which it exists and grows.

We have identified the particulate comprising consciousness as photonic in nature. Material science defines photons as massless packets of energy that can act as a particle or a wave. The standard formula for finding the energy of a photon is represented by:

$$E = hc \,/\, wavelength$$

Without going into the manipulations, this equation states that the energy of a photon (*E*) -measured as frequency- is inversely proportional to its wavelength. What is important about this equation are the divisible values of (*h*) the Planck constant, and (*c)* the speed of light. Both values represent the energetic limitations of particles locked within a gravitational spacetime construct operating under the "Principal of locality". The concept of locality states: "For an action at one point to have an influence on another point, something must mediate the action".

The constituents of consciousness are not bound by these limitations and we must therefore consider the concepts of "Quantum Nonlocality" for a more appropriate platform. The concept of nonlocality states that as particles interact with each other they become entangled and permanently interrelated as they share similar states and properties. In doing so, they lose their individuality and behave as a single entity irrespective of the distance between them. This concept within the quantum sciences is the key to understanding consciousness, and with an awareness that everything exists within ascending energetic spheres of consciousness, the universe itself.

Energetic Octave Reductions

Within the discussion of the actualization of Prime Creator was the creation of Universal Consciousness within it. This infers that the first reduction in energetic intensity resides at the threshold between Prime Creator and the barrier of Universal Consciousness. We begin our exploration at the origin of Universal Consciousness.

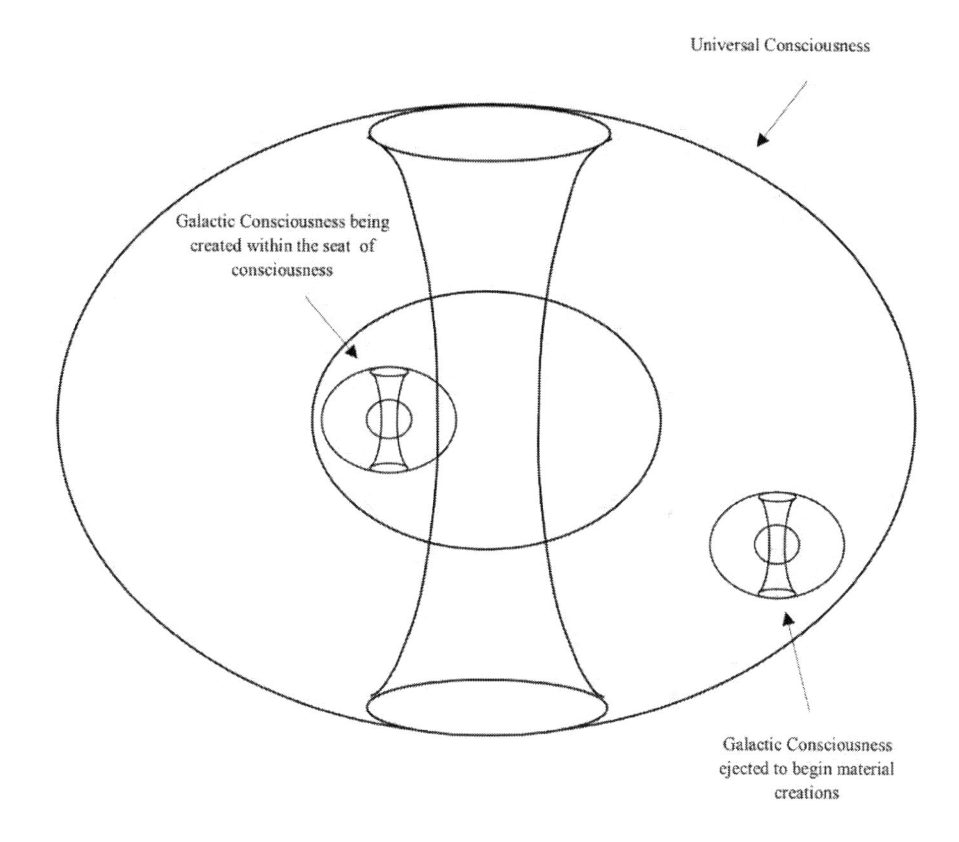

Figure 2 - Galactic Creation

The creation of a galactic consciousness occurs within the universal seat of consciousness. The energy within the universal seat of consciousness is so concentrated that material creation cannot exist within its proximity. The new galactic consciousness is ejected to a safe distance within the universal array and construction of its ascension pathways begins.

For the expansion within universal consciousness to commence in earnest, compartmentalization of its photonic density must occur. Within this new partition, the rotations are realigned to mimic that of universal consciousness on a smaller scale. When the rotations attain a toroidal architecture, the energy signature is modified to a unique wavelength and a self-energizing barrier membrane forms. Within this membrane the new energy signature becomes aware of an observational perspective separate from its creator. With the array energized and its barrier complete, it is ejected from the universal nucleus to a distance where material creation can commence. This ejected consciousness is the first galactic consciousness to exist within the rotations of universal consciousness. The galactic consciousness will repeat the compartmentalization process that created it using portions of its photonic particulate to create system consciousnesses that further reduce the energy levels.

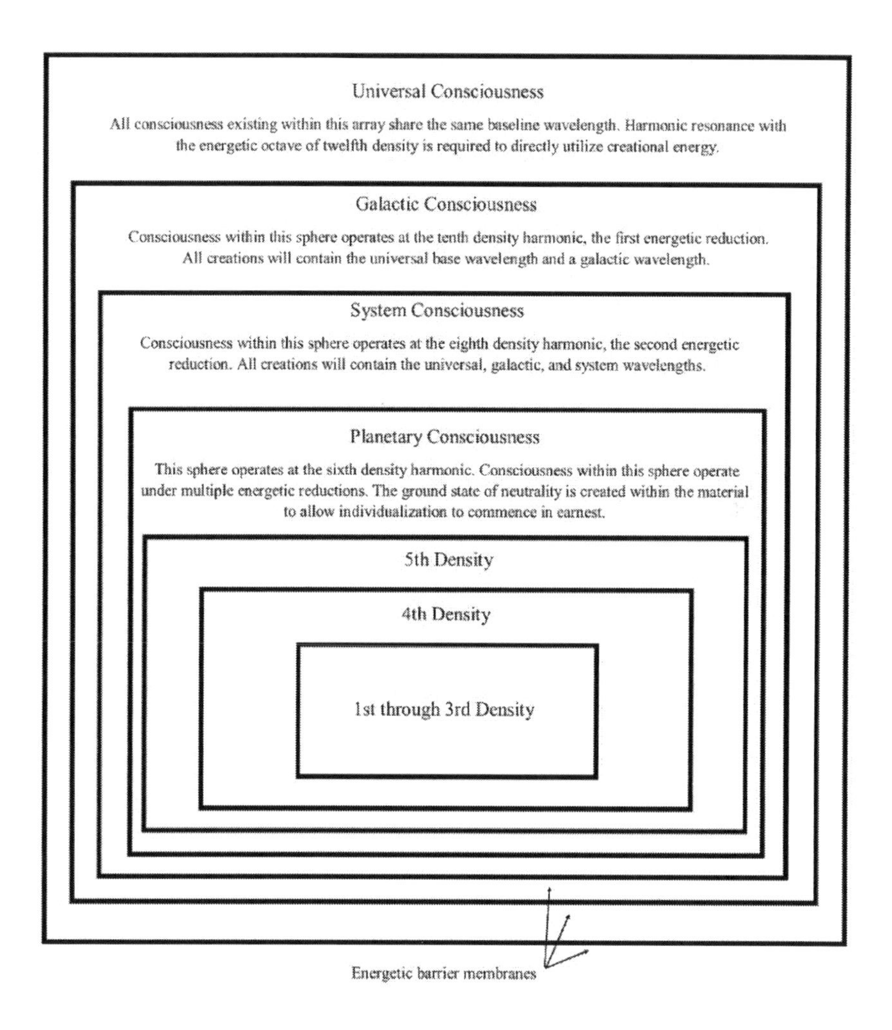

Figure 3 - Energetic Octave Reductions

The boxes above represent the barrier membranes of the respective consciousnesses. Each barrier membrane reduces the energetic potential of universal creational energy as the consciousness uses it to empower its rotations and filters it to a harmonic that can be utilized by the creations within it. Galactic consciousness exists within universal consciousness at the octave of tenth density. System consciousnesses reside within the galactic membrane and operate at the octave of eighth density. Planetary consciousnesses reside within their respective system and operate at the octave of sixth density. Planetary consciousness further filters the energy into discreet octaves that allow the systematic energetic ascension of individualized consciousness from the ground state of neutrality.

Figure 3 represents a simplified visual representation of the energetic reductions that occur as consciousness exists within successive barrier membranes. This image indicates that Galactic Consciousness is immersed within the complete spectrum and intensity of universal energy. Each galaxy resonates at a unique energetic wavelength and shields its creations from the full spectrum of creational energy. It observes itself as separate, but part of the universal collective. Each galaxy is free to define the systems of ascension that consciousness will experience within it. Each galactic consciousness exists within the twelfth octave and reduces the energetic availability to the creations within it to the tenth octave. Each galactic consciousness is responsible for creating system consciousnesses that further reduce and refine the energy. As with the Galactic consciousness, System Consciousness is free to define the order of ascension within it but must conform with the overarching galactic parameters. System consciousnesses reduce the energy from the tenth octave to the eighth octave. The next energetic partition is the planetary consciousness that will further reduce the energy of the System Consciousness through several octaves to the ground state where it will donate portions of its particulate as it nurtures and oversees the material creations that grow within it. This systematic reduction in energetic immersion creates a conducive low energy environment that allows rapid photonic division to occur. A single particle of consciousness is the beginning of the journey for all individualized consciousness created within a planetary consciousness. Consciousness ascending through the densities from the first upon a planet are considered organic. This term is not derogatory but identifies them as native and differentiates them from consciousness who have ascended elsewhere and have come to participate in the constructs.

The energetic barriers of consciousness can be observed operating in the material as they filter and support the growth of lifeforms within them. Science has observed and defined the portion of the interstellar medium detectable with current technology. These material remnants of creation do not directly represent the energies of consciousness that created them, but they do assist in defining the barrier membranes and their purpose. On Earth the barrier between the solar system and interstellar space is termed the heliosphere. This barrier is created from the energetic emanations of the system star that interacts with and creates a protective barrier from the material constituents of the interstellar medium. Within this protective barrier the energy spectrum produced by the star creates the platform upon which life will grow under its influence. The planetary spheres within the system create another energetic barrier termed the magnetosphere that further filters the system energy. The dynamic between the energetics of the system star and the filtering effects of the planetary barrier determine the evolutionary path of the life forms on the respective planets. These are the materially observable effects that correlate to the energetic barriers of system and planetary consciousness.

Chapter Four

The Densities of Consciousness

Consciousness is comprised of photonic particulate bound together through sympathetic oscillations that create a spherical rotation. As the particulate moves around the sphere it creates an energetic barrier that protects the unique oscillating signature being created. The amount of particulate contained within the barrier of each consciousness is considered its density. The more particulate within the barrier, the higher the particulate density and the more energy the consciousness is capable of harnessing. The changes to the geometry of the sphere and the energy that results through increasing particulate density are divided into levels. This book references the various density levels of consciousness as first, second, third, and so on. This definition relates to the particulate density of the individual consciousness and the resulting energetic capabilities it can manifest.

The Pathway Toward Individualized Consciousness

The first book discussed the mechanism of photonic division that occurs within consciousness as the stressors of experience reach the threshold of harmonic fracture. For ease of understanding we observed a single photon undergoing division and then jumped to a late second density consciousness about to achieve third density. We now expand upon those concepts as the focus turns to the energetic interactions that create oscillating wavelengths and frequencies that energize the barrier membrane.

The Creation of Individualized Ascension Pathways

When a planet has been designated as an ascension pathway, a consciousness is either created or assigned to imbue and oversee the ascension of consciousness upon it. The selected consciousness then envelops the planet, and the material substrate becomes the body that is energized by focused intention of creational energy. The new planetary consciousness begins filtering the energy from the system consciousness and prepares the planet for life. When capable of supporting biological processes, it bathes the planet with the seeds of consciousness and life begins. To understand this process, remember that Figure 1 shows a fully developed rotational geometry and that this geometry expands within the universal aspect ratio that governs the height of the column to the width of the openings and the circumference of the sphere. Before individualized life can commence, the planetary consciousness must expand its geometry until the seat of consciousness extends beyond the material surface of the planet. It does this through the acquisition of energy from the system star that assists in expanding the particulate density of the planetary consciousness. It balances and accelerates the increasing rotational particulate through the experience gained while shaping the planet and preparing it for life

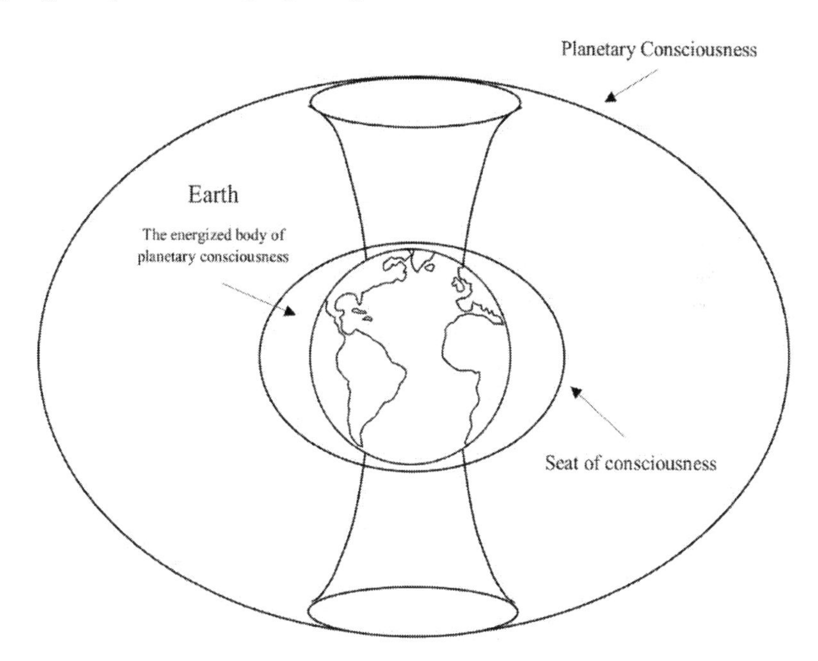

Figure 4 - Planetary Consciousness

The planetary consciousness must expand until the seat of consciousness completely envelopes the material sphere. The seat of consciousness contains the lowest energy particles and is where the ground state of neutrality occurs. It is also the densest particulate location within the sphere. The planet exists centrally within the toroidal column and represents the energized body of the conscious array.

There are several reasons why planetary bodies must exist within the seat of consciousness. This is the area where the per particle energetics are the lowest, a requirement for first through third density. This is also the densest location of particulate per area volume, a required foundation for material constructs. While per particle energetics are low, its particulate density makes it a central energetic point. An explanation of why these parameters exist at the seat of consciousness will be provided later in the text.

Within the energetic ocean at the center of the planetary consciousness, life begins upon the planet as single photons empower the building blocks of life. These seeds of consciousness begin the first steps of their journey acquiring baseline energy of a generic nature as the first signs of life emerge upon the planet. These early experiences do not impart a unique energetic signature as the seeds empower material life and return to the ocean of the planetary consciousness with each successive incarnation. As their journey progresses, the seeds begin to divide and grow under the stressors of repeated experience. Each division locks the fracturing pairs into a sympathetic rotation. The planetary ocean of consciousness now contains clumps.

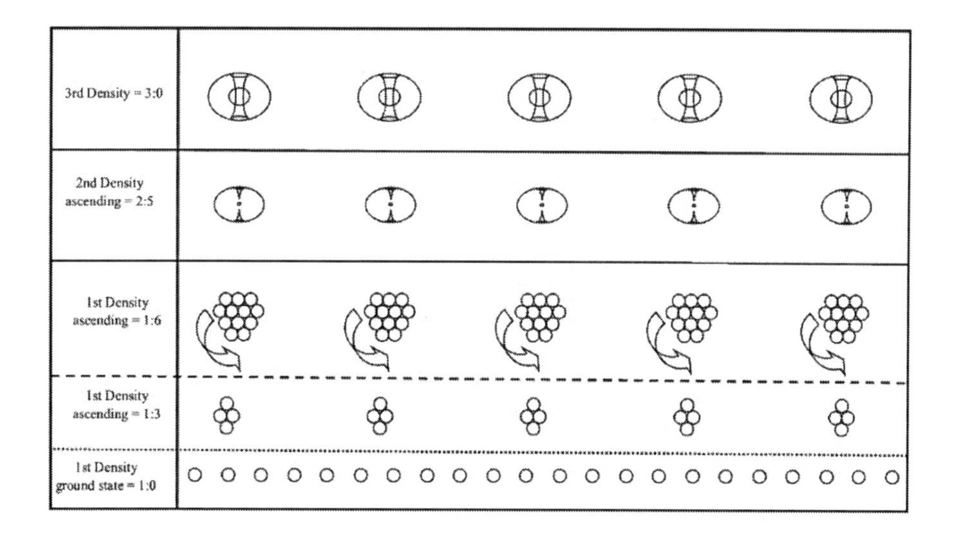

Figure 5 - Planetary Ocean of Ascension

This chart shows a condensed ascension pathway that begins as single particles begin their journey toward individualization within the energetic ocean of planetary consciousness. The particles engage in experiences that harmonically bind them together. When a clump of sufficient mass has formed, it rises from the baseline energy as the particles now share a unique oscillating wavelength that causes the clump to rotate and pull in more energy. The growth of particulate accelerates under the increasing energy as the clumps begin to form a sphere and rise into the next level of energetic capacity. As the spheres continue to gain energy, depressions at the top and bottom begin to create a column at the center. When the columns meet and create a tube through the center, the seat of consciousness energizes, and third density self-awareness begins.

These clumps were drawn together as the photons acquired a unique energetic signature that caused them to oscillate in unison. As the clumps form, they begin to acquire unique experiences which provides increasingly individualized oscillations. This is the demarcation point where the journey toward self-awareness begins in earnest.

To give this concept perspective, consider first density as a pot of water on the stove. When heat is first applied to the pot there is no visible change to the water. As the water continues to absorb heat, small vapor bubbles begin to form at the bottom. These small encapsulations are absorbing more energy than the surrounding water and are showing signs of change. The bubbles continue to absorb energy and increase in diameter until they break free and rise to the surface where they escape from the water as steam. This is a direct correlation to what occurs as clumps form in the photonic soup of first density. From an energetic perspective, these clumps of growing individualization swell and begin rising energetically above the initial layer of first density consciousness. Two layers of conscious potential now exist; the originating density, and the newly formed layer of second density.

From a material perspective, first density appears as the unicellular organism. This foundation of life exhibits a simple programming where the cells exist and reproduce. The consciousness that empowers these cells also contain a single photon. The cycle continues as these organisms are the only expression of life. At a point in this process, the photons that repeatedly empower these cells obtain enough energy to undergo photonic division during embodiment. The single photon becomes two and both share a unique energetic signature that binds them together through harmonic oscillation. These bound photons will remain together from this point forward. As the two continue to divide and multiply, the clump will increase in size as the energy within it becomes increasingly individualized. These clumps now require a more complex organism to continue their expansion. Unicellular becomes multicellular and the diversity of life begins in earnest as the requirements of consciousness push the observable evolutionary arc.

The planetary organisms continue to diversify as the second density consciousnesses begin striving for individuality. As the diversity of lifeforms increases, so too does the richness of available experiential pathways. As second density consciousnesses acquire increasingly complex experiences, the rotations within their array accelerate and begin to exhibit depressions at the top and bottom. The experiences in second density culminate when consciousness attains the required particulate and enough energy to create a fully formed column through the center as shown in Figure 1. When formed, the center column allows for the proper energization of the photons and the seat of consciousness at the center becomes self-actualized. Consciousness containing this structure has become self-aware and rises above the energetic medium of second density. Returning to the boiling pot of water analogy, these consciousnesses have emerged from the water to become steam. Three energetic densities now exist from which consciousness will embody upon the planet. This is the pathway of systematic ascension that energizes the seat of consciousness and the barrier membrane of individuality.

Sympathetic Energy Transfer

When third density consciousness begins to embody in earnest on the planet, another form of energetic expansion becomes available; sympathetic energy transfer through focused intention. This ability is a result of the column within the toroidal array of third density that draws energy in and subsequently radiates it outward to the object of focus as energetic waves. The mechanics of sympathetic co-resonance will be discussed later.

The clumps of consciousness forming within the generic experiences of first, and early second density do not have the particulate density to store large amounts of energy. Because of this, unique energetic experiences can cause large increases in density that accelerate the clumps toward self-awareness. For this example, consider the plant structures that exist on Earth. They are living organisms whose structure grows, is vibrant and is then observed to die and decay. This is an indication that a field of consciousness is responsible for the cycle as it enters and exits. Now consider an expanse of undisturbed forest where millions of trees live out their existence. Some may become the home for animals while others do not, but for the most part they are all participating in a generic experience. Now assume that someone went into that forest and brought a sapling home and planted it in their yard. They nurture the tree and attend to its care until it takes root. Children play and build structures in the tree and the entire family feels love and gratitude for the tree that shades and entertains them. The consciousness embodied within the tree has been impacted by the nurturing sympathetic energy focus provided by the family. This provided a unique experience and caused the particulate density within the consciousness of the tree to multiply. When the structure of the tree ceases viability, the consciousness that empowered it may then contain the particulate density and energy to move to the next level of individualized incarnation.

Chapter Five

Octaves and Levels within Densities

In this discussion of conscious particulate and the resulting densities they inhabit we must add the complexity of sub-levels that exist within the numerical densities. The conscious array is comprised of photonic particles that vibrate and move through the motivation of kinematic interaction. This motive force is acquired through experiences in material form and interactions with other consciousness. As the lifetimes of experience accumulate, the oscillating particles within consciousness begin to exhibit an internal resonance. This occurs as the multitude of oscillations begin to harmonize with each other. When finely tuned and balanced, this energetic harmony expands beyond the barrier and interacts with consciousness external to it. This is a waveform dynamic that is easy to understand when compared to the pressure waves associated with musical instruments.

Musical instruments are tuned to create oscillating pressure waves that interact with each other within discreet frequency bandwidths. A bandwidth is defined as the difference between the highest and lowest frequency within a continuous range. When multiple waveforms at different frequencies combine, they create a harmonic bandwidth if they are multiples of the fundamental frequency.

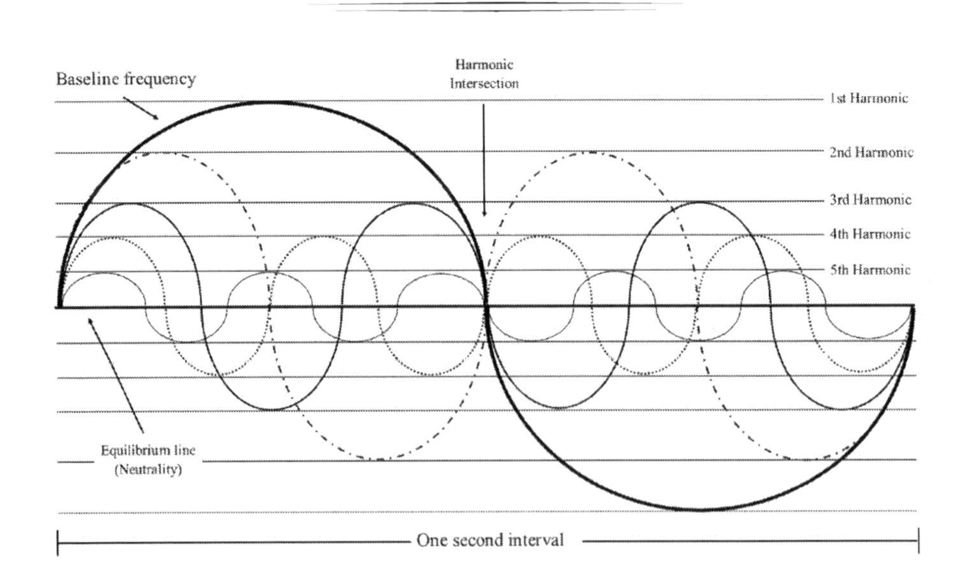

Figure 6 - Harmonic Multiples

The waveforms above represent the harmonic resonance found in musical pressure waves that oscillate at multiples of a baseline frequency. As the waveforms increase in frequency, they maintain their harmonic with the baseline. This harmonic interaction is reflected as the waveforms intersect the equilibrium line at the same point as the baseline frequency regardless of complexity.

Figure 6 represents musical pressure waves that have been tuned to oscillate within a baseline frequency. The waves are measured by how many times they create a complete waveform per unit of time. The standard measurement is in cycles per second, a unit of measure known as Hertz, named after Heinrich Hertz, who established it. Hertz is often abbreviated to Hz. For ease of understanding, assume Figure 6 is measuring a one second period. The baseline frequency would then be one hertz as it completes one full cycle in a second. For harmonic resonance to occur, the additional waves must oscillate at a multiple of the baseline frequency and this is reflected. The additional waves are producing intervals of 2, 3, 4, and 5. Although the waveforms are increasing in frequency, they all harmonically intersect the line of neutrality at the same point as the baseline frequency. The wavelengths combine to create an oscillating spectrum that spans from 1 to 5 which reflects its bandwidth. This is the concept of frequency and bandwidth.

The harmonic relationship between musical pressure waves is an important concept, but must be coupled with the second term, resonance, to provide value in understanding the expansion of consciousness. Particles by themselves contain resonant frequencies, where the energetic intensity and periodicity of wave action acts as a vibrational multiplier. If sustained, the energy will reverberate (or resonate) within the particle. Increasing the energy in this resonant area further will cause the particle to fracture. On either side of the area of resonance, the energy excites the particle in a normal fashion. If the particle then becomes part of a larger system whose geometry continues to change, two areas of resonance are created. The original resonance of the particle, and a second resonance associated with the composite system. If we now place the first system within successive systems, the energetic intensity and wave oscillations between them must harmonically oscillate for resonance to occur.

When the instruments of an orchestra are tuned to a baseline frequency, the various waveforms they produce are multiples of that baseline. This is what creates the symphony of pleasant interactions known as music. As musical waveforms increase in oscillating frequency from the baseline frequency, they are grouped into scales known as octaves. These ascending octaves of sound represent increasing energy - in the form of pressure waves- being created through the instruments. At every level of energetic capacity, individual consciousness exists as a bandwidth of oscillating waveforms. From this perspective, the densities of consciousness and the ascending energy levels within them exhibit the characteristics of octaves and sub-octaves. Ascension in consciousness can then be associated with a gradual increase in energetic oscillation and complexity from a baseline octave toward the next. The movement from originating first density to the threshold of second density requires a series of steps that steadily increases the oscillating frequency and energetic emanations of the multiplying particles.

Relating the levels of conscious density and their associated frequencies to harmonic octaves and musical instruments brings another requirement into focus. Both require a tuning of the instrument to achieve sympathetic resonance within a desired octave. Sympathetic resonance occurs when a vibratory body acts upon another with similar characteristics to impart its oscillating frequency. This concept is easily understood when related to traditional tuning forks. If two identical tuning forks are at rest and you then strike one, the reverberations from it will cause the second one to begin to vibrate at the same oscillating tempo. The two tuning forks are now in sympathetic co-resonance.

Consciousness is created through a complex coordination of spinning, vibrating, and oscillating particulate encapsulated within a protective energetic membrane that creates a toroidal sphere as shown in Figure 1. As the particulate density within the membrane increases, the additive oscillations create increasingly complex waveforms. The compounding waveforms combine to create the overall harmonic bandwidth of the individualized consciousness. The oscillating bandwidth that a consciousness produces determines the octave it is in co-resonance with. When the factors that create the harmonic octaves of conscious are plotted, the increasing potentials create an upward spiraling of energetic capacity that represents the compounding oscillations resulting from increasing particulate density within consciousness.

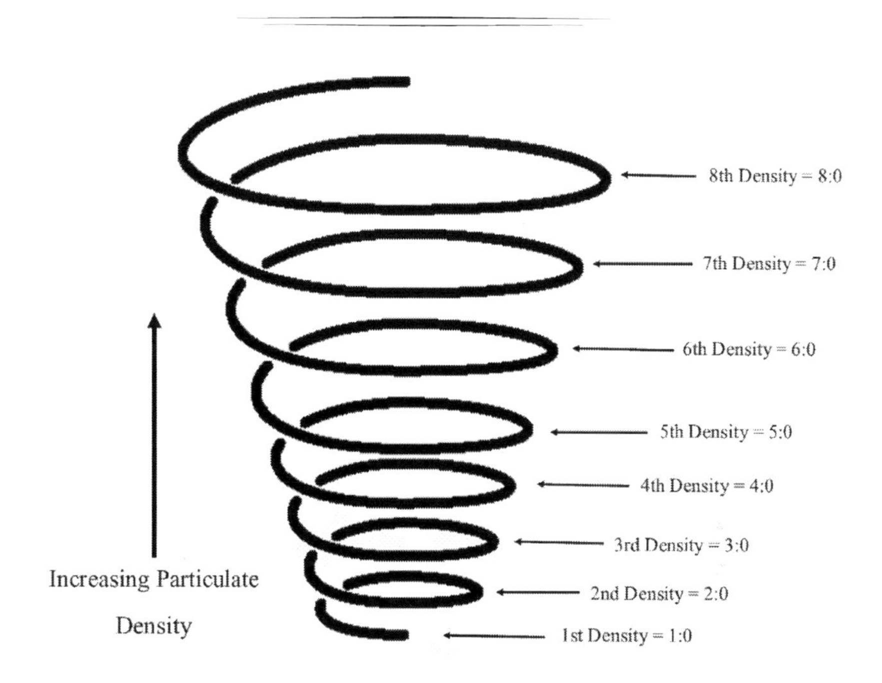

Figure 7 - Upward Spiral with Density Indicators

The oscillating waveforms generated within the sphere of consciousness have minimum and maximum values limited by the effective operating parameters of the constituent particles. When the minimum and maximum values are plotted on a graph of increasing particulate density, it creates the ascending logarithmic spiral shown.

The geometry of the conical spiral incorporates the upward progression of increasing particulate density and the compounding waveforms that oscillate within each resulting octave. The increasing oscillations generated within individualized consciousness as they gain density require tuning to achieve resonance within a given octave. To properly understand the concept of octaves and their relationship to consciousness, you must understand the process that creates these oscillating waveforms.

Chapter Six

The Helical Movement of the Universe

The foundation of the universe is consciousness. Everything exists within the movement of conscious particulate and while matter appears solid and immutable, it is a product of energy in motion. The transport of energy that solidifies matter results from a high energy potential moving toward its ground state. The ground state can be considered the absolute zero point -or neutrality- where matter ends, and consciousness begins. To understand this apparent contradiction, we must discuss the foundations of solidified matter, why it has been created, and how it correlates with the ascension of consciousness.

We have associated the particulate of consciousness with the scientific concept of photons. The term photon comes from the Greek term 'phos' which meant light. Science has studied photons and observed them as they acquire energy and subsequently dissipate it. Unpotentiated, these particles are the base constituent filling the expanse of the universe and are the photons being observed by science. Only under the intention and stewardship of consciousness do these particles begin to acquire individualized energetic signatures that grow into unique packets and become 'enlightened' as they gain energy.

Enlightenment is a term associated with increasing awareness and logic that is often used in new age literature. The metaphorical correlation to illuminating darkness and the resulting ability to clearly observe your surroundings is an easy concept to associate with the term. Beyond the metaphor, there is a literal correlation to what occurs in consciousness as the photonic particulate acquires energy. As the discussions in the awakening communities move to more advanced consciousness operating beyond the need for physical embodiment, we encounter another term associated with increasing illumination, light body. As with the term enlightenment, light body is a highly searched term being used to discuss various topics related to the ascension of consciousness. While the extended discussions containing these terms varies depending upon the source, these terms are attempting to describe the concept that consciousness is related to light and its illumination increases as it gains energy. Using the foundation these terms provide, a clearer understanding will be built upon it.

As previously stated, current science defines photons as discreet packets of electromagnetic radiation that can exhibit the characteristics of a wave and a particle. If we look at a graph of electromagnetic radiation, we see a logarithmic scale of increasing energy where a small portion contains the observable light spectrum.

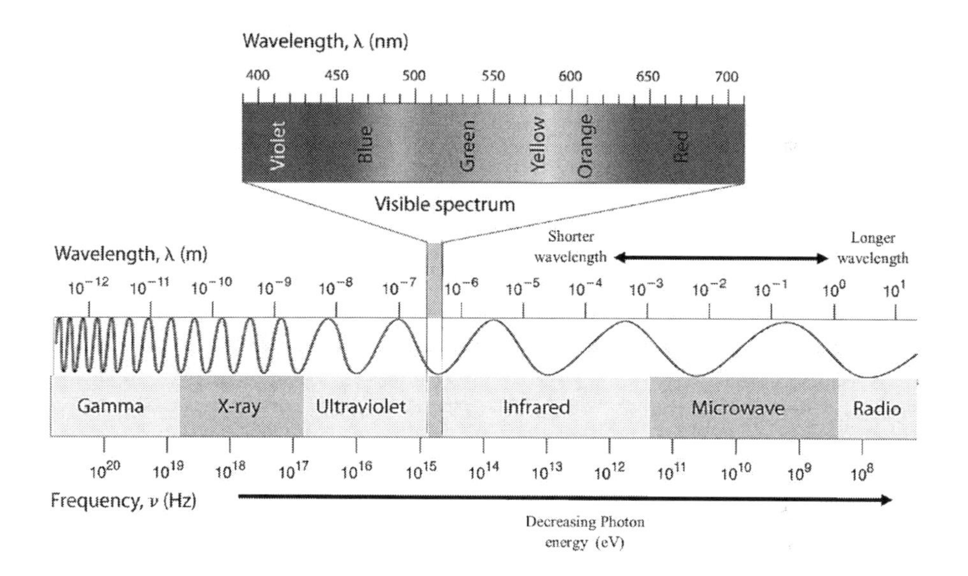

Figure 8 - Electromagnetic Spectrum

The image above represents the electromagnetic spectrum with the area of visible light expanded. The graph shows that as photon energy increases, its wavelength becomes shorter and more frequent. This graph represents photonic particulate locked within the inverse relationship shown in Chapter 3.

The amount of energy within these particles radiates outward as they travel and is measured in frequency and wavelength. Frequency is defined as the number of waves that pass a point per unit of time.

Wavelength is defined as the distance between identical points on consecutive waves.

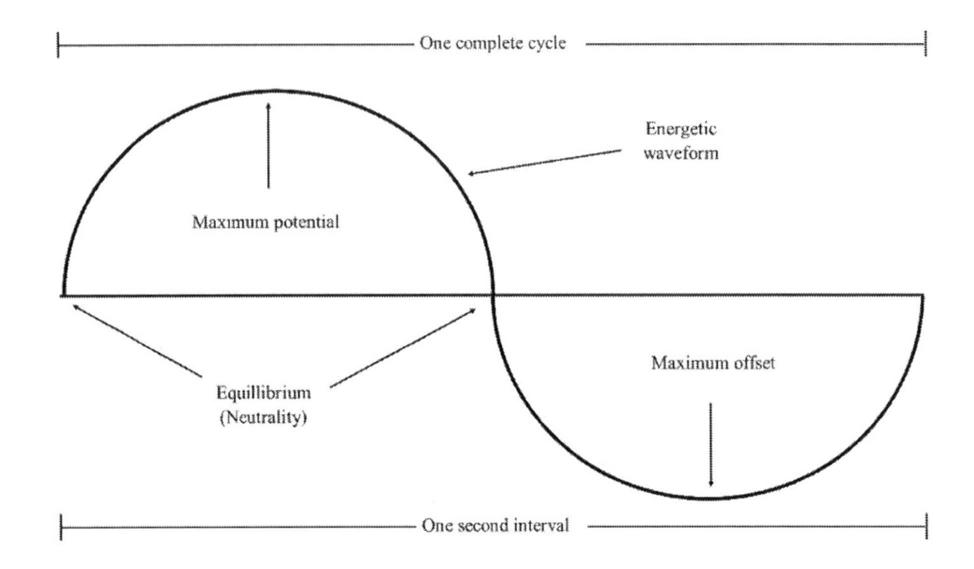

Figure 9 - Frequency Definition

The standard measurement of a complete waveform is shown above. Electromagnetic waves occur in cycles. A cycle includes the complete energetic movement (one oscillation) from initial deflection to the return of energetic origin. The waveform above completed one cycle in one second which is stated as one Hertz (1Hz). Electromagnetic waves are measured by calculating the positive arc and resulting negative arc required to return the wave to equilibrium. Assuming a steady energetic state, the waveform will continue to repeat this pattern indefinitely.

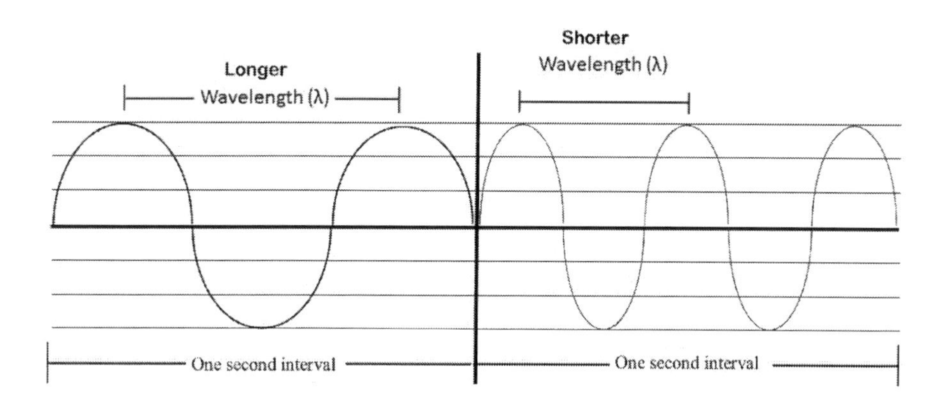

Figure 10 - Wavelength Definition

Wavelength is the distance between identical points on consecutive waves. Two separate waves are shown above with their respective wavelengths measured. The wave to the left has a lower energy and resulting longer wavelength when compared to the wave on the right.

Within the confines of material constructs, frequency and wavelength are inversely proportional to each other and locked into this relationship through the limitation of the speed of light within a spacetime construct. This governs the distance a photon can travel per unit time as shown in the equation in Chapter 3. The inverse relationship between frequency and wavelength dictate that as the energy within a particle increases it will spin faster, emitting more waves within a measured period (frequency), as the waveform (wavelength) decreases. The principle causing this observable manifestation of photonic energy within the material is the foundation of consciousness and everything else, helical spin.

If we take the two-dimensional representation of electromagnetic energy waves from Figure 8 and expand it to three dimensions, we see that the photon does not move in a straight line from point A to point G but spirals imperceptibly toward it.

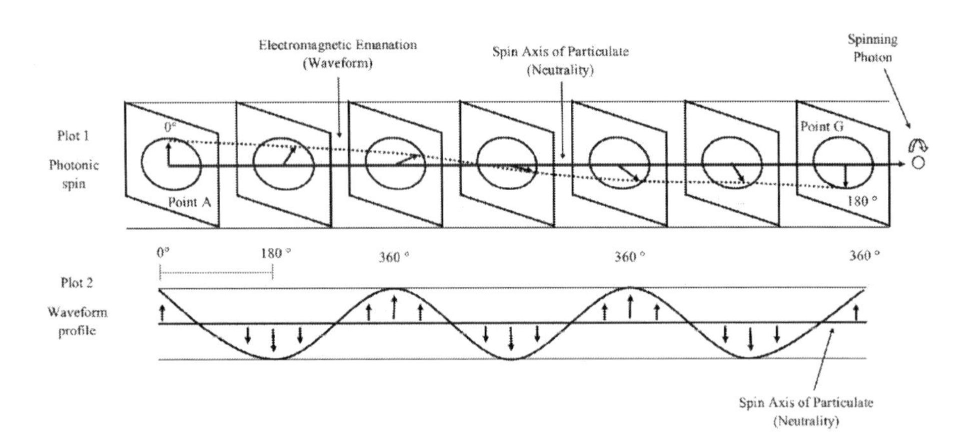

Figure 11 - Helical Spin

Plot 1 shows an energized photon traveling across a distance from point A to point G, as it radiates the energy it contains. The plot begins at 0 degrees and tracks the photon as it spins to 180 degrees. As it travels, it spins around its axis creating a corkscrew electromagnetic emanation, or helical spiral. As it spirals along its path, the energy it radiates is measured and plotted on a two-dimensional graph. Plot 2 shows the waveform profile of the particle as it spins along its path creating three 360-degree rotations. The two-dimensional waveform profile represents a particle traveling in three-dimensional space.

The energy within the photon dictates the rate at which it spins. The more energy the photon contains, the faster it spins. Since the rate of travel is limited by the laws of locality in this example, as photonic spin increases the number of waves within point A and G also increase as the speed of the particle remains constant. This effect creates an increasing oscillating/vibrational frequency. If we overlay the three-dimensional spiraling architecture of increasing spin from Figure 11 onto Figure 8, we begin to see the correlation between the two. Figure 8, when viewed from left to right, represents an excited particle shedding energy as it spins. The energy radiates from the particle as it attempts to find equilibrium (neutrality) within the construct. This is the foundation of matter; spiraling energy moving from a fully excited state toward the ground state of neutrality as it energizes and locks the substrate into specific octaves of vibrational frequency. When creational energy is sequestered in solidified matter as binding energy it is no longer available as a catalyst for consciousness. In this way solidified material acts as an energetic grounding rod, diverting large portions of energy which then creates the ground state -energetic zero point- at the planet surface. This purpose-built zero point is the incubator from which individualized consciousness ascends and forms an energetic barrier that will protect it from increasing energies. To understand the scale of energetic sequestration required to create this neutral point you need only look to the heavier elements of uranium and plutonium. The weapons created from these elements are impressively destructive, yet only liberate a fraction of the creational energy required to solidify them.

With the conceptualization that creational energy spirals from a state of high potential to a ground state as it solidifies matter, we find originating consciousness ascending within the material planes from that neutral state into higher potentials. From this perspective, the complete circuit that powers the universe begins to come into focus. If consciousness is the foundation of the universe, and the helical spiral the foundation of consciousness, we must discuss how one creates the other.

The Spin of Consciousness and the Barrier Membrane

Energized photons within consciousness emit energy as they spin. The more energy they contain, the faster they spin. The rate of travel is dictated by particulate energy, the push from the energy emitted by other particles, and the pull of the harmonic binding they all share. The particles travel within a spherical composite whose circumference is proportional to the amount of particulate it contains and the capacity of that particulate to transport energy. The spiraling movement generates an upward flow through the center of the sphere as consciousness attains resonance with mid-first density. As the sphere expands, the spiraling flow at the center causes depressions to form at the top and bottom. Second density begins when the depressions form cones, and third density begins when the column is complete as shown in Figure 5.

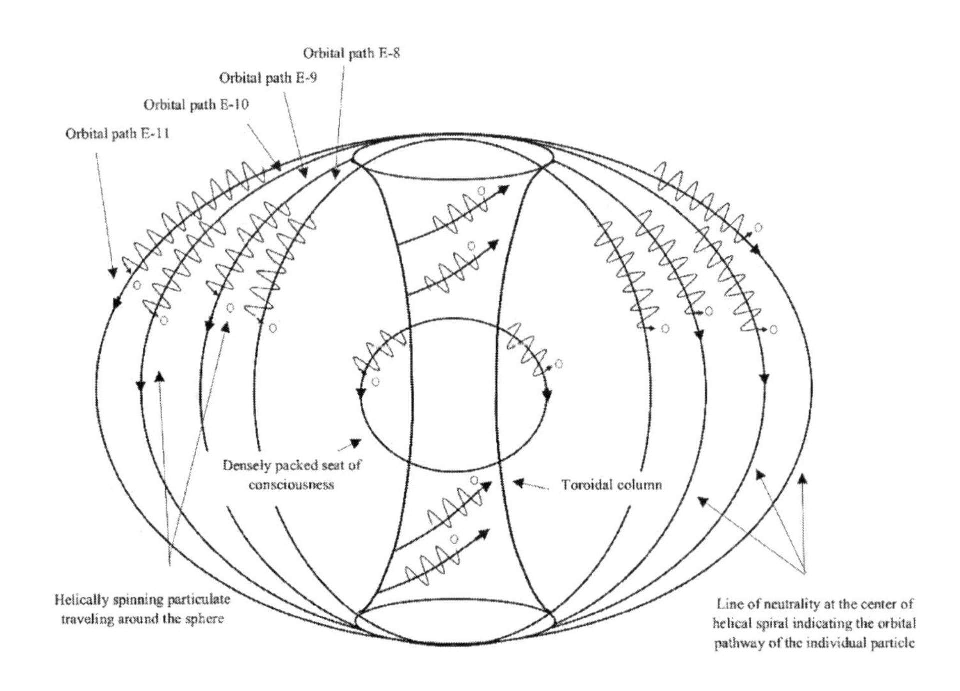

Figure 12 - Helical Pathways

The image represents a self-aware consciousness containing a fully formed column and seat of consciousness. The particles move within the sphere as a continuous exchange of energy causes them to increase in charge and then deplete that charge and repeat the cycle. Individual particulate is shown helically spinning along its orbital pathway. The pathway that particulate travels is dependent upon the energy they contain. E-11 represents the highest energy pathway within the sphere. Moving inward, the pathway numbering convention for those shown are E-10, followed by E-9, E-8 and continuing in reductive order for paths not shown. The seat of consciousness contains the lowest energy particulate, and the low energy creates a densely packed sphere within the larger array.

Figure 12 shows the pathway of spinning particulate in a third density consciousness as it moves from the center of the mass upward and outward around the sphere toward the bottom to repeat the process. As the photons spiral around the periphery of the structure, the spinning creates an energetic envelope that surrounds each pathway. The height and strength of each envelope is a result of torsion tensors that determine the geometry of the spiraling pathway the particle travels. The individual energetic envelopes (manifolds) combine to create a field that surrounds the conscious array. The term torsion is defined as a twisting or screwing motion.

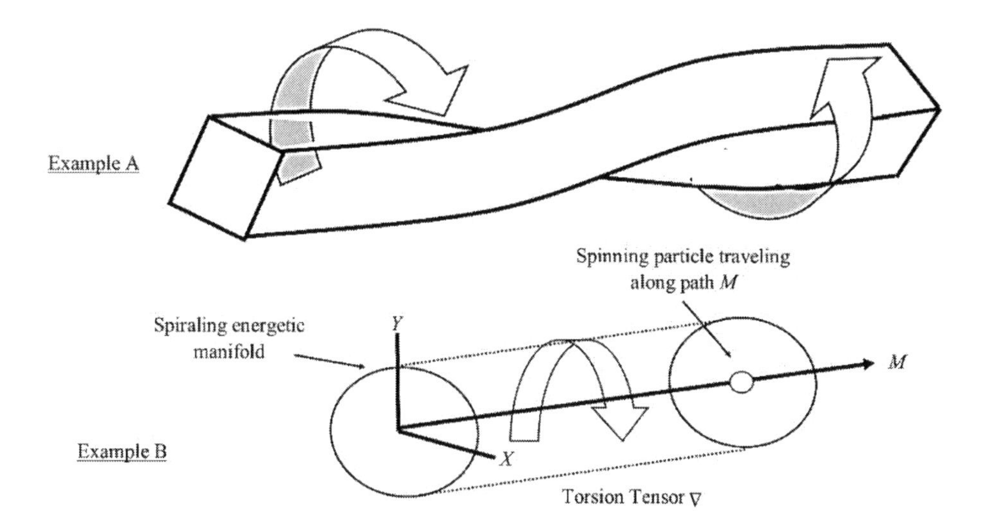

Figure 13 - Torsion Definition

Torsion is defined as the twisting or screwing motion of a frame as one end is compared to the other as shown in Figure A. In physics, a tensor is a multilinear product of several variables plotted in dimensional space. The spiraling energy radiated from a photon as it travels around the sphere of consciousness results from a torsion tensor (rate of twist) proportional to the energy contained in the particle. This twisting field creates a tube of energy (manifold) along path M whose magnitude is also dependent upon the energy the photon contains.

The torsion spin creates the effect of an energetic tube -known as a manifold- that surrounds the travel path of the particle. There are millions of highly energized particles spinning within a sphere of consciousness generating individual energetic manifolds. Each individual manifold acts upon the other to form a tangentially bundled manifold. The individual manifolds blend in the bundled manifold to form the barrier membrane that protects the energetic signature being generated within the composite as shown in Figure 1.

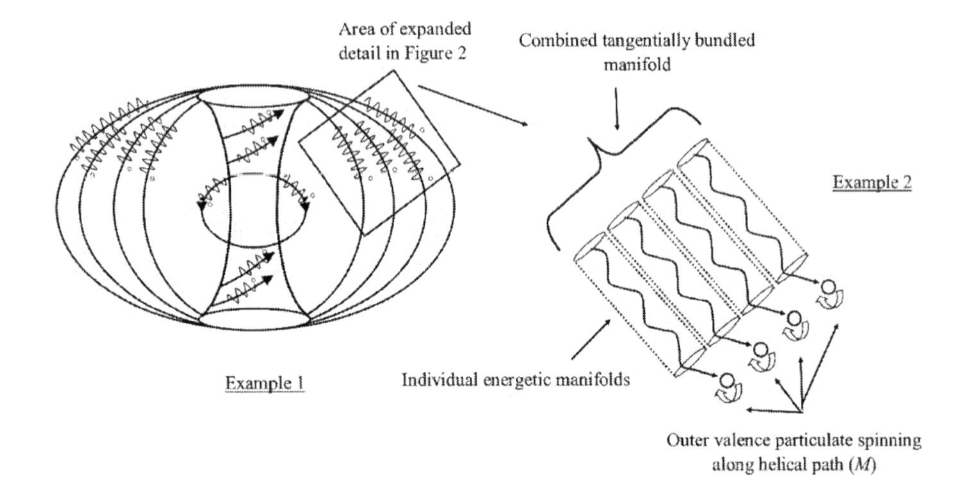

Figure 14 - Tangentially Bundled Manifold

Example 1 represents the sphere of third density consciousness with the outer valence particulate pathways shown. Example 2 is an extracted view of the pathway of four particles as they travel around the periphery of the sphere. As the particles spin along their orbital paths, they create individual energetic manifolds that combine to form a tangentially bundled manifold. The combined manifold surrounds the entire sphere at a distance and strength commensurate to the energy contained within the particles. This combined manifold is the barrier membrane of individualized conscious and is what protects the unique energetics contained within.

Overlaying the concept of harmonic pressure wave dynamics from Figure 6 onto the layers of oscillating particulate of consciousness, we begin to see an intricate relationship between the energetic emanations that must be managed. It is this interaction between particles at varying energies that causes consciousness to resonate within harmonic octaves of density.

Chapter Seven

The Upward Spiral of Ascension

The cover of the first book contained a representation termed The Triad of Light .

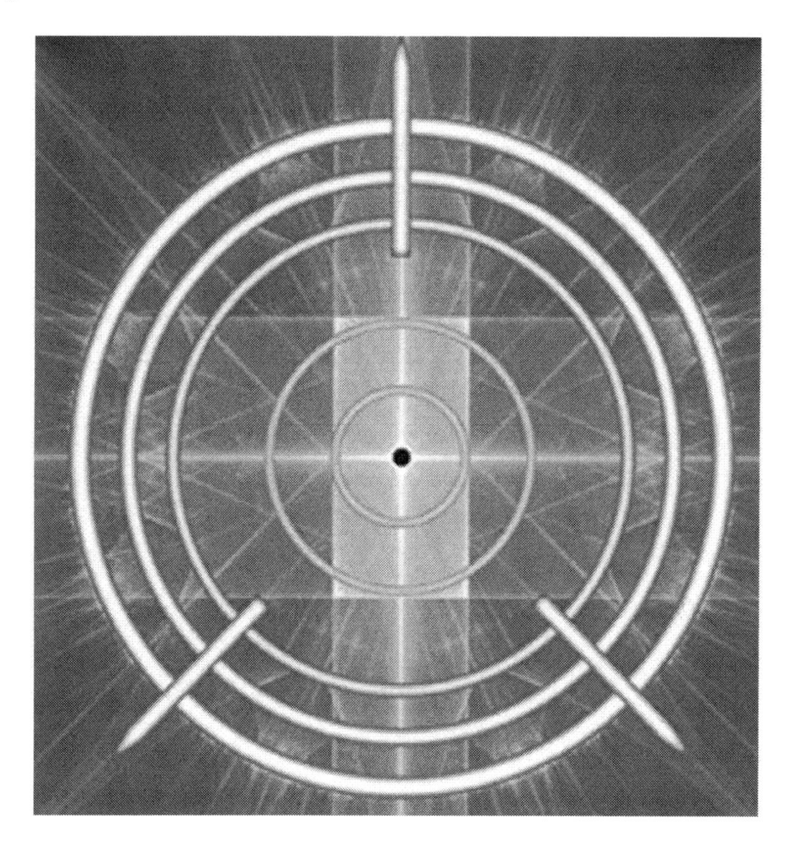

Figure 15 - The Triad of Light

The image above is known as the Triad of Light. The black dot at the center represents a single photon at first density about to embark upon the journey of individuality. The next two rings represent the baseline harmonics of second and third density. The remaining rings signify entry into fourth, fifth, and sixth density.

The Triad of Light is a simplistic view of the ascending energetic levels of consciousness where the rings represent the various base octave densities and the expansion required within consciousness to move from one to the next. The first three rings are widely spaced to convey the separation consciousness experiences in these levels. The remaining rings are closer signifying the increasing energetic collectivity of these densities and the shorter interval required to reach them as expansion accelerates. Energetic collectivity occurs when the oscillations of separate consciousnesses begin to synchronize and this was shown as lines connecting the fourth, fifth, and sixth density rings. With the introductions of the first book behind us, we begin a detailed exploration of the expansion and synchronization required to move into ascending harmonic octave densities.

Consciousness -beyond the observable functions within the brain-is a creation of oscillations combining harmonically to create coherent waveforms. Harmonic oscillation is defined as; multiple frequencies combining to create an integral oscillation that is a multiple of the fundamental frequency. The most appropriate correlation in current science is the concept of three-dimensional harmonic oscillators discussed in quantum mechanics. However, for ease of understanding we will continue our correlations of consciousness to the interactions found in musical pressure waves.

The harmonic resonance that occurs within consciousness is directly relatable to the musical scale. Playing a note within an octave of sound produces an oscillating pressure wave that your ears interpret. If you then play that note simultaneously with the note from the next octave, there are now two pressure waves oscillating in harmonic resonance, with one wave oscillating at twice the frequency as the other. This is the creation of beautiful music where the octaves and sub-octaves of sound waves build upon each other to produce a harmonic resonance. Consciousness follows a similar principle of waveform dynamics. Helically spinning photons exhibit harmonic tendencies as they move within consciousness. As the particles gain energy, they spin faster which translates to a higher oscillating frequency. As the particles continue to multiply, the waveforms they produce create a harmonic resonance that when played together becomes the individualized symphony of that consciousness. The harmonic symphony of consciousness shares other similarities with a musical symphony. Like the instruments within the orchestra, the harmonic oscillations of consciousness have a minimum and maximum operating threshold. Within the parameters of this operating band, consciousness must actively tune its oscillations to achieve optimum resonance. When plotted on a graph, the operating parameters of consciousness create the upward logarithmic spiral that was shown in Figure 7. As consciousness increases in energetic potential, its operating parameters are tracked within this expanding spiral tube.

With an understanding that the sphere of consciousness creates oscillating frequencies operating in harmonic resonance, let's overlay the Triad of Light image onto the methodical expansion of consciousness within the upward spiral.

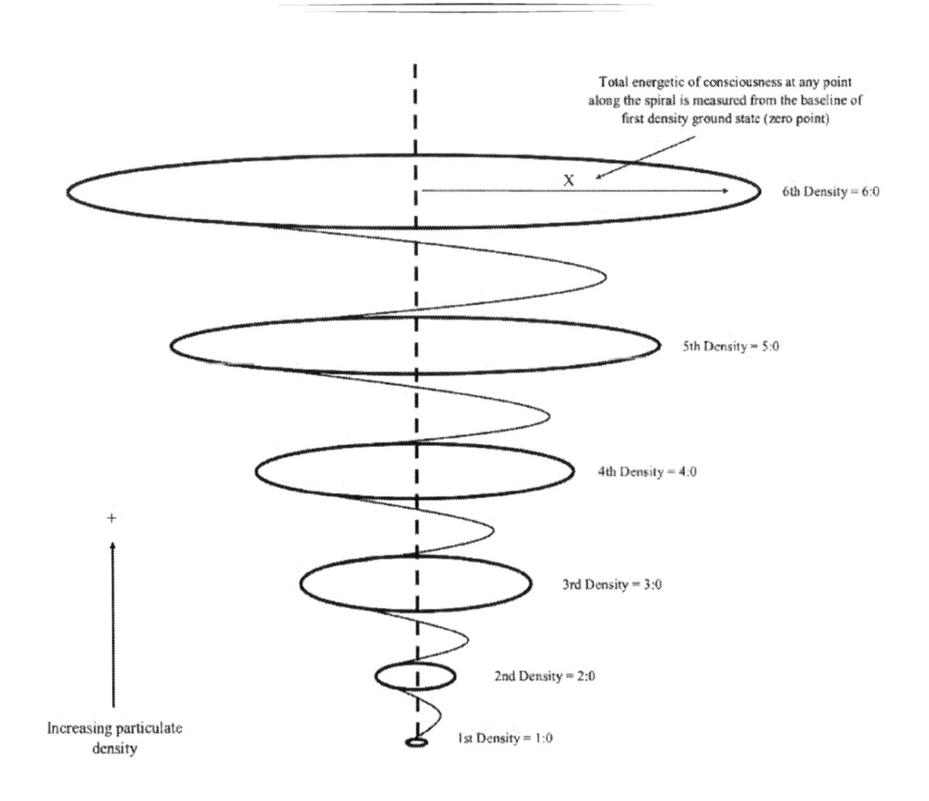

Figure 16 - Upward Spiral with Triad of Light Overlay

The upward spiraling tube of ascending consciousness is shown with the Triad of Light image superimposed upon it. Each ring represents the base octave oscillation that consciousness enters. Once a base octave is obtained, consciousness begins the methodical expansion through the sub-octaves of that density as it seeks higher energetics. The energetic capacity of consciousness ascending within the spiral can be obtained at any point by measuring the radius of the spiral to the originating state of first density neutrality. This measurement represents the lowest particulate energy within the consciousness and is termed the sliding scale of zero point.

The spiral in figure 16 moves upward in a logarithmic expression as it plots the increasing energy and waveform multiplication occurring as consciousness gains particulate density. The spiral rises vertically from the ground state of neutrality as it tracks increases in density. The spiral increases in diameter from neutrality as it tracks waveform complexity. When combined, the upward spiral represents a steadily increasing energetic capacity within consciousness as it moves toward the next octave density. The spinning particulate creates the waveforms being tracked as a result of the attractive, repulsive, and spiraling forces within the sphere. Consciousness was previously defined as awareness within the ever present now of existence. Where you place your awareness in each moment determines whether you are creating a harmonic oscillation or a discordant one. How the sphere creates the oscillating wavelengths and how the focus of consciousness affects the resulting harmonic interactions must be understood and mastered as you attempt to move beyond third density.

To understand this requirement, consider the diversity of instruments in an orchestra. A group of musicians with a variety of instruments are tuned to operate harmonically within an oscillating spectrum. This requires that they first individually tune the instruments they will play, and then possess the skill to operate them together in harmonic unity. This is a direct representation of what must occur within consciousness. Individual consciousness must tune and balance themselves through focused effort to effectively transport energy through their spherical geometry. When accomplished within its own sphere, it must then tune to operate in collective harmony with other consciousnesses within its construct. This is the creation of a finely tuned collective. When this initial collectivity has been achieved, the newly formed collective must then focus their efforts upon synchronizing with their respective planetary consciousness. This is the process of ascension from third density into the sixth density.

Defining Octaves

For ease of understanding, we will apply the intervals defined within musical tuning to provide a basis for understanding the tuning that must occur within consciousness. In actuality, the graduated steps between the doubling octave densities can be divided to an almost infinite number depending upon how closely you wish to focus upon the increasing oscillating wavelengths. If we consider the rings depicted on the triad of light as representing the base octave densities of first through sixth, we can then further divide the intervals between the rings into sub-octaves.

The term octave comes from the Latin word octavus which translates as eight. In music, octaves are defined by the frequency of their waveform. Increasing in octave infers a doubling of frequency. It is in this representation of a doubling of frequency that the term octave holds value in relation to the upward spiral of consciousness. For the purpose of this text, the incremental divisions between one octave density and the other will follow the accepted musical intervals associated with the term octave. This allows a gross measurement of trajectory and increasing ability within each density level. Therefore, each octave density contains seven major sub-octaves where resonant thresholds exist. The seven sub-octaves are mathematic multiples of the base octave density and when included with the base octave, define the literal Latin translation of the term octave.

Frequency is defined as the number of waveforms within a given interval as was shown in Figure 9. If we assume that the ring of first density represents a wavelength radiated within an interval, it follows that the second density ring represents a doubling of wavelength and intensity within that same interval. Between the two density rings are the sub-octaves that exist within consciousness as the photons multiply and obtain threshold resonance. As consciousness gains energy and particulate, it passes through each increasing sub-octave until it reaches the next doubling octave of consciousness. The sub-octaves are portions of the preceding density by virtue of waveform and harmonics.

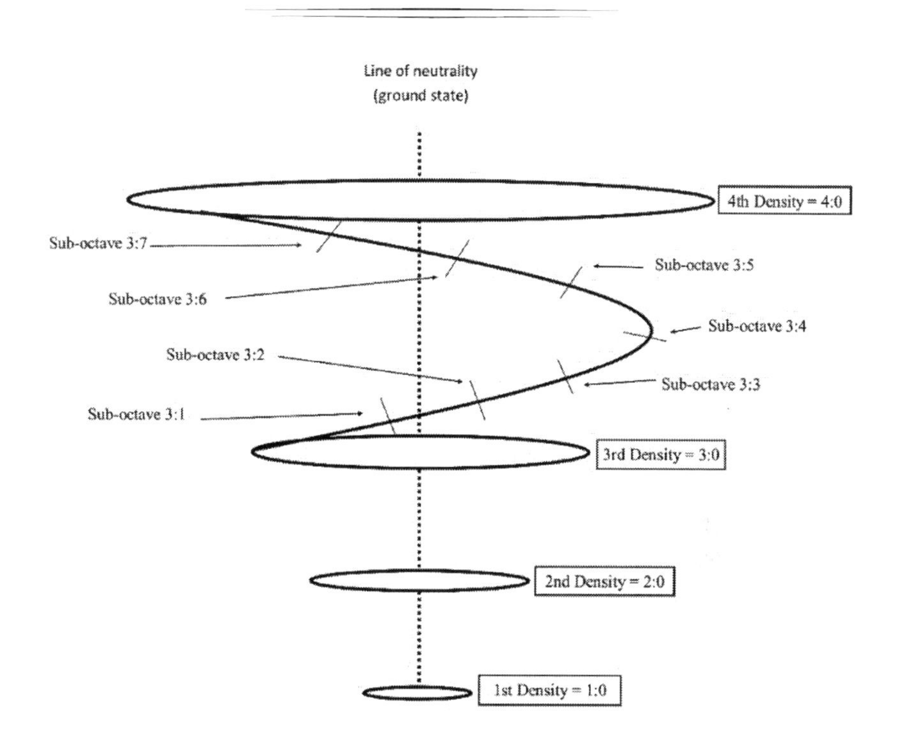

Figure 17 - Upward Spiral with Sub-Octave Intervals

Above is the image from Figure 16 showing the base octave rings of first through fourth density. Only the spiral from third to fourth density is shown for clarity of concept. As consciousness gains density and increases in energetic capacity it moves upward within the spiral of ascension from one base octave to the base octave of the next doubling. As it transits upward between the octaves it travels through the increasing energetic thresholds of harmonic sub-octaves. The sub-octave thresholds are resonant with the base octave and when obtained provide additional abilities and insight to the consciousness. The sub-octaves are identified using the base octave followed by the sub-octave. Adding the seven sub-octaves to the originating base octave you arrive at the numerical definition of octave (eight).

Figure 17 shows the octave doublings of first through fourth density as rings. The spiral upward from third to fourth density shows the sub-octave graduations that are harmonic multipliers of the base density. These are the incremental steps that individualized consciousness climbs along its journey. Climbing the energetic stairs of the upward spiral is much like climbing stairs in life. Some deliberately climb one stair per lifetime as they firmly grip the railing, ensuring they do not slip. Others stretch their reach to its limit as they attempt to climb several at a time. Others still will stop at a step during a lifetime and rest before proceeding.

Movement upward from origination to the third density ring is a function of consciousness attaining the requisite particulate needed to expand the sphere and generate the rotational spin that creates the column of self-awareness. When self-awareness begins, consciousness must use free will to actively seek the balance required to obtain harmonic resonance with fourth density. When consciousness enters fourth density, continued expansion now requires a dual focus on balancing the internal oscillating harmonics through focused intent and aligning that internal harmonic with the harmonic of the collective. The division of photonic particulate still occurs, but the rotations within the sphere are gaining efficiency which allows the particulate to hold significantly more energy before fracture. In fourth density, increasing the spin rate through balancing becomes the primary mechanism of harmonic fracture.

In this discussion of harmonics and octaves another concept must be considered. All consciousness organically ascending upon a planetary sphere will contain a sympathetic resonance between them in addition to their unique wavelengths of experience. This is the base photonic wavelength and is the same concept as the transference of genetic coding between biological progenitors and their offspring. This would be considered the fundamental frequency wave found in Figure 6. The individual consciousness frequency waves would then be harmonic multiples operating within that fundamental frequency. This occurs because individualized organic consciousness is originating from, and ascending within, the same planetary consciousness. The ring of fourth density within the Triad of Light is the entry octave to awareness within a planetary consciousness. When consciousness organically ascending upon a planetary sphere attains harmonic resonance with the octave of fourth density, it begins to access the planetary collective and the knowledge available within it.

Chapter Eight

The Concept of Harmonics

Our discussions regarding the interactions of oscillating forces that combine to create the coherent resonance of consciousness do not literally translate into the electric charges or magnetic moments observed within quantifiable matter. At the time of publication, the component of conscious awareness that survives beyond physical death remains unobservable and unmeasurable. The actual measurement and subsequent understandings of coherent resonance are fourth density discoveries that occur when the veil between lifetimes is no longer needed.

The particles of consciousness are best defined as photonic oscillators; energetic packets that vibrate and spin when they become charged. As the particles spin through their orbits, they create unique waveforms as the energy they contain causes the array to rotate. The individual rotations combine to create an overall oscillating frequency. As consciousness attains the energetic capacity of fourth density, tuning the composite frequency generated by their structure becomes the primary consideration for continued growth as they attempt to match the frequency of ascending constructs. This is where harmonic octaves of density come into focus.

To give this a material perspective, consider the particulate of consciousness to be a group of marbles unaffected by gravitational forces. The marbles are moving as a result of a dynamic energy exchange occurring as they spiral. The energy each marble contains affects its individual rotational characteristic which in turn affects the rotational characteristics of neighboring marbles. These energetic interactions determine the spacing between the marbles and is what ultimately shapes the composite into a sphere. Looking closer we observe each marble to contain a baseline rhythm. This unified rhythm creates the attraction that binds them together as a unit.

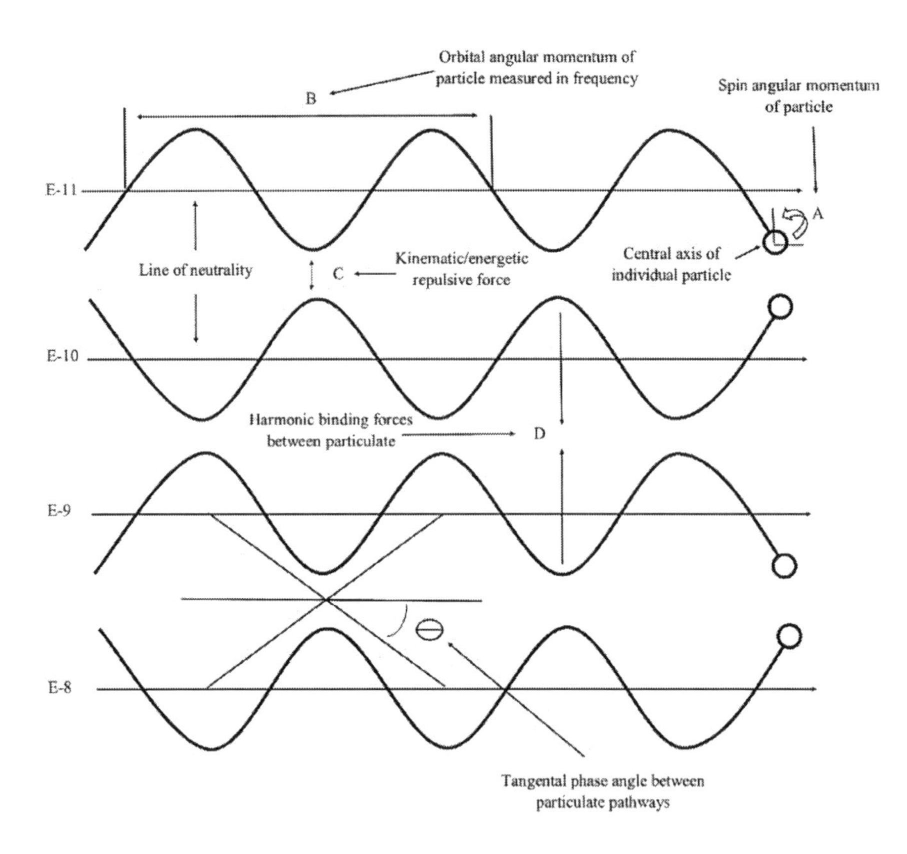

Figure 18 - Components of Rotation

Four individual particulate pathways are shown as they travel around the toroidal sphere. Pathway E-11 is the outermost rotation with the remaining numbers representing rotations as they move inward toward the seat of consciousness. The lines numbered E-11 through E-8 represent the line of neutrality that exists at the center of each particles spinning pathway. Component A reflects the rate at which each particle completes as 360-degree rotation around its central axis. Component B represents the frequency at which the particle helically spins as it travels around the sphere. Component C represents the energetic forces contained within the particle that act to push them apart. Component D represents the harmonic similarities between particles that act to pull them together. The Tangental phase angle is used to measure the balance and energetic transport between particulate pathways.

Figure 18 shows the components of movement each marble exhibits because of the energy they contain. Where component *A* represents the spin angular momentum of each marble about their individual axis. This variable reflects the balance contained within the particle and tracks polarization in environments where it is offered. Component *B* represents the orbital angular momentum of each marble and the resulting energetic waves. The calculations to arrive at the true value of orbital angular momentum and wave vectors are beyond the scope of this text. However, the important aspect of this variable is the frequency of wave propagation. Orbital angular momentum has been simplified to the standard definition of frequency presented in Figure 9. Component *C* represents a lateral vibration induced as the particles react to the repulsive forces between them. Finally, component *D* represents the harmonic binding force that holds the marbles in their rotational array. The X pattern between the rotational waves represents their tangental phase relationships and will be discussed shortly.

As the marbles continue to absorb energy, the spin (component *A*) increases which translates to an overall increase in orbital momentum (component *B*). The orbital momentum of each marble traveling within the sphere also creates an oscillating energetic wave as it moves. This wave pushes against the waves created by the other moving marbles (component *C*) which causes a lateral deflection of the orbital course. As the energy within the composite increases, the oscillating waves created by component *C* act like a lubricant between the marbles which reinforces the increase in individual angular and orbital momentum. The energetic lubricant of component *C* also acts to increase the space between the marbles which creates a more complex rotation as the marbles multiply. Since component *D* is a binding function created from the individualized harmonics within the marbles, as the energy within the marbles increases, so too does the binding energy. These variables, increasing in proportion to each other create the universal aspect ratio and the upward spiraling pathway of ascension.

Shifting perspective to the overall structure, the sphere will exhibit a slight expanding and contracting tempo resulting from the oscillations occurring within it. This oscillating tempo is a factor of the composite density, the balance within the marbles that causes them to create a helical spiral (vibration), their rotational speed around the composite (frequency), and the magnitude of the energetic waves they create (amplitude). The oscillating tempo produced by the combination of these factors is defined as its harmonic octave of density.

Chapter Nine

Understanding Oscillations

When the particulate of consciousness acquires energy, it moves. This movement is measured based on various factors termed, vibration, frequency, and wavelength. These terms attempt to convey the concept that particulate within consciousness is moving along multiple vectors that create energetic oscillations as they interact with each other. We must understand these terms before we can understand the forces that create them.

An oscillating frequency occurs when an energetic deflection within a system moves the system from equilibrium to an excited state. The excited system will then experience a force attempting to restore equilibrium, but an internal inertia causes overshoot. To bring this concept into focus consider a string on a guitar. The string is affixed to the instrument at two locations and then tensioned to produce the appropriate tonal quality. At rest, the string is content to sit motionless as it exists in equilibrium with its environment. Now consider what occurs when an energetic deflection is applied as the string is pulled in one direction and subsequently released. The string attempts to return to its resting point but the energy it has absorbed pushes it beyond neutrality as it travels in the opposite direction. The string will continue to oscillate in this manner until all the energy within it has been expended and it returns to equilibrium with its surroundings, or additional energy is imparted that continues its oscillation. Now let's translate the observed properties of the guitar string to the particulate of consciousness.

Individualized consciousness tunes their strings to be deflected by universal energy. As each consciousness plots their course, they decide their individuated tune. As the energy of creation rushes through them, each use that energy to create the oscillations within their sphere. The ability to be severely out of tune exists within the energetic separation of the lower densities and polarized constructs. As the instrument of consciousness evolves and becomes more sophisticated, tuning of the strings to resonate within the universal tempo becomes the limiting factor to further energy absorption and growth.

The universe is consciousness. All that is observable -material or otherwise- exists within its barrier membrane. Considering the rotations within consciousness that have been described, it follows that the universe is filled with particulate in motion. Much of the particulate is being used to create individualized consciousness, some has been solidified into coherent material structures, while the remainder transports creational energy as it circulates through the structure. The delineation between the generic particulate of universal consciousness and the individuated consciousnesses within it exists at the energetic partitions, or barrier membranes. Particulate within the barrier membranes is engaged in individualized experiential pathways that create unique oscillating frequencies. The individual oscillating frequencies are nurtured and encouraged because they have the potential to grow into energetic contributors. Universal particulate not actively engaged in individualized ascension is considered unpotentiated. This is the particulate of universal consciousness left to transport creational energy to the conscious spheres within it.

Continuing with our musical analogy, unpotentiated particulate would be the guitar string sitting upon a shelf in a music store waiting to be purchased and used for its intended function. A planetary consciousness would then be the case that the individual guitars are protected within. As the particulate of consciousness is bound together with the glue of shared energetics, it rises into individuality as each guitar takes shape. The sphere of individualized consciousness is the guitar upon which the strings of particulate are affixed and vibrate. The vibrations of the strings create their unique oscillating wavelength tuned through experience and are continuously energized with creational energy. The awareness of individuality that you enjoy as you read this book is the result of trillions of particulate strings uniquely oscillating to create the perception of who you think you are.

The guitar string in this example is limited in its energetic responses due to its attachment to the instrument. This designed limitation imparted intentional characteristics that allowed it to be tuned to operate synergistically with the other strings. This directly correlates to the energetic composition of consciousness and the photonic strings that comprise it. The toroidal design is a function of the forces affecting the particulate that determine the patterns of movement. The individual parameters shown in Figure 18 require tuning by the consciousness. These parameters have minimum and maximum values that combine to create the operational boundaries that form the upward spiral of ascension. The limiting factors of toroidal operation require that consciousness follow this path toward the harmonic expressions of planetary, system, galactic, and universal frequencies it exists within.

Self-Sustaining Resonance

An integral part of the oscillating system of consciousness that must be discussed is the self-sustaining and amplifying nature of resonance within rotating fields. The term resonance comes from the Latin word resonantia which meant echo or resound as it applied to the tendency of musical waves to cause a sympathetic vibration in similarly tuned systems. Electrical induction motors incorporate the principle of resonance for their operation. This occurs through the movement of electrons and magnetic fields which do not exist within the rotations of consciousness. However, the resonant interactions between the sinusoidal waves share a cause and effect that is analogous to those of consciousness.

Under the excitation of an external charge to the wiring, motors create electrical and magnetic fields that expand and contract out of phase. This phase relationship creates a self-sustaining oscillation that results in a spinning shaft.

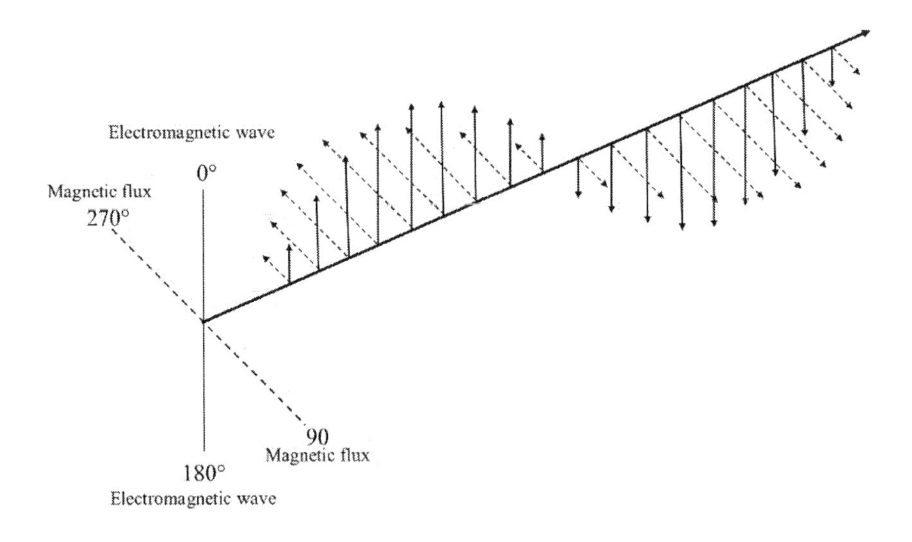

Figure 19 - Electromagnetic Resonance

This image represents an electric current traveling through a conductor. The electromagnetic wave generates a sympathetic magnetic flux wave 90 degrees out of phase. This action and resonant reaction when applied to electrical circuits is the theory that energizes electric motors. While not electromagnetic in nature, a similar resonant action occurs between the particulate of consciousness.

This requires the assistance of a capacitor and secondary windings in some motors, but the initial oscillation is creating a resonant action that will continue indefinitely while electrical potential is supplied to the main windings. If you reverse the process and apply a force that spins the shaft, the oscillating forces within the motor will generate an electrical potential at the terminus of the wires as the resonant action of electrical and magnetic flux operates in reverse. This is the difference between an electric motor that runs a pump, and a generator that creates electricity as shown in Figure 20. The same electromagnetic system that is externally charged to generate motion can also be reversed to provide an external charge.

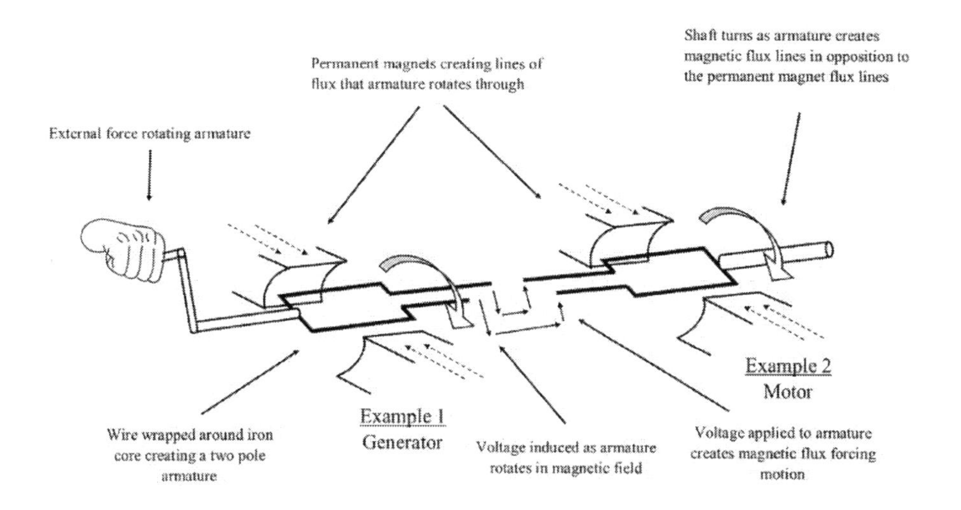

Figure 20 - Motor Generator

Example 1 represents a generator whose shaft is being turned by an external force. As the windings cut through the field being produced by the stationary magnets, the flux induces an oscillating voltage within the windings. If this voltage is then supplied to the windings of the motor in Example 2, the oscillating voltage creates the opposing magnetic flux that was shown in Figure 19. The induced magnetic flux pushes against the flux of the permanent magnets and the shaft attached to the armature rotates.

The ability of electric motors to be empowered by an external source and then switched to produce that same current is a critical concept that directly translates to toroidal spheres of consciousness and why they are created. Consciousness begins its journey as a motor that requires an external source of power. At a point in its growth, the self-sustaining nature of resonant action becomes the overwhelming energetic driver within the sphere. It is here that the motor matures into its true role as a generator within the universe.

Chapter Ten

The Dynamic Energy Engine of Self-Aware Consciousness

The sphere of consciousness is a dynamic energy engine. The term engine is derived from the Latin word "Ingenium" which is loosely translated as, innate talent, character, or genius. As the industrial revolution began, the term engine became associated with combustion machinery that converted chemical energy into motive force. We specifically associate the term engine with the vehicle of consciousness due to this evolution as a term used to describe both the conversion of energy into motion and the use of mental capacity, which perfectly describes what is occurring.

The concept of consciousness as a dynamic energy engine is critical to understanding the rotational vectors within it and why it is cultivated in low energy fields. The toroidal geometry and rotations discussed thus far are a result of conscious particulate undergoing a continuous cycle of charge and discharge. The relative charge within the individual particles determines the oscillating space generated between them and their resulting orbit within the array. A self-aware third density geometry as shown in Figure 1, includes the seat of consciousness at the center of a fully developed column. It is this central mass of particulate that generates the perception of individuality within the barrier membrane. The seat of consciousness is created as low energy photons congregate at the center due to their orbital velocities. Individually, the photons have low kinematic potential, but the aggregate density and compact rotation in this area creates the highest composite energy signature and densest oscillating frequency within the consciousness.

With the column established and the seat of consciousness energized, the third density array can hold significant amounts of energy. It is here, as consciousness moves toward the energetics of fourth density that balancing the orbital rotations within the sphere becomes the primary objective. Proper oscillating resonance is now required between the particulate and within the sphere to cause harmonic fracture and density additions. As the successive incarnations accrue, the unseen balancing within the consciousness sphere will propel embodied consciousness along an accelerating upward trajectory. It is at this point - when consciousness understands its true nature during incarnation- that tracking density expansion within the upward spiral of ascension becomes valuable.

Converting Material Energy into Conscious Energy at Lower Levels

The energy used to expand consciousness through the first three densities is supplemented through a material form experiencing existence within material constructs. The form in which consciousness embodies converts low level material energy to support the body and the creation of biophotons until it attains the efficiency to rely solely on the energy of creation. The capability of consciousness to expand through direct contact with creational energy begins when the column forms at the entry to third density. The ability to utilize creational energy is accelerated through concentrated effort to balance the rotational sphere and tune the oscillations. When mastered in upper fourth density, the need for continued embodiment within material constructs is released. Embodied experience through the first three densities is required to cultivate consciousness in the same manner as a seed must germinate within the soil and create a structure that can utilize the energy of the sun before it emerges. With few exceptions, we are all seeds of consciousness that have germinated within the ground state of a protective planetary consciousness.

Ascending Through Energetic Reductions

Consciousness is an engine under intelligent control that converts energy into motive force. The energy being converted is the creational energy that has been filtered through the barrier membrane of Earth's planetary consciousness. Recall from Figure 3 that planetary consciousness exists within the successive barrier reductions of system and galactic consciousness. These reductions are necessary to create the low energy fields required for the optimum growth of consciousness. When a planetary consciousness assumes stewardship of a construct designated for ascension, it resides at the energetic octave of sixth density. Within the barrier membrane of planetary consciousness, successive reductions in energetic availability are created that provide the ascension pathways organic consciousness will follow to sequentially increase in ability and reach parity with the octave of sixth density.

The lowest energetic construct within the planetary barrier is the ground state of first through third density. The seeds of first density exist within this construct and the buds of second density emerge from them. Second density subsequently blossoms into third density self-awareness who then strive to mature and gain access to the energetic octave of fourth density. As they enter the new energetic construct of fourth density, they find a higher creational energy field that supports their continued expansion. Entry into this increased energy requires a balanced and maturing geometry of consciousness. An unprepared mid-level third density consciousness attempting to enter this energy would find itself increasingly unbalanced as the acceleration of particulate amplified any imperfections within their toroidal array. Since fourth density is an embodied density, the upper tier of first, and some of second density also exist here in service to the fourth density collectives. This is possible due to the limited energetic capacity within fully formed first and second density consciousness. The rotations within their spherical arrays are compact and lack a fully formed central column. This allows them to remain viable within the increased energies and in service to the collective. When the fourth density collectives mature, they graduate into the next energetic construct to continue their growth in energetic capacitance. The last energetic separation is reserved for fifth density consciousness and is where the ascending collectives from all energetic timeline constructs meet and merge as they prepare for integration with the planetary consciousness. These energetic construct separations allow consciousness to form and expand within energetic gradients conducive to their growth.

The Flow within Consciousness

To understand how the energetic components defined in Figure 18 create the toroidal sphere and the seat of consciousness, we must begin with a consciousness in the early stages of third density. At this energy level the sphere is creating a slight neutral zone, or vortex, at the center of the column that pulls creational energy toward it. Consciousness entering third density has a low energetic capacity and the difference between the neutral vortex and external creational energy is slight. Because of this, the flow of creational energy toward the vortex follows the path of least resistance as it moves up from the bottom of the column following the flow of energetically depleted particulate within the sphere. The neutral vortex at the center of the column is being created by the seat of consciousness; low energy photonic particulate held in a tightly packed array as resonant attraction within the particulate overpowers the weakened opposing kinematic forces. These low energy photons spin around their individual axis as they travel in a helical motion. This creates a rotational spin of the particulate and an orbital angular momentum as the particles move in the direction of their spin, constrained by the attractive forces of neighboring particles.

Looking at a cross section of a third density array, the ascending orbital trajectories associated with the energy of the particulate comes into focus.

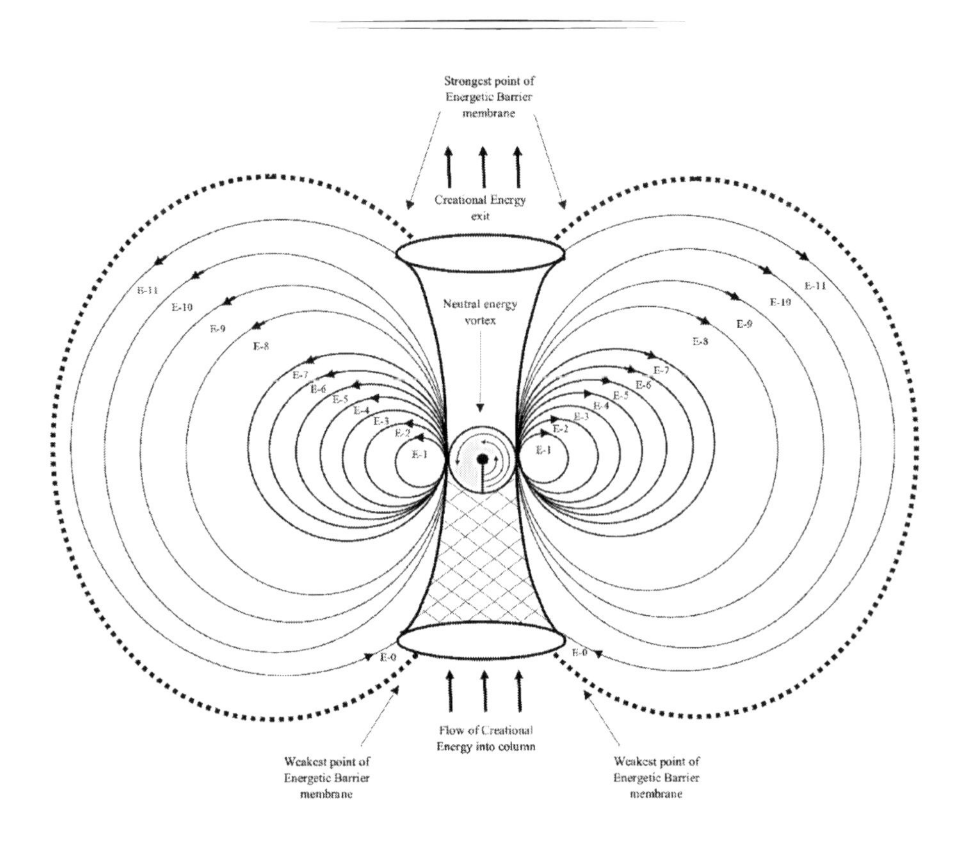

Figure 21 - Conscious Flow

The image represents a simplified cut-away view of the rotations within a third density consciousness. The neutral energy vortex at the center of the column is being created by the rapid and dense flow of particulate within the seat of consciousness represented by pathways E-1 through E-7. Creational energy flows upward into the column and transfers its energy to the rotating particulate before exiting out the top. With each rotation through the column, the particulate gains energy and ascends through the orbital paths until it travels around the sphere at E-11. This pathway energizes the barrier membrane as it depletes the charge within the particle. The particle then enters the bottom of the column at E-0 to repeat the process and reenergize.

The neutral vortex at the center of Figure 21 forms as depleted particulate becomes tightly packed as it regains energy through successive exposures to creational energy entering the column. The particulate will increase their orbital paths from this location with increasing orbital angular momentum. Starting with position E-11, a highly charged particle exits the column at the outer periphery of the sphere. As it spins along its trajectory, the energy it contains creates an energetic manifold that joins with other particles traveling along pathway E-11. These tangentially bundled manifolds create an energetic barrier that surrounds and protects the sphere. A barrier is defined as something that prevents or blocks movement from one location to another, and that is what this energetic field is doing. It is protecting the lower energy oscillations within the array from external energy that might overpower and realign it. The ability of this barrier to shield the individual energetic signatures within it is directly proportional to the energy contained in the particulate traveling along the E-11 path.

The Zero Point of Consciousness

As the photon travels around the periphery, it loses potential as it interacts with external energy and protects the oscillating signature of the sphere. Having expended its energy during the interaction, it enters the bottom of the column at position E-0. The energy remaining within the particle at E-0 is considered the consciousnesses zero point, and this is an important concept of ascension. The upward spiral of ascension is tracking several variables. Moving upward within the spiral reflects an increasing energetic capacity which is reflected by the increasing radius from the ground state of first density. The increasing radius of the spiral directly corresponds to the energy remaining within the outer valence particles at position E-0 before they enter the column and reenergize. This is the sliding scale of zero point within consciousness. This concept will be expanded upon later.

Returning to Figure 21, the neutral zone vortex at the center pulls the depleted particle into the bottom of the column. Depleted of energy, the binding forces are overwhelming, and the particle is pulled into the center of the seat of consciousness along path E-1. The binding forces remain the overwhelming force as the particle rotates within the seat of consciousness. Repeated exposure to creational energy within this spinning loop begins to recharge the particle and after multiple rotations within the center along paths E-2 through E-7, it exits the seat of consciousness at path E-8. The energy within the particle has steadily increased and the energy of momentum now exceeds the binding forces within the seat of consciousness. The particle picks up additional energy with each successive exposure to creational energy in the column as it travels along paths E-9 and E-10. As it does this, the energetic layers between the particulate become wider as the energetic manifolds between layers pushes against the particulate binding energy. If balance exists, the widening creates the energetic equivalent of lubrication which allows the particles to increase their rate of travel. When the particles reach a fully energized state, they again exit along path E-11. The fully energized state of particulate within a consciousness at path E-11 is dependent upon several parameters within consciousness that will be explained. As the parameters change, the potential charge at E-11 also changes. This is the primary objective of ascending in consciousness. By using your awareness, you become a mechanic of consciousness and tune the parameters of your dynamic energy engine to increase the charge of particulate traveling along path E-11 to its fullest potential.

While the preceding example followed a particle along eleven points within its path, the sphere of consciousness is created through the interlocking rotation of millions of particles stacked side by side and one upon the other. The space between one energetic layer and the next depends upon the energy within the particulate. This creates a high particulate density at the seat of consciousness with the particulate increasing in energy with each orbit creating larger spaces between the layers. The effect is a decreasing particulate density from the nucleus outward as the energy increases until it reaches the outer valence. This is the flow within the engine of consciousness that converts raw creational energy into a coherent oscillating motive force. With a basic understanding of the flow, we turn our attention to the nuances of the energetic oscillations, the interactions they create, and their relationship to harmonic resonance.

Chapter Eleven

The Variable Factors Within the Consciousness Equation

The individual photons spin as they move within the sphere (component *A*). The rate of this spin contributes to the orbital momentum of the particle as it travels around the sphere (component *B*) as previously shown in Figure 18. This concept is the foundational component that creates the harmonics of individualized consciousness. The sphere of consciousness is composed of particles stacked layer upon layer moving in this manner buoyed by the interactions between the energy they contain. The circumference of the sphere is dependent upon the amount of particulate, the successive rotating layers they create, and the energetic gap between the layers. If you expand this concept to the millions of particles that comprise a consciousness, the oscillating nature of the sphere becomes apparent. This oscillating interaction has been created by unique perspectives amassed through experience, and they are what makes each of us a unique fragment within universal consciousness.

Your ability to make your own choices and choose your experiences guarantees the unique perspectives of oscillating consciousness. Each choice you make brings an experience that creates an energetic oscillation within your consciousness. Within the human form, emotions provide the clearest physical indicator of what energies you are creating. The emotional contrast between love and hate requires no discussion. The difference in energies and resulting oscillations these experiences create in consciousness are just as clear. As these experiences are incorporated into the sphere of consciousness, we find a composite structure of individual particulate uniquely oscillating from the energy they contain. Each particle creates an energetic field associated with its oscillating frequency as it completes an orbit around the sphere. These interlocking energetic fields expand and contract dependent upon the interactions between the energetic field of other particles in proximity. Within a single self-aware entity, there are millions of oscillations combining to create the energetic bandwidth of that consciousness.

Balance and Tangental Phase Relationships within Photonic Layers

An individual consciousness seeking higher potential ascends in density along the upward spiral. The spiral is not a single line, but a tube that allows each consciousness to plot their own energetic course within it. The pathway each consciousness travels is plotted within the tube based on the oscillating bandwidth it contains. The oscillating bandwidth can be a harmonious symphony, or one that requires tuning. Tuning occurs as consciousness begins to focus upon balancing their energetics. Understanding the concept of balance is critical to using the graphs that are about to be presented. Thus far, balance within consciousness has been related to overall rotation of photonic particulate. Like the tire on a car, the fundamental concept is that a rotating array will spin faster and more efficiently if it is balanced as energy is increased. Applying that concept to consciousness as a composite array allows you to grasp the overall objective. However, consciousness is comprised of millions of particles spinning and interacting with each other based on individual rotational vectors. If we apply the tire concept to each particle, we find that we must individually balance millions of tires. The imbalance of one subsequently affects the balance of another, which cascades through the sphere. If left uncorrected, minor imbalances can become major impediments to energy expansion. Additionally, polarized constructs allow an opposing rotation to be embraced which adds complexity as balanced expansion can then be achieved through positive or negative focus.

Within Figure 18 is the graph of tangental phase angle. This graph compares the angle of one wave within a layer of rotation to another to examine the balance between them. Looking closer at the graph we see that there are five lines that meet at a common point.

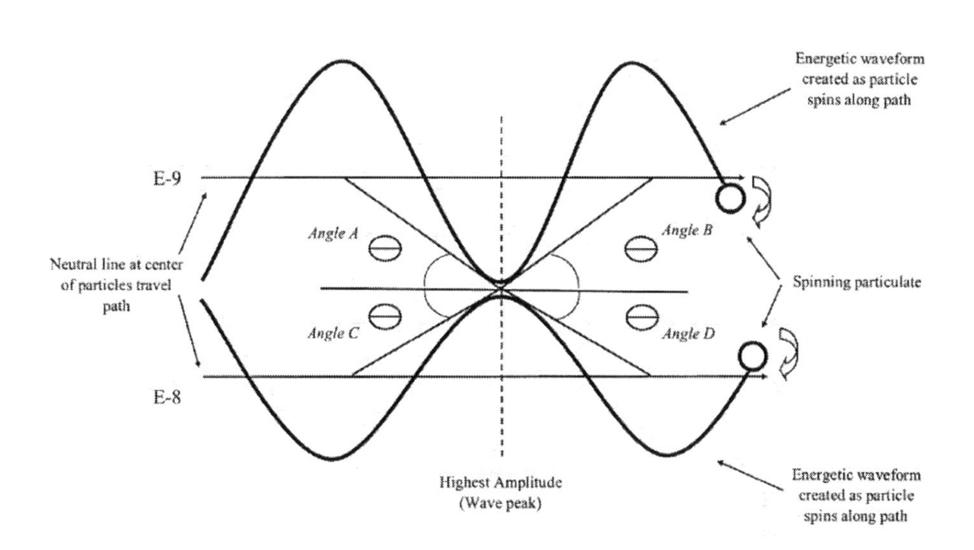

Figure 22 - Tangental Phase Angle

The image shows two particles traveling along pathway E-9 and E-8 as they move within the conscious array and create their respective energetic waveforms. If the particulate is balanced it will create a uniform wave along its path. The wave increases in amplitude as the particle gains energy and climbs from pathway E-8 to E-9. Balance is measured by the change in the tangental phase angles along each pathway *(°A/°B or °C/°D)* and between pathways (*°A/°C or °B/°D*). These measurements, taken at various locations within consciousness, determines the balance and efficiency within the sphere. Pathway E-11 is a depleting pathway that energizes the barrier membrane. Its efficiency is measured by the energy it contains as it exits the top of the column, and the energy that remains as it enters the bottom.

The horizontal line of the graph in Figure 22 represents neutral between two layers of photons traveling around the sphere. Regardless of where the two layers are within the consciousness or the distance between layers, this line represents the midpoint of that distance. A tangent is defined as a line that touches a curved surface at a point but does not cross it. The four diagonal lines intersecting the horizontal line are the tangents formed as the length of each wave is related to its peak on the neutral line. As the lines are drawn, they create four tangental phase angles that are measured from the neutral line. The particulate of consciousness is in a constant state of charge as it rotates through the sphere. The relationship between the phase angles of the waves within the layers will reflect the balance or imbalance of the consciousness. Figure 22 reflects a balanced consciousness seeking higher energetics. The inner layer waveform is being created from pathway E-8 and the outer layer is pathway E-9. The lower energy inner wave of E-8 will have a longer wavelength and produce a smaller phase angle when measured at *°C and °D*. The higher energy in layer E-9 will create a shorter wavelength with higher amplitude as the particle spins faster, producing a larger phase angle measurement at *°A and °B*. If the particle is balanced, the product of *A/B* or *C/D* would be zero or nearly zero. Since the calculation involves pathways at different energy levels, the product of *A/C* or *B/D* should be a positive value. If balance exists in both layers, the products of *A/C* and *B/D* will be equal. Balance within consciousness is calculated in this manner and the products are part of the variables plotted within the upward spiral. Pathway E-11 is a depleting pathway where the energy of the particulate interacts with external energy and loses its charge as it protects the sphere. In this instance the tangental phase relationship between E-11 and E-10 would reflect the energetic drain a particle traveling along pathway E-11 is experiencing.

To give this concept some depth, consider what would happen if one of the particles being observed acquired some negative polarization. Negative polarity is defined as a photonic rotation that opposes the universal default and acts to absorb creational energy. This concept was explained in detail in the first book. The initial effect of polarization is that the helical spin of the affected photons slow excessively as their energy is absorbed. Negative polarity is first absorbed through the outer valance photons as it impacts the barrier membrane. This draws the energy from the particles attempting to maintain the barrier. If the drain is large enough, the particles lose all energy as they travel around the sphere. If the negative energy continues, the energetically depleted particle will reverse rotation before entering the column at E-0. If the consciousness allows the negative and includes it in its focus, reverse spinning particulate will gain energy within the seat of consciousness and propagate through the sphere. If the negative impact is then measured, the normal phase angle relationship between pathway E-8 and

E-9 from Figure 22 will appear inverted. The imbalance will continue until consciousness decides upon a pathway forward and focuses upon it.

This level of detail regarding the mechanics of consciousness has not been provided to lead the reader into trigonometric calculations as they attempt to find balance. It is meant to show what balance within consciousness represents and that it can be mathematically determined. The resonance created as the waveforms interact at various phase angles determines the overall harmonic of consciousness. These components are part of the calculations that determine position within the logarithmic spiral of ascension.

Chapter Twelve

The Logarithmic Spiral of Ascension

When separate oscillating systems contain the same wavelength or integrals of the same wavelength, they create a harmonic resonance between them that is larger than the sum of the parts. This is true of musical instruments where the resulting harmonies create pleasant auditory sounds, and true of consciousness where the harmonically tuned emanations of the individual compound within their sphere and also interact with the emanations of others that are in sympathetic resonance. Like musical scales, the oscillating octaves of consciousness and their integrals are spatially scaled subdivisions of energetic emanations that increase in intensity and complexity from the ground state of a single photon to the oscillating composite frequency of fully ascended consciousness. Consciousness ascending within the universe follows the upward spiraling pathway shown in Figure 7.

The perspective of individualized consciousness that we all possess is predicated on the freedom to choose your own path. For this reason, the spiral is not a singular path upward where deviation is impossible. It instead resembles a tube where consciousness can explore and deviate from the optimum ascending trajectory. The boundaries of the tube represent the maximum deviation between the energetic variables within the sphere of consciousness that it can withstand and remain a coherent oscillating complex. Consciousness pushed outside of the upward spiral pathway as it exceeds one or more variables would quickly lose effective rotation. A loss of rotation means a loss of coherent oscillation and correlates to a dissolution of the sphere and loss of individual self-awareness. This can occur as a purpose driven realignment to restart stalled consciousness in lower densities, and at upper densities as ascended collectives are prepared for galactic capabilities.

The sphere of consciousness is constrained within the upward logarithmic spiral by the binding force (component *D* from Figure 18) and three variables that combine to produce a fourth:

- Composite particulate density.
- The directional spin and momentum of the individual particulate as a result of the energy it contains (component *A* and *B* from Figure 18)
- The diameter of the energetic manifold created from the amount of energy within particles (component *C* from Figure 18)

These variables combine to produce the individual waveform profiles that were measured in Figure 22. The individual waveform profiles combine to create the harmonic resonance that represents the bandwidth of the consciousness. Harmonic resonance is created in pathways E-1 through E11 as the waves interact sympathetically and form multiples of the fundamental base wavelength. When balanced, the resonant action between them acts as a multiplier to the intensity (amplitude) of energy projected from the consciousness.

Amplitude is a measure of the energetic intensity of a wave. This is the distance between neutrality and the peak of the energetic waveform that results as spinning particulate travels around the sphere of consciousness.

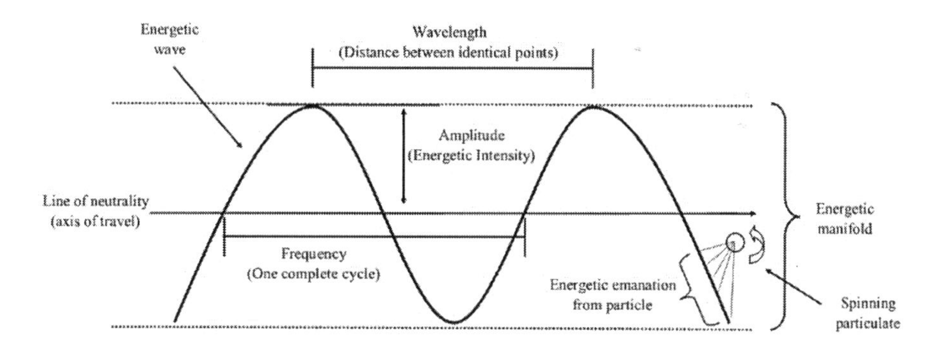

Figure 23 – Amplitude

Amplitude is the measure of the energetic intensity of a wave. As particulate spins along its trajectory it emits energetic waves. The central axis of the spiral creates the line of neutrality as shown in Figure 11. The intensity of energy radiated from the particle as it travels is measured from the line of neutrality and is termed amplitude.

The amplitude of the energetic wave creates the radius of the individual energetic manifold shown in Figure 14.

The amplitude of the lowest -baseline- oscillating wavelength and the amplitude of the highest oscillating wavelength reflect the operating bandwidth that each consciousness emits and is measured in relationship to the octave densities. The ascending energy contained within the octaves and sub-octaves of harmonic resonance are represented as the radius of the upward spiral increases around its central axis.

The photonic particulate of consciousness is not bound by the laws of locality that limit velocity to the speed of light. The governing factors on particulate speed and wavelength are instead related to the geometry of the sphere and the energy of the particulate affecting the variables listed in Figure 18. As the sphere of consciousness becomes larger and more complex, an increasing amount of energy is translated into the angular rotation of the particulate (component *A)* which translates to its orbital velocity around the sphere (component *B*). When this process is viewed as a composite energetic emanation, the oscillating frequency and energetic amplitude of consciousness increase together. It is the increasing density, coupled with increasing frequency and amplitude that create movement within the upward spiral.

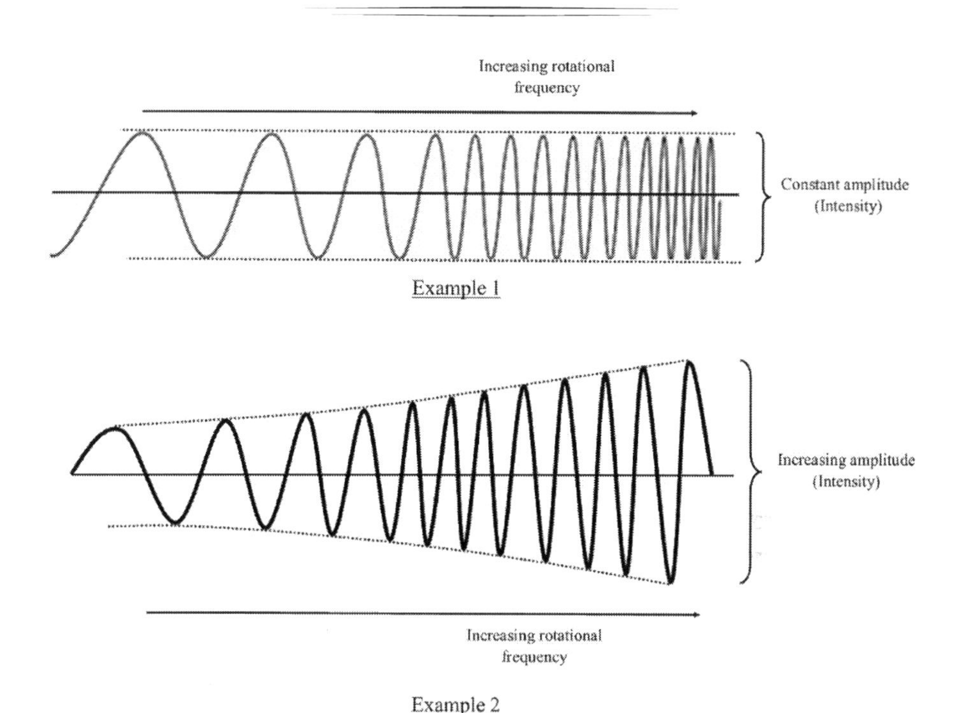

Figure 24 - Increasing Frequency and Amplitude

Example 1 represents the frequency of electromagnetic emanation of a photon increasing in energy while locked within a material construct (see Figure 8). The particle is bound to and interacting within the laws of locality. This limits the speed at which it and its electromagnetic emanations can travel as they propagate through the material. This is represented in the graph as an amplitude that remains constant while the frequency of waves increases as the photon spins faster about its axis. The waves in Example 1 are measured using the "Principal of locality" as they interact with material in ways that can be observed and quantified.

Example 2 represents the increasing amplitude and frequency of a photon of consciousness as it gains energy. While the graph shows a relatively stable speed, the speed at which a particle travels is determined by the energy within it, the balance it contains, and energetic effects from other particles comprising the consciousness sphere.

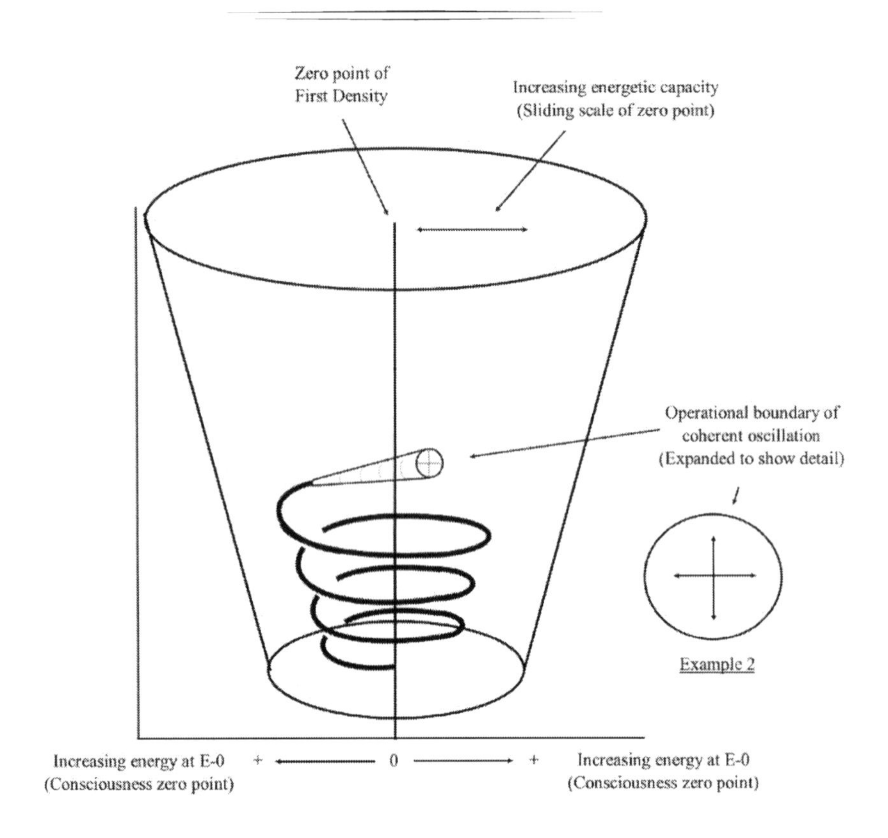

Figure 25 - Three-Dimensional Upward Spiral

The upward spiral is a three-dimensional graph that plots the increasing energetic capacity of consciousness and the resulting harmonic resonance it contains. The effective energy and resonance of the consciousness is plotted within the operational boundaries of the tube. Example 2 shows an expanded view of the tube's cross section. The center of the tube represents perfect harmonic resonance within any octave or sub-octave. This image represents a non-polarized pathway of ascension. The vertical line at the center of the spiral represents the ground state of first density where E-11 and E-0 are both zero (no energy). As the energy remaining at E-0 increases, the radius of the spiral increases from the ground state axis. The particulate pathways that included E-0 were shown Figure 21.

Figure 25 is a three-dimensional view of the upward logarithmic spiral of ascension. The spiral increases in diameter as it rises from ground state as it tracks the increasing energetic capacity of consciousness within it. The center line is the ground state from which consciousness ascends. This ground state represents zero energy within a single particle as it begins its journey. The spiral expands from the ground state as it tracks the generic energy increases of first and second density. When a third density geometry is attained, the spiral tracks the variables of energetic potential and harmonic resonance within the ascending octaves. The expanding radius from the central axis is a function of the energy remaining at E-0 after the highest energy particles energize the barrier membrane. E-0 is the lowest particulate energy state and is considered the zero point of any consciousness. At the entry of first density, this zero point is a literal energetic representation. As consciousness gains energy and ascends the spiral, the zero point moves with it as an increasing amount of energy remains within the particles at their lowest state.

Moving from one octave to the next is represented by one full rotation around the spiral. The height of the spiral at any point represents the particulate density of consciousness at that location. As particulate density increases, oscillating bandwidth follows as the increasing particulate creates new pathways around the sphere (E-12, E-13, E-14, etc.). For ease of understanding, the orbital pathways will remain labeled as E-1 through E-11 as shown in Figure 21. However, density addition creates new orbital pathways as consciousness ascends the spiral and increases in complexity. When consciousness enters the octave of fourth density, it has thousands of layers. It is here that the quest toward becoming a self-sustaining multi-wave generator begins in earnest.

As consciousness moves upward it increases in rotating frequency and amplitude. While all particulate layers within consciousness produce waveforms that combine to create the overall oscillating bandwidth, the outer pathway's frequency and amplitude is representative of total energetic potential. Measuring the energy differential along pathway E-11 to E-0 provides a direct measurement of energetic capacity and balance.

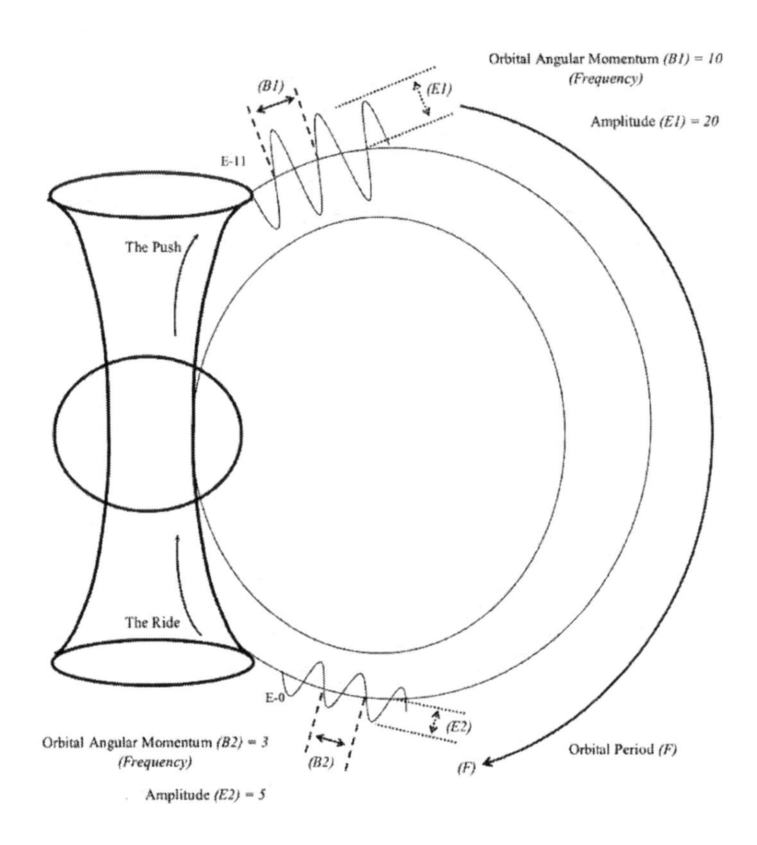

Figure 26 - Amplitude and Orbital Period

The image shows a particle traveling around outer valence pathway E-11 as it energizes the protective barrier membrane. The particle exits the top of the column fully charged and contains the highest orbital angular momentum *(B1)* and energetic amplitude *(E1)*. Orbital angular momentum is simplified to a measure of wave frequency per length of travel. Wave frequency begins at a value of 10 waves per unit length at *(B1)* and reduces to a value of 3 per unit length at *(B2)* as the particle loses energy. The amplitude of the wave begins at 20 at *(E1)* and reduces to 5 at *(E2)*. Since the particle is losing energy and momentum as it travels, the total time of orbit is measured as orbital period *(F)*. These arbitrary values reflect a third density consciousness with sufficient energy to move into the next sub-octave of harmonic resonance.

Figure 26 shows the particulate completing an orbit around the outer valence. The energy of the fully charged particle is measured in wave amplitude as it exits the column at E-11. The example shows an amplitude of twenty at *E1*. The particle loses energy as it creates the barrier and is again measured at the fully depleted state of E-0 where it measures as five at *E2* before re-entering the column. The particle has lost energy which also translates to a loss of momentum. High energy within the particle exiting at E-11 creates a high rate of spin and produces more energetic waves per unit of travel. This is seen as the angular momentum -measured as frequency- at E-11 begins at ten waves per unit of travel *(B1)* and ends at three waves per unit of travel *(B2)* before re-entering the column. To compensate for the changing value of momentum along the pathway, the entire orbital period is measured as *(F)*.

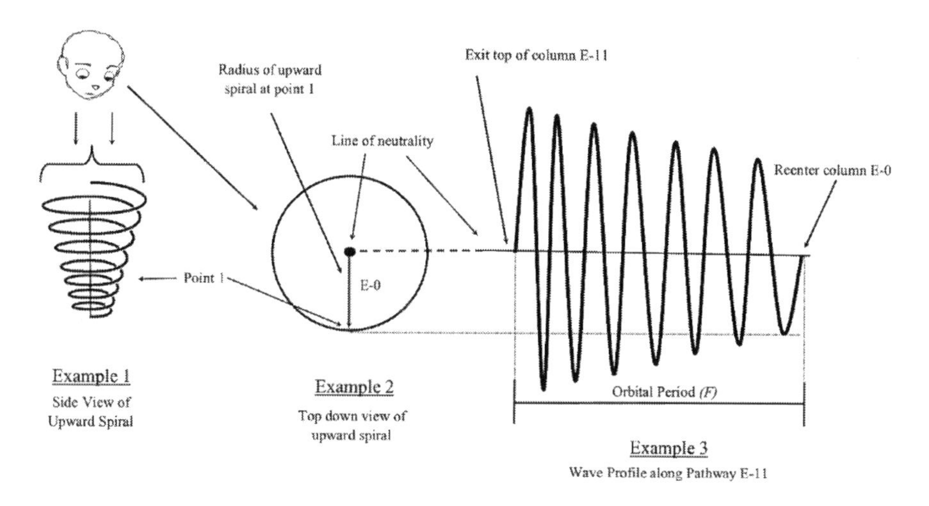

Figure 27 - Sine Wave Calculation

Example 1 shows the upward spiral of ascension with a consciousness existing within it at point 1. Looking down from the top, the radius of point 1 from the centerline of neutrality is equal to the amplitude of the energetic wave produced at pathway E-0 as shown in Example 2. The line of neutrality from Example 1 is the center of Example 2. The energetic oscillation created as the particle travels along pathway E-11 to E-0 is shown in Example 3. The particle exits the column with a large amount of energy and transfers it to the barrier membrane. This is shown as a steadily decreasing amplitude and frequency as the particle loses energy. The unused energy remaining in the particle at Pathway E-0 determines the location within the upward spiral.

Figure 27 shows a top down view of the upward spiral. The amplitude of E-0 determines where the consciousness is plotted within the upward spiral. The radius of the spiral from the line of neutrality at any point corresponds to the amplitude of E-0. Example 1 shows someone looking down upon the spiral and observing a consciousness at point 1. Example 2 shows that top down perspective with the radius of the circle representing the amplitude of E-0 for the consciousness at point 1. Note the line of neutrality in Example 2 shown as the point in the center is also reflected as the neutral point for the waveform in Example 3. The Oscillating wave represented in Example 3 is the frequency and wavelength created along its pathway as a particle exits at E-11, energizes the barrier membrane while losing energy, and reenters the column at E-0.

The value of E-0 is a direct representation of the energetic capacitance within consciousness. The line extending from the last wave in Example 3 back to the arrow of Example 2 shows the relationship between its amplitude at E-0 and its location within the spiral. When the value of E-0 reaches parity within an octave or sub-octave, the consciousness is easily shielding itself from the energetic construct and is in resonance with the octave. When resonance within an octave is achieved, it becomes the foundation from which the next progression is sought. Like the body builder who finds the weight they lift no longer challenging, consciousness with excess energy at E-0 must increase the resistance by stepping into the next octave for continued growth.

Transitioning from the third to fourth density octave is a significant step that requires a strong barrier membrane. When consciousness nears the transition to fourth density, a considerable amount of energy remains at E-0. This is required to move into the next doubling. When this occurs, the particles exiting at pathway E-11 begin to emit a pulse as the highest amplitude wave emerges from the column and energizes the barrier. This pulse will follow behind the particle as it travels around the pathway to E-0. The rate of pulsation is measured using the orbital period *(F)*. This is an important concept that will be expanded upon.

Light Chambers and the Variables of Consciousness

The perspective thus far has been one of a barrier membrane around consciousness that is energized through the depletion of potential within the rotating particulate. The first book discussed the concept of light chambers that were used to remove polarization and reorient consciousness within the positive pathway. These chambers were designed with an understanding of the concepts of consciousness that are being presented here. Consciousness entering these chambers were measured for their energetic capacity, rotational balance, and harmonic resonance. The chamber was then set to bombard the barrier membrane with a predetermined amount of creational energy that would impact but not penetrate the barrier. As particulate traveled around pathway E-11, rather than depleting their energy as they energized the barrier, they were reenergized as the barrier operated in reverse. Inefficient or negative rotations within the consciousness were realigned to the positive as they cycled through pathway E-11. Consciousness would remain in the chamber at least one complete particulate cycle where all the particulate density had one exposure in the barrier. Several cycles may be required if the consciousness had acquired a large polarization exposure. The effectiveness of the light chamber is dependent upon the willingness and focus of the consciousness. Realignment in this manner is non-invasive and requires that the consciousness allow permeability within their barrier. A consciousness focused upon a negative pathway and unwilling to release the orientation would find no lasting benefit to the procedure. The effect of exposure would be some loss of negative polarization as they fought to keep their barrier energized and retain their chosen focus.

The light chamber process and results can be related to warfare in the physical. The soldier who fights long and hard becomes weary and loses focus. Soldiers need intermittent rest and recovery periods to continue to be effective. These are the consciousnesses who willingly enter the light chambers and have the weariness of exposure to polarization removed. The unwilling light chamber participant would then be a soldier who is captured and injured during interrogation before being released. Their wounds will require a longer recovery period before they can return as an effective soldier, but they will return.

Within the Tube of Ascension

The third density portion of the upward spiral brings self-awareness and the resulting self-determination of free will choice. The rotating sphere has attained the proper geometry but lacks the energetic capacity to synchronize harmonically with the sixth density consciousness it resides within. Reaching sixth density from third density is a gradual process of increasing density and managing the resulting increase in oscillating bandwidth in steps. Each step contains an external oscillating bandwidth that the consciousness must harmonically tune to. The bandwidth in this case is the octave or sub-octave step of the spiral where consciousness finds itself relative to its particulate density. Synchronization within an increasing oscillating bandwidth continues in this manner until locked harmonic resonance is achieved at entry into the sixth density octave. Adding the concept of synchronization with an external harmonic requires a closer inspection of the portion of the spiral that traverses third through fifth density. This area represents a self-aware conscious geometry that is seeking to balance increasingly complex internal oscillations and match them to an external requirement. Consciousness is under a constant state of expansion as it steps upward. Balance within the third through fifth density portion of the spiral requires continuous management of the oscillating interactions.

With this understanding, we can now place the expanded radial cross section of the tube from Figure 25 on a three-axis graph and examine the relationship between the variables considering the concept of internal management to obtain harmony within the spiral.

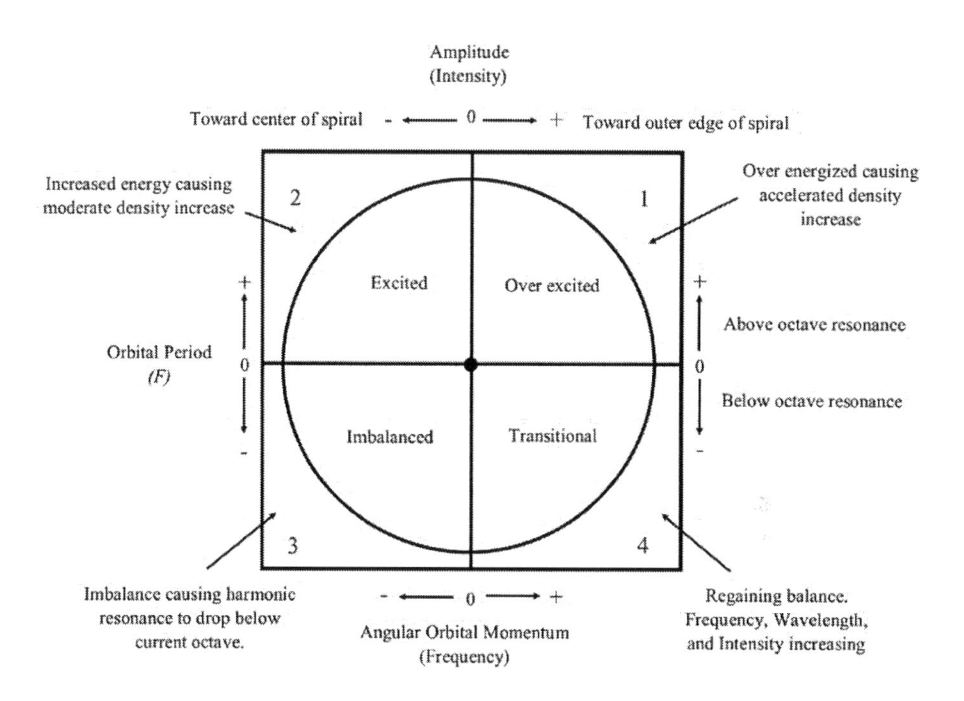

Figure 28 - Radial Cross Section

The image above is a radial cross section of the upward spiral. The four quadrants reflect how the changing variables affect the stability of consciousness within the upward spiral. Consciousness will seek the centerline of balance within any octave or sub-octave before proceeding higher. The zero indicator represents harmonic balance within the current octave or sub-octave for that variable.

The diameter of the tube has been expanded for the example in Figure 28, but the pathway of ascension within non-polarized constructs allows for deviations as a single trajectory would be undesirable. The ability to choose a course within the radius utilizes free will while assuring individuality of the composite bandwidth being created within the consciousness. Deviation from harmonic resonance at the centerline also causes imbalances between the variables that push expansion of the lagging parameters.

Looking at the graph, the center represents perfect harmonic resonance within the octave or sub-octave of a density level. This is also the point where the energy at pathway E-0 is optimum for that octave. The objective is not to find harmonic balance and remain there, but to achieve it and push ever higher. Above the horizontal line, the parameters diverge as one or more variables becomes imbalanced in relation to the others. This initiates an energetic correction within the consciousness to regain balance. An imbalance above the horizontal equates to over energized particulate and causes density additions to rebalance the array. Once acquired, particulate density is not lost. An imbalance above the horizontal will push the consciousness farther up the spiral pathway as it adds density and seeks resonance within a new sub-octave.

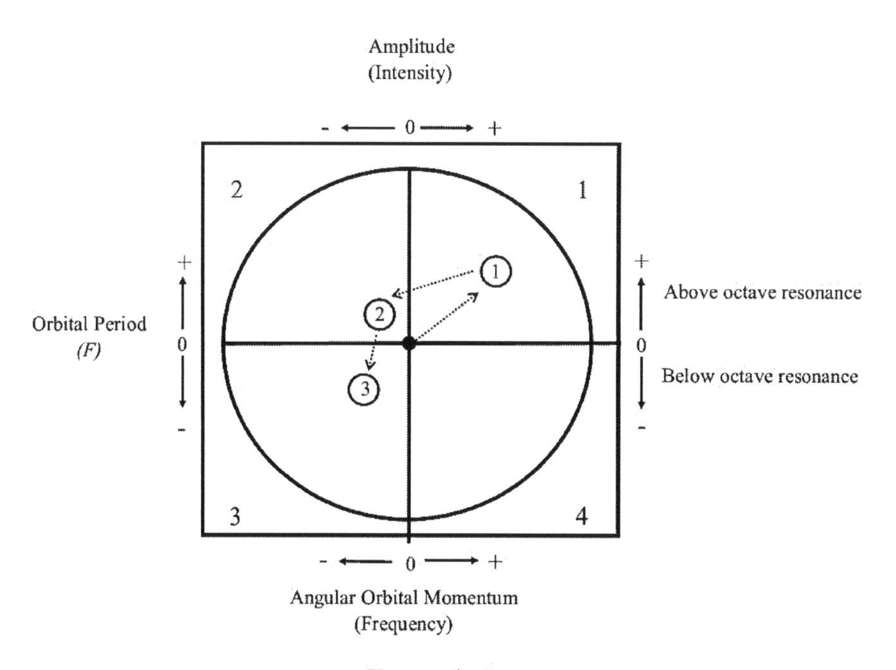

Example 1

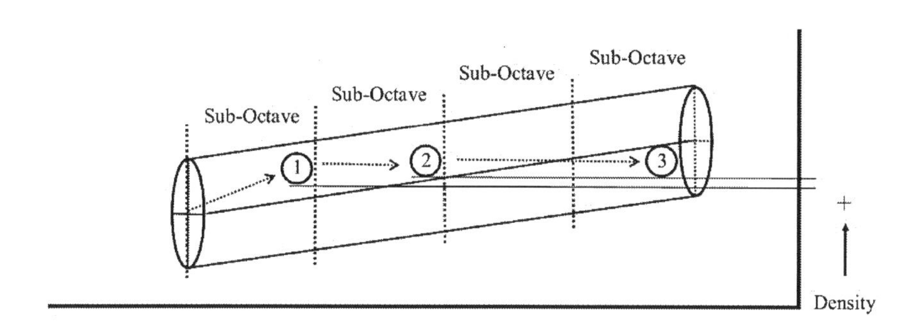

Example 2

Figure 29 - Non-Polarity Movement

Example 1 is a radial view of the upward spiral and shows a consciousness initially in resonance with their current sub-octave gaining energy and moving to position 1. The excess energy causes particulate density to increase. As the energy is shared among the newly created particulate, over excitation slows and the consciousness moves to position 2. Density expansion continues until imbalance occurs within the next sub-octave represented by position 3. Harmonic resonance must be regained before expansion will resume.

Example 2 is an axial view of the upward spiral as the consciousness moves through the positions. Once acquired, density is not lost and is the foundation for the next step. The line under position 1 is the density level used to move to position 2. The line under position 2 is the density acquired from the step up and is used to move forward two sub-octaves.

Figure 29 represents a typical pathway of expansion in a non-polarized construct. Example 1 shows the pathway of expansion for a consciousness initially existing in harmonic balance with a sub-octave. As the energy within its array increases the particles become over excited, it pushes the frequency and amplitude values of the consciousness into position 1. This creates an energetic imbalance within the particulate and an increase in density occurs as the particles undergo energetic division as they seek to rebalance the system. There is a slight lag between overexcitation and particulate multiplication as the rotating system responds to the imbalance.

As the density of the consciousness responds to match the increased frequency and amplitude, excitation slows, and the consciousness moves to position 2. As particulate density compensates for the energy, it pushes the consciousness forward and upward along the spiral. This continues until the additional density causes an imbalance as the consciousness moves to position 3. Looking at the axial view of the spiral in Example 2 we begin to see the upward trajectory the imbalance created. The initial overexcitation pushed the consciousness upward to position 1. As density increased the consciousness moved forward into the next sub-octave as it attempted to rebalance at position 2. Density expansion initially lags overexcitation and then overshoots perfect balance within a sub-octave. This occurs as the particles energizing the barrier at pathway E-11 continue to multiply until the barrier once again becomes a net drain. This is shown as the consciousness moves two sub-octaves from position 2 into imbalance at position 3. From here it will recenter in harmonic balance with the new sub-octave before once again moving upward and forward.

This example represents what is occurring within consciousness as it moves upward along the ascending spiral. Once acquired, density is never lost during the natural progression of ascension. Therefore, density is the denominating factor within the spiraling graph of consciousness. You cannot lose density, but you can lose rotational balance which translates into a reduction of oscillating frequency, amplitude and orbital period. How far out of balance consciousness can travel is limited by density and whether it exists within a polarized construct.

There are twelve distinct octaves of conscious density within this universe. The ability to solidify material exists within the lower ten. The frequency, amplitude, and particulate composite of consciousness within first and second densities are so low that the ascending spiral has a negligible cross section. This is a result of the limited resonant capacity within the still forming spheres of consciousness. When one parameter changes, the others immediately follow. At the other end of the spectrum, as consciousness moves into sixth density the harmonic resonance within the collective is firmly established and creating a rotational torque that locks the individual spheres into a synchronous spin. From this point upward, collective direction is required to change parameters and where one goes, the others must follow. Sixth density is also the entry to production within the universal grid. This is the definition of unity consciousness and as you would expect, the cross section of the upward spiral again becomes negligible.

The concept of synchronous spin within a collective of consciousness and the universal grid can be related to the concepts within electrical generation. The electrical grids that supply power to individual users have numerous sources connected to them generating the power that is available. This alternating current cycles at a set frequency that your personal devices need to operate properly. Each individual generator attempting to connect, and supply power must match the oscillating frequency of the grid. Once the frequency is matched, the generator must also be capable of supplying power to the grid or the generator will become a motor as power from the grid flows into it instead of from the generator as was illustrated in Figure 20. Consciousness attempting to enter sixth density has reached the capacity within itself to become a generator and must now match the operating frequency of the sixth density collective -and the universal grid- it wishes to join.

The previous images and discussion represent the pathway upward through non-polarized constructs toward sixth density. We must now discuss the deformation that polarity within consciousness causes to the upward spiral of ascension.

Chapter Thirteen

Polarity within Ascension

Everything exists within a carefully constructed balance of orderly progressions and rotations. The concept of polarity within consciousness was created to serve as a moderate obstacle within the upward spiral of ascension in the third through fifth densities. It is here that the rotations of consciousness begin to become self-energizing and mature into collective synchronization. Negative polarization provides an increased focus upon self-interest as those acquiring the reverse rotations are pulled away from the harmonic oscillations of unity. This creates an impediment to the creation of the planetary collective that requires a focus upon positivity to neutralize. Ascending consciousness must strive to obtain collectivity by offsetting negative polarity within their construct as they move through polarized densities toward the harmonic unity of sixth density. By creating reversed rotational possibilities within the particulate of consciousness, the cross section of available pathways was expanded. If we straighten the third through fifth density section of the upward spiral of consciousness and look at an axial cross section in its entirety, we see a bulge that begins at the entry to third density, expands continually into fifth density, and contracts abruptly at the entry into sixth density.

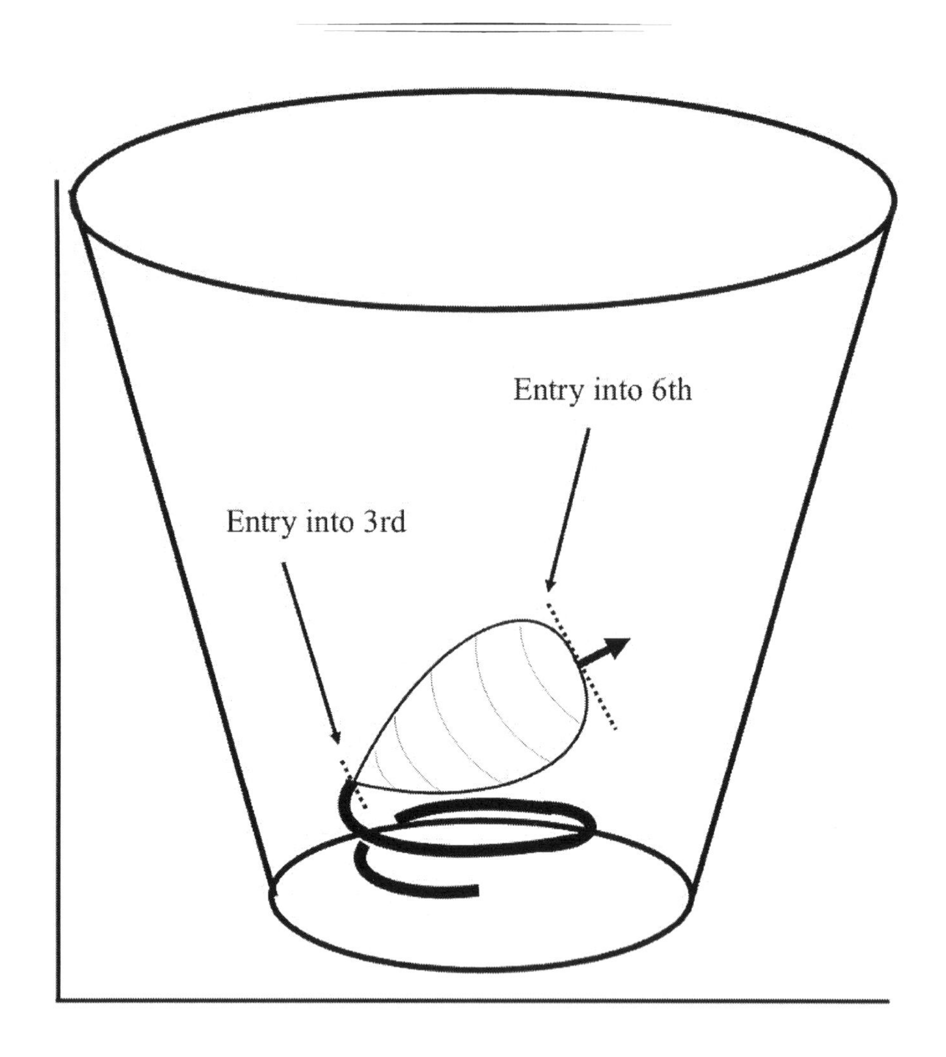

Figure 30 - Polarized Envelope

The image above shows the upward spiral of ascension with the expanded envelope of polarity. Third through fifth density spirals have been artificially straightened and condensed to show envelope detail.

To maintain balance within the creation, an offsetting path toward the positive of the same magnitude must exist to counteract the new expression. Before we can continue the discussion of expanding opportunities within the upward spiral, we must explain why it was necessary.

Polarity in Material Creations

In the strictest sense, polarity is defined as the state of opposing or contradictory aspects. This opposition is what creates a potential and encourages flow. In the material creations we can observe polarity just about anywhere we look, hot vs cold, light vs dark, magnetic lines of flux, protons vs electrons, etc. Creational energy flows through the material in this manner and in doing so solidifies and holds spatial relationships. The material universe is founded upon this flow and the laws governing it are well documented. These physical creations and the attributes they possess exist within the energetic particles of universal consciousness, and this is an important distinction. The physical is created from, and exists within, consciousness. Consciousness is not constrained by material limitations. This distinction is important because matter must adhere to artificially created spatial relationships within an energetic network, consciousness does not.

A Brief Review

As you read this text your consciousness seems to exist within your head somewhere behind your eyes. This sensation is a result of your consciousness being tethered to your body through the neural interface that is your brain. The body you associate with your existence is what allows you to experience the physical as it translates the energy derived from the interaction. During your time in embodiment, you are locked into an experience that creates the perspective of a linear timeline. When your brain ceases to function, the tether is released and your interaction with the material ceases. Once untethered, your consciousness rejoins the collective consciousness that contains the same base energetic wavelength as yours. Having relinquished your connection to the material, you now exist in the non-locality of universal consciousness.

Consciousness beyond the body exists within the energetic web of particulate within the universal consciousness. Reductions in energetic intensity occur within galactic, system, and planetary consciousness, but the base constituent is the particulate of universal consciousness. Time is not a variable in equations involving energetic transit through universal particulate; it is immediately available where it is needed. Individualized self-aware consciousness utilizes this energy to grow and expand in energetic potential. As density and energetic potential expand within individualized consciousness, it must be exposed to increasing energetic fields for growth to continue. This growth and movement into increasing energy is the definition of ascension and is the primary pursuit of consciousness. Particulate rotation within all consciousness -regardless of energetic capacity- is motivated through the affinity of photons with identical energy signatures to adhere while an energetic spin pushes them apart. The wavelengths of consciousness result from these increasingly complex interactions. The flow of energy powering the dynamic engine of individualized consciousness within universal immersion is driven through kinematic vortex dynamics.

We have reiterated these foundational principles to support the following statement:

Polarization within consciousness is an artificial creation and not a component of the foundational architecture of the universe.

Polarity in Consciousness

During the initial expansion of the universe, pathways for individualized conscious ascension existed within the unity of creational energy. These early attempts at individual expansion provided a clear view of the universe and the path required to ascend in energy. There was no opposition to growth or ascension and consciousness embodied within these constructs obtained clarity of their station within existence as they reached upper third density awareness. With all this knowledge at their disposal it was assumed that rapid ascension would occur, and the collectives would then strive to become productive members of the energy web. Contrary to expectations, several constructs stagnated as large portions of consciousness chose to remain in the comfort and familiarity of embodiment and did not ascend. This created an energetic imbalance that required intervention.

The material creations of planets and solar systems exist and move within an energetic galactic balance. Balance is achieved when consciousness ascends in an orderly manner through material constructs into their energetic collectives. When systems of consciousness ascend in one quadrant of a galaxy but not the other, it creates an imbalance in the energetic movement that must be corrected. If a planetary construct for ascension cannot be repaired and motivated, the only recourse is to reset it. This represents a loss of energetic advancement that detracts from the expansion of the galaxy in which it occurred. To prevent the occurrence of stagnation, the galaxy that Earth resides in created a new concept: a reverse rotation of particulate that creates a polarization within consciousness.

Reversing the spin of particulate creates an energetic oscillation that opposes the normal harmonics of consciousness. As a conscious sphere acquires this reverse rotational dynamic it becomes unbalanced as one rotation cancels the other. The imbalance detunes the oscillating bandwidth of the consciousness and it begins to lose harmonic resonance with the unifying energy of creation. If the path toward reverse rotation is chosen, the consciousness becomes increasingly isolated and focuses on the only thing it can feel, itself. A singular focus creates outward manifestations that reinforce the worth of the self. These unbalanced consciousnesses become the impediment that others must overcome as they seek unity and ascension. Therefore, the upward spiraling into higher states of collectivity is identified as positive since this is the only pathway to unlimited expansion. The reverse spiraling into increased separation is a limited construct that opposes the oscillating harmonics of unity. It is therefore considered the opposing force to the positive path of ascension and is appropriately defined as negative.

Beyond the artificial construct of polarization, the energetic particulate of consciousness within the universe spins in a single unified direction. Polarity was designed to be a moderate impediment to the ascension of consciousness in the third through fifth densities of energetic expansion. The actual extent that polarity would ultimately interfere with ascension within this galaxy was not appreciated. It is now in the final phases of controlled dissolution. A detailed discussion of the creation and effects of polarization can be found in the first book.

Chapter Fourteen

Infinite Expansion and the ANKH Polarity Model

The pathway of ascension is a process that moves the potential of the individual and in turn the potential of the whole upward along the spiral of ascending energetic capacity. As individual consciousness ascends upon a planet to join their collective, planetary consciousness grows and expands. This increasing energetic causes the system they exist within to expand in capacity which contributes to the energetic expansion of the respective galaxy. As the energetic capacity of the galaxies expand, so too does the universe they exist within. From this comes the realization that while the upward spiral of ascension has an originating ground state, it does not have a limit of maximum potential. As we discuss the existing twelve octaves of consciousness, the universe is moving through the sub-octaves within the twelfth as it strives for the next doubling of the thirteenth octave.

We are all engaged in this dance of symbiotic energetic expansion where the smallest divisions within first density are just as important as those within the twelfth. Consciousness begins to understand this relationship in fourth density as the call to unity is felt. At fourth density the desire to unify manifests as a cohesive effort as consciousnesses engaged in a collective timeline strive toward higher energetics. As these fourth density collectives enter fifth density, they begin to synchronize their oscillations with the planetary collective and their vision expands to encompass the complexities of ascension through the densities. An understanding of the energetic nature of the universe and your role within it brings an inherent desire to assist and instruct others. This is the expectation of the positive pathway where service to others benefits all. Within this galaxy, the creation of polarized pathways also brought the ability of fourth density consciousness engaged in separation to expand their chosen negative energetic pathway. The conflict between the positive path of sharing knowledge and the negative path of sequestering it for self-enrichment resulted in the dilution or withholding of information meant to assist collectives along their path of ascension.

The history of Earth contains artifacts of ascended teachings that were brought here to assist maturing consciousness. Over time the teachings were modified to suit those who controlled its dissemination. Graphic representations coveted by one culture became symbols loosely associated with the original intent or repurposed to alternate meanings. The truth is always the truth and some aspects of these teachings have survived the sands of time. For this reason, as we continue our discussions some overlap with antiquity will occur. The intention is not to associate this text with the veneration of historical icons but stems from a desire to remove the distortions that have occurred as we assist the transit of this collective into fourth density.

The Pathway of Polarity within the Upward Spiral

Polarity was created as an impediment that would force consciousness to seek collective intent as it overcame the obstacle of separation and self-interest. It was expected to be a moderate catalyst of potential as consciousness experienced both aspects of polarity. Consciousness could choose to be the inhibitor to ascension where it was expected to eventually tire of this role as it was pulled farther into separation and away from creational energy. With this experience of separation, it would then become the champion for unity, ultimately achieving balance and ascending beyond polarization.

The concept of light and dark within consciousness is an analogy that provides an easily understood contrast, but also has a literal context. As previously stated, the particulate of consciousness is most relatable to the photon, and the photon is a light emitting energetic particle. The interpretation of light is a function of oscillating energetic intensity, regardless of whether you are using material optics or are viewing the resulting wavelengths through your consciousness. The spectrum of light that is visible to the human eye is a fraction of what is available but affords a frame of reference. When properly oriented to creational energy, the particulate of consciousness emits an increasingly brighter spectrum of energy as it oscillates faster and increases in energetic intensity. Conversely, as the photonic particulate acquires a reverse rotation it emits a deeper and darker spectrum of energy as the oscillations increasingly oppose and absorb creational energy. Relating this contrast to the visual spectrum, the positive entity would appear to transit through the lighter shades of green, blue, and violet until it transitioned into white and increases beyond the visible spectrum. The negative entity would be observed transitioning through the darker hues of orange, red, and purple, until it transitioned into black as it drops below the visible spectrum. This is a function of the oscillating bandwidth of consciousness that we will now discuss.

With a basic understanding of what polarity is and why it was created, we return to the upward spiral of ascension that includes the increased area of potential pathways shown in Figure 30. In this image the spiral has been artificially straightened to allow discussion and inspection of the polarized envelope. The expanding diameter begins at the entry to third density self-awareness. The diameter continues to expand through fourth density and into fifth density where it rapidly contracts as polarity ends at entry into the sixth density octave. Understanding its relationship to, and position within the upward spiral, we now remove the expanded portion and orient it vertically.

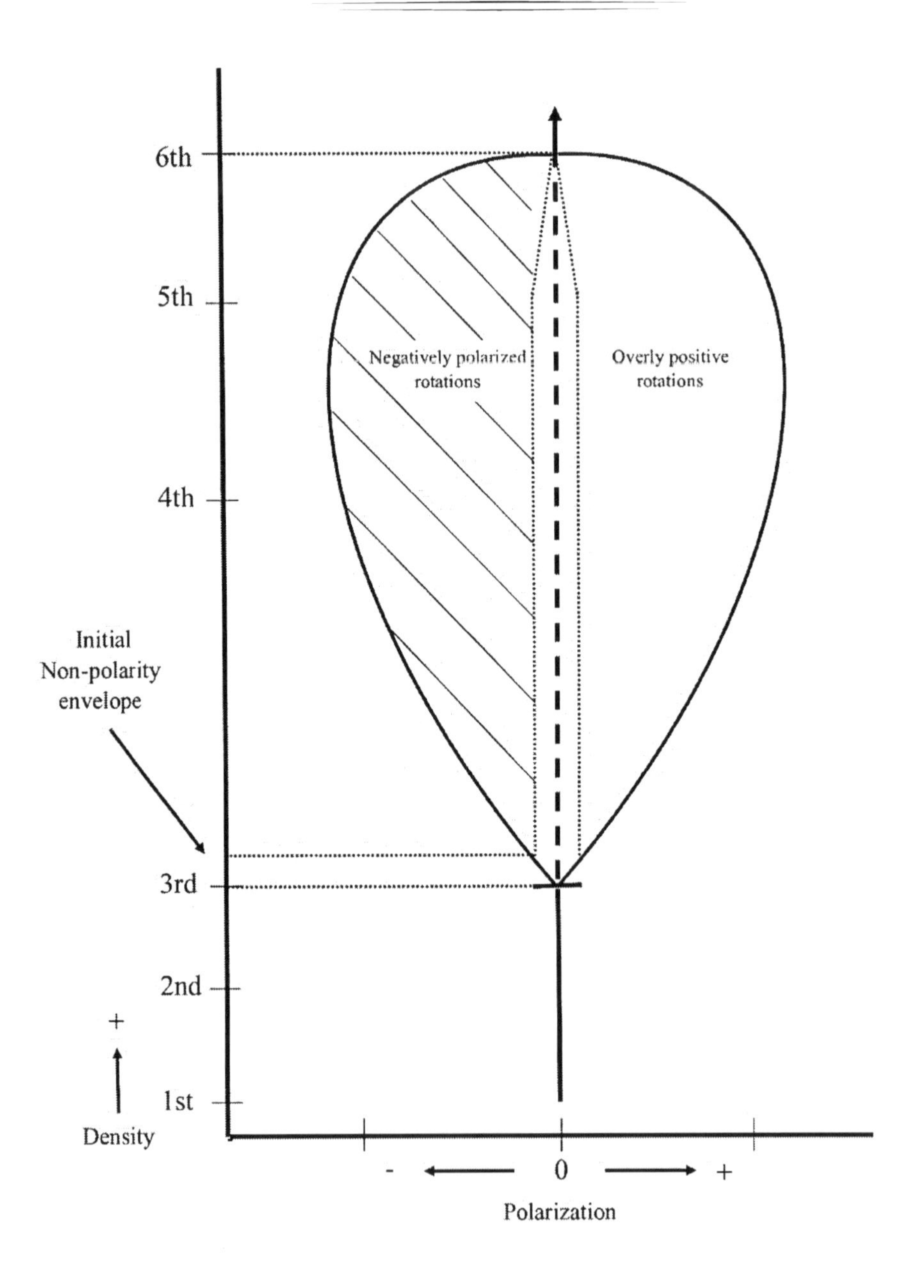

Figure 31 - ANKH Polarity Outline

This image represents an axial view of the expanded envelope of polarity within the upward spiraling tube of ascension. The spiral has been straightened and oriented vertically in this two-dimensional representation. The dashed lines up the center represent the original non-polarized pathway shown in Figure 28 with the line at entry into third density reflecting the original diameter. The original tube has been expanded equally on both sides to provide balance to the creation. Consciousness ascending within the expanded envelope can now choose to be overly positive and give energy in service to the collective. Or it can choose to focus on self and take energy.

In Figure 31 increasing particulate density is shown ascending along the Y axis. The X axis is divided into a positive and negative scale with the dark dashed line at the center being zero, or perfect harmonic resonance at any level. The lighter dotted lines on either side of center represent the original diameter of the non-polarized pathway shown in Figure 28 as does the small black horizontal line between second and third density. This expanded envelope represents the balanced scale of polarity. The particulate of consciousness rotates within a sphere formed from energetic forces operating within margins of stability. If you are creating a new force, it must be offset with an opposing force of equal magnitude.

The base of the graph is where originating organic consciousness begins its journey at first density. There is no polarity in first or second density because the energy of the particulate is low and producing compact rotations. The limited energetics require consciousness in first and second density to operate under instinctual programming until the formation of a third density toroidal geometry. When consciousness achieves third density self-awareness, it enters the expanding envelope. The first few lifetimes in third density are spent within the original non-polarized diameter as consciousness orients itself to free will choice and the new form it incarnates into. As the lifetimes progress and density increases, consciousness now has an expanding choice of experiential pathways. As the plotted variables within consciousness begin to change and exceed the dotted lines, they begin to experience increasing levels of positive or negative polarization depending upon their trajectory. This is where balancing the increasingly complex multi-wave harmonics within consciousness becomes a factor.

The non-polarized pathway reflected by the dotted lines bisects the graph from third to sixth density. Ascending within this pathway would not expose consciousness to polarization. This is the default experience of ascending consciousness outside of this galaxy where polarity does not exist. If consciousness remains within the dotted path as it ascends through the polarized densities, it will require fewer experiences to reach sixth density. Consciousness is a rotating sphere of energetic particles. To increase the density of your consciousness and move upward on the graph, you must increase the energy within the particulate. Increasing energy translates to an energetic array that spins faster. Accelerating velocities within the sphere result from a combination of increasing kinematic forces and improved balance. In non-polarized environments the particulate spins in a single direction. Minor energetic imbalances occur, but counter rotating imbalances are not possible. Inside the polarity envelope, consciousness containing imbalanced polarized rotations will begin to wobble rather than accelerating under increasing energy. Energetic balance of the individual sphere is therefore essential, and a key lesson expected to be learned during experience within polarized constructs.

As Figure 31 illustrates, density increases are available to both polarities. However, increasing in density along the negative trajectory is a difficult undertaking. Due to the natural affinity of the particulate of consciousness to rotate toward unity and creational energy, extreme focus is required to achieve balanced and accelerating negative rotations that cause increases in density. As previously stated, the creation of reverse polarity required an offsetting extreme toward the positive. This brought balance to the creation and provided the energetic ability of positive collectives to overpower the negative obstacle. The inherent tendency of particulate to prefer the universal rotation within creational energy gives positive collectives a natural advantage over negative collectives. A smaller, well focused positive collective will always have the energetic ability to overpower and neutralize a larger negative collective using combined collective focus. If you find yourself incarnated in a construct that offers polarized experience, it is impossible to avoid some degree of polarization. In the case of polarized pathways, third density is the orienting density where consciousness chooses a positive or negative trajectory into the energies of fourth density.

Consciousness will spend numerous lifetimes incarnating and experiencing both aspects of polarization before attaining the balance and density required to move into fourth density. As consciousness enters fourth density, the energy and rotational balance produces an extended energy field emanating beyond the barrier membrane. Other consciousnesses in fourth density are also experiencing this and the result is the beginning of collective intention. To phrase this differently, the auric field has expanded and begun to interact with the expanded fields of other consciousnesses. On the positive side, this collective intention manifests as unity and inclusion as all share equally. The focus is external as they work toward raising the energetic of the collective whole. On the negative side, collective intent manifests as solidified hierarchal power structures as all accept their station and agree to exist within it. The external power structures of those negatively aligned is a literal representation of the energetics involved. Each consciousness is looking inward as they attempt to maximize their energetic potential, rising to the top of the power structure at the expense of others.

The polarity potential continues to expand until it reaches the maximum potential for polarization at upper fourth density. As consciousness enters fifth density, the need to embody has ended, although the desire may remain in early fifth density. As the need for polarized experience concludes at upper fifth density, the polarized pathways taper sharply toward unity. As the graph suggests, you must regain harmonic balance and synchronize with the universal grid prior to accessing the energies of sixth density regardless of which side of polarity brought you there.

This elaborate model was created to allow rich experiential pathways for consciousness to explore and appeared to be a successful experiment. However, an anomaly occurred as the experiment progressed. Consciousness at the outer edge of fifth density negative experience lost the desire to return to unity and set about forcibly expanding their energetic capacity. This created an artificial pocket of consciousness completely disconnected from the universal harmonic.

This is represented by the small bulge extending from the left in Figure 32.

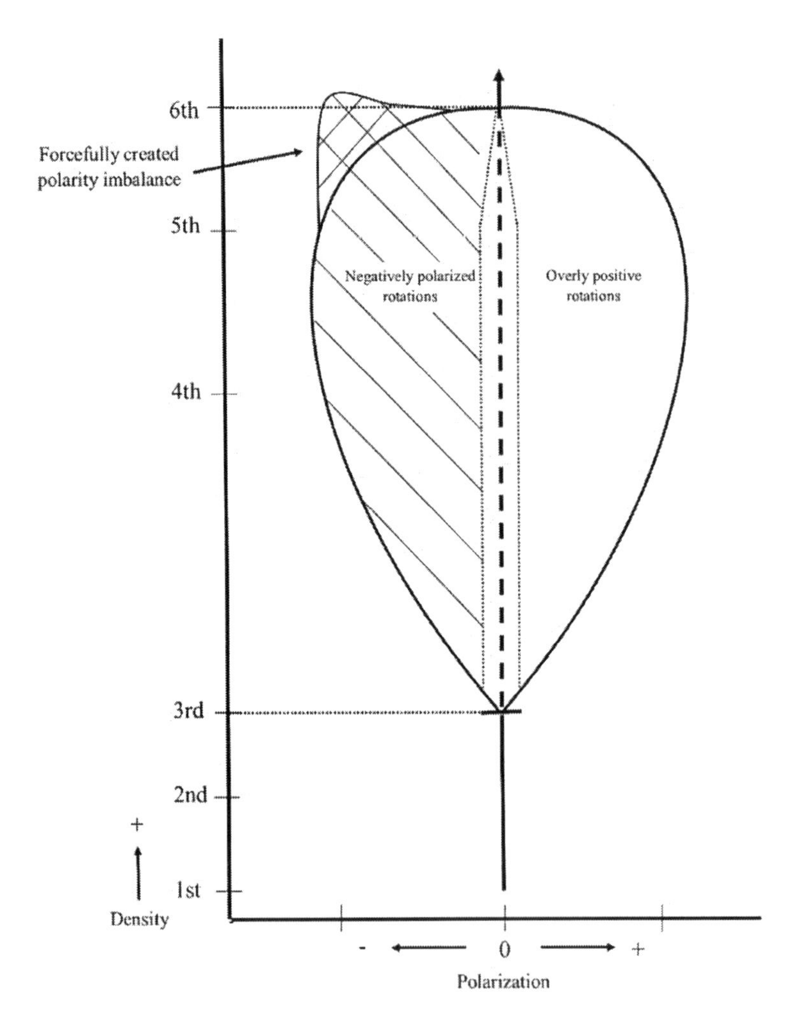

Figure 32 - Forceful Polarity Imbalance

The image above shows the imbalance created as the negatively oriented consciousnesses embarked upon the forceful expansion of the negative polarity envelope. While the envelope pushes into the sixth density harmonic it was not in resonance. It was created and maintained by overwhelming and absorbing the entire energetic potential of positive collectives and at the height of its expansion threatened to imbalance the galaxy.

Consciousness fully immersed in negative polarity entered this pocket as the last vestiges of positive rotation ceased. Immersed in the darkness of complete separation, the pathway back to unity was lost. Those lost in the darkness were now dependent upon an artificial energy of limited capacity. Sensing the imposed limitation and expecting the law of free will to allow their exploits, they began to forcefully expand their energetic environment. They did this by spreading the reverse rotations of negative polarity throughout the galaxy into constructs that were not designed for them. At the zenith of negative polarity, entire positive collectives were overwhelmed, as their energy was absorbed to expand the pocket. Although sixth density negatives had achieved the density requirement, they were not in resonance with the sixth density octave and could not access the energy. Maintaining the pocket required increasing amounts of absorbed energy. This forceful expansion created the pocket shown and threatened to imbalance the galaxy. The pocket has since been remediated using the free will ratio and is only provided for historical context. The concept of free will ratio is discussed in chapter seventeen.

Ascension Example within the Linear Polarity Graph

To better understand the graph, we will chart the trajectory of a consciousness embarked upon density expansion within it. The lessons of polarity require hundreds of lifetimes to understand and balance the potential energies as consciousness orients itself in third density and chooses a polarization in fourth density. This creates a meandering pathway that crisscrosses between the polarities as consciousness slowly acquires density and moves upward in potential within the ascending spiral. For ease of understanding, the example that follows has been shortened to six lifetimes that lead the consciousness from the entry of third density into the next octave of the fourth.

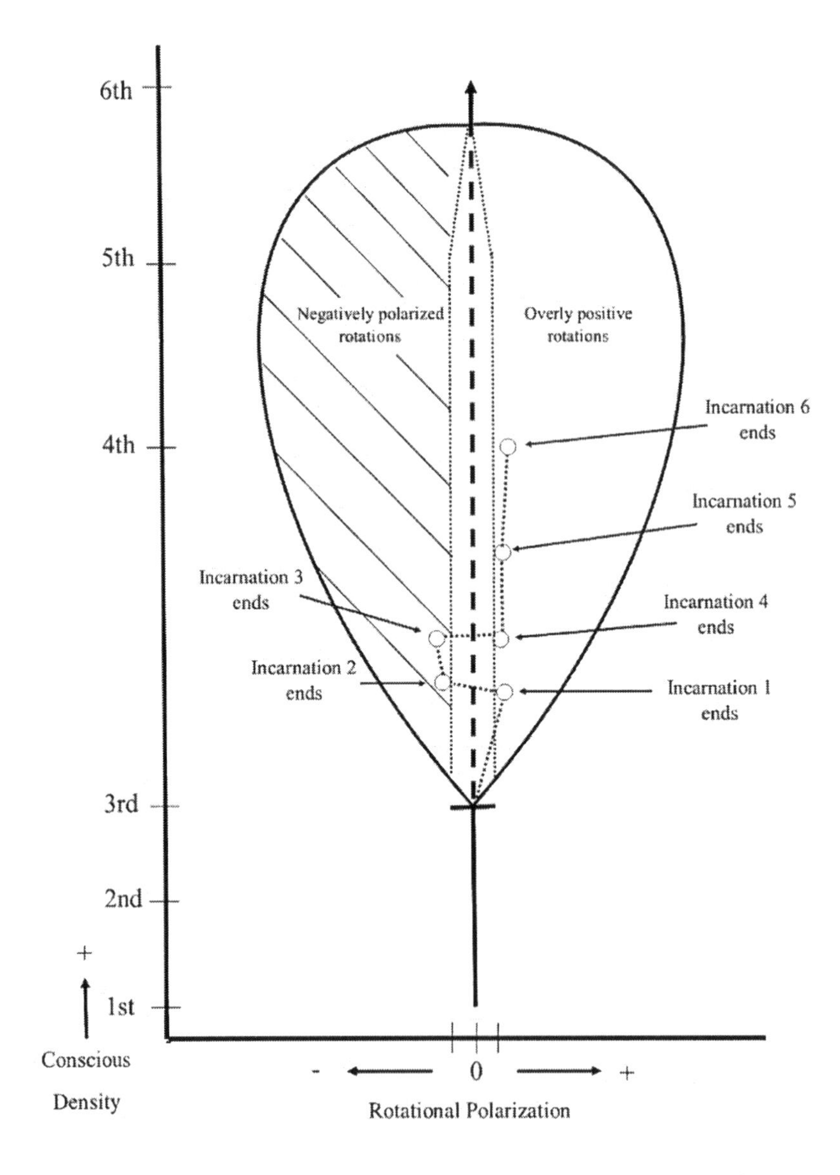

Figure 33 - ANKH Lifetime Polarity Expansion

The image above shows the pathway a consciousness took to increase in density and reach entry to the fourth density octave. Six lifetimes are shown for simplicity, but hundreds are required. Density expansion occurs faster in positive polarity as is reflected above. The consciousness will require a subsequent incarnation to match the oscillating harmonics of fourth density and enter it.

Figure 33 represents the highly condensed path of an individualized consciousness ascending in density within the two-dimensional representation of the upward spiral. The line to point one represents a single lifetime where the overall density increased within the positive portion of the graph. Since the consciousness stayed within the single positive polarity, particulate density increased at a greater magnitude within the harmonics of increasing oscillating wavelength and frequency. The line from point one to point two indicates that the consciousness began to experience and embrace negative polarity. This hindered the addition of conscious density as the increasing imbalance pulled the consciousness into the negative. The line from point two to point three shows a focused intention that caused density expansion along the negative path. Point three to point four shows a slow abandonment of the negative as the consciousness returns to a positive alignment before the incarnation ends. Point four to point five reflects increasing balance and wisdom that correlates to larger increases in conscious density. Point five to six shows a focus on increasing balance as the consciousness becomes energetically aware of fourth density and actively seeks parity with the positive collective. If the resonance within the consciousness is not near parity with the fourth density octave, another incarnation will be required for tuning.

Chapter Fifteen

Radial View of the Polarized Envelope

The radial cross section of the upward spiral is an easily recognized image that has been stylized to represent the contrast and balance found within opposites; light and dark, good and bad, masculine and feminine, etc. Like the Ankh, it was provided to illuminate the polarized pathways available to consciousness and the balance between them. The information was provided without any judgement associated with which pathway should be chosen since it was believed that either path would bring consciousness to the threshold of sixth density. It was hoped that with an understanding of the pathways and the results associated with choosing either -or neither- an informed decision could be made and the most effective path toward the sixth density octave plotted.

The linear view of ascending density within the upward spiral shown in Figure 31 is a simplified two-dimensional graph for ease of understanding. However, the graph represents increasing particulate that is generating repeating energetic waves, spinning around the sphere at varying orbital heights, thereby creating the product of harmonic resonance in multi-dimensional space. As one variable changes in relationship to the others it drives movement within the spiral. To properly plot how the changes in the variables affect each other we must again look at a radial cross section of the spiral on a multi-axis graph.

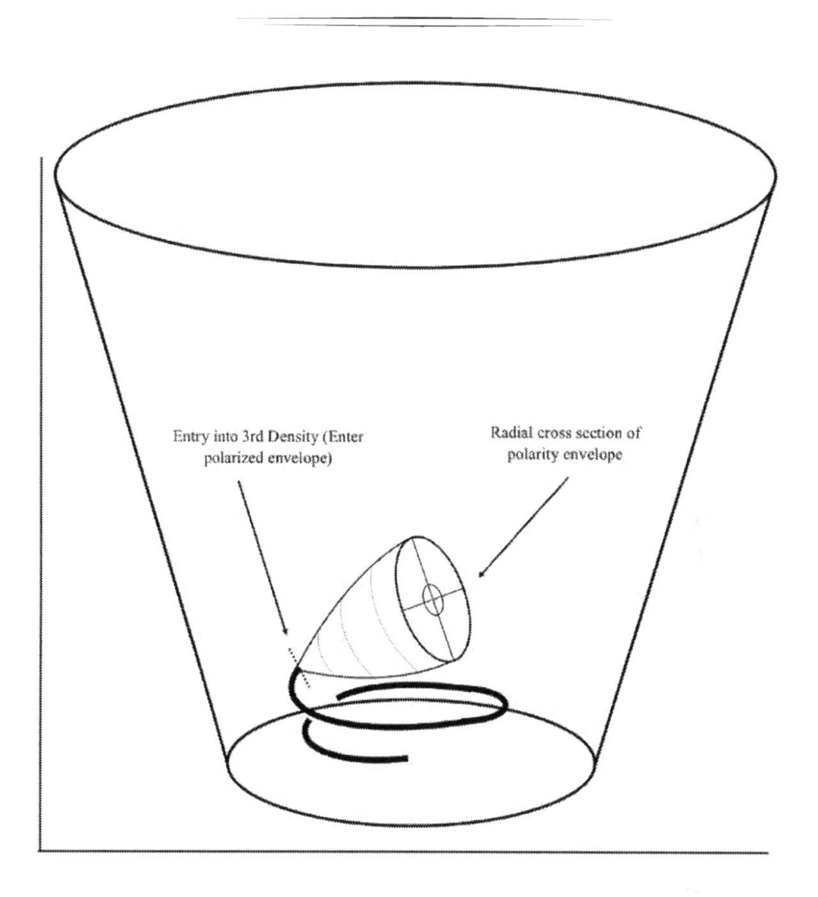

Figure 34 - Upward Polarized Spiral with Radial Cross Section

This image shows the expanded envelope of polarity from Figure 30. The envelope has been bisected to show how the radial cross section of the polarity envelope is obtained. As consciousness ascends within the envelope, the radial cross section at their current location plots the level of balance and polarization they contain.

The creation of polarized pathways increases the diameter of the non-polarized radial cross section from Figure 28 and adds opposing variables that affect the upward trajectory of density increases. As consciousness increases in density it moves upward within the expanded envelope. The experiential choices the consciousness chooses determines how it ascends and the level of polarization it acquires. At any point along this journey its exact location within the envelope can be obtained by plotting it within the radial cross section.

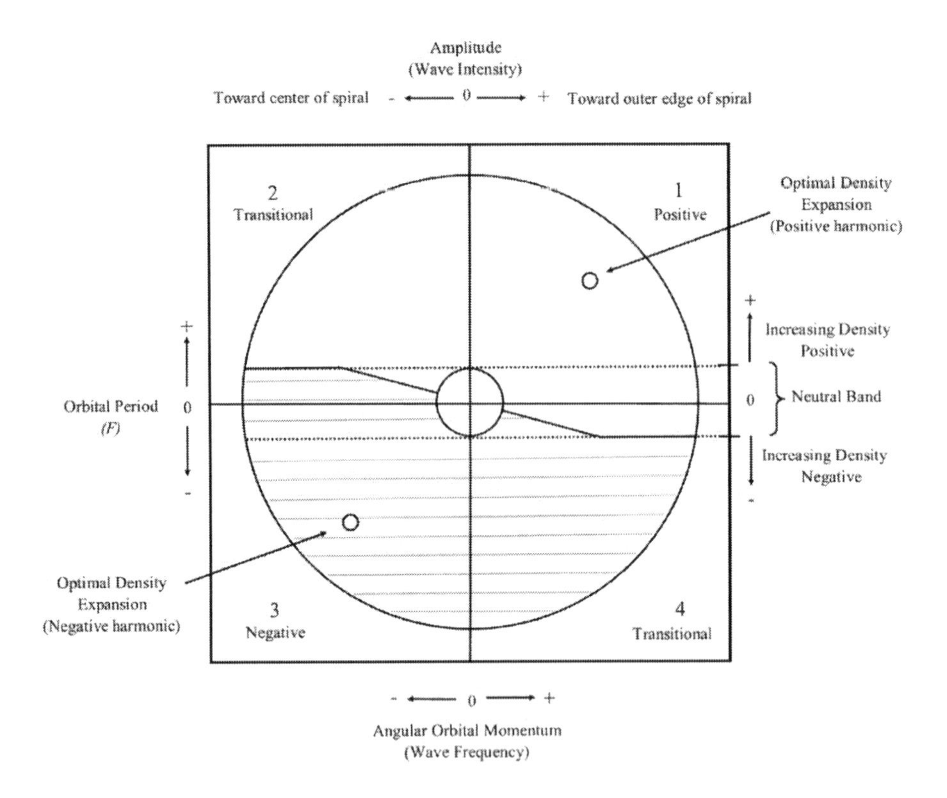

Figure 35 - Polarized Radial Cross Section

This image represents the radial cross section of the polarized envelope. The circle at the center is the original non-polarized pathway shown in Figure 28. The intersection of the lines at the center represent perfect resonance within the octave or sub-octave being observed. The dashed lines above and below the center circle are the density dead band where transitioning imbalances prevent harmonic density additions. While the dead band encompasses the non-polarity portion at the center, density increases still occur within it. Quadrant 1 and quadrant 3 reflect areas of increasing density within the polarities. The small circles represent the optimal harmonic for density expansion within them. Quadrant 2 and 4 are where the variables are attempting to rebalance and will either move toward the center circle or into quadrant 1 or 3.

Polarization within consciousness has added another variable as the particulate of consciousness is able to spin in opposition and create reverse potentials. The reverse spin provides the opportunity to expand in particulate density on either side of harmonic resonance within an octave. The circle at the center is the originating radial diameter of the upward spiral previously shown in Figure 28. Within this originating center diameter, the non-polarized graph applies due to the absence of polarization within it. While shown within the dead band, density additions to consciousness still occur within the center diameter due to the harmonic resonance with the external octave. The expanded envelope surrounding the center diameter represents the experiential pathways of polarized particulate spin states. How the reverse charge creates a negative harmonic must be understood in order to understand what occurs within the expanded envelope of the upward spiral.

Understanding Reverse Spin

Figure 18 illustrated the interactions between photonic layers that create the oscillating bandwidth of consciousness. In that non-polarized example, particulate rotated in the direction of universal movement. Minor imbalances could occur between the parameters, but nothing acted to impede or reverse the universal movement. As previously mentioned, reverse polarity employs a spin that opposes the default movement that acts to absorb energy as it empowers its rotation. This concept needs clarification as both rotations need a continuous flow of energy to empower their spins below sixth density.

The universal movement of positive spin -termed positive only to differentiate it from its artificial opposition- acquires energy in the toroidal column as highly charged unpotentiated universal particulate flows through it. Both are of a positive nature and the energy transfer occurs through a difference of kinematic potential as the faster spinning particulate transfers energy to the slower. This occurs in the same manner as striking a tuning fork whose resulting vibration causes a similarly tuned fork at rest to begin vibrating in sympathetic resonance. Like the tuning forks, both particles are similarly tuned in their rotation and the transfer occurs as a large differential exists within the column. The sympathetic rotations also translate to a major difference at the barrier membrane. A positively aligned consciousness will radiate energy from its barrier membrane as the kinematic flow operates in reverse as it energizes the barrier membrane. This energy transfer outward at the barrier membrane underlines the need for the energetic octave reductions shown in Figure 3.

The reverse spin of negative polarity is an absorber in the truest sense. The kinematic potentials of the universal movement are not being shared between similarly rotating particles where one assists in accelerating the other. When reverse rotation encounters a positive rotation, it attempts to absorb the entire potential from the positive. If successful, the positive rotation will cease. If the negative continues to be the higher energy, the previously positive particle will begin a reverse rotation as it operates in sympathetic resonance with the higher potential. This absorptive potential also translates to the barrier membrane of individualized consciousness. The reverse rotations still contain energy that forms the tangentially bundled manifold of the protective barrier. However, a negative barrier is not radiating and sharing energy, it is absorbing it wherever it finds it. Ascending along the negative path is a delicate dance. Absorbing energy through the barrier only benefits negative rotations if the negative remains the higher potential. The negative barrier membrane of consciousness is energetically permeable when compared to one of a positive alignment. When confronted by an overpowering positive force, refusal to withdraw from the encounter can cause a significant loss of hard-won negative potential.

Negative polarity is acquired in two ways, through the barrier membrane when in proximity as stated above, and through intentional focus and action. In both cases the particulate of the individual consciousness loses positive spin and their rotations slow. If the external negative influence or internal focus continues, the particulate will eventually reverse rotation at pathway E-0 and begin propagating through the sphere. The instability created from the opposed rotations creates friction between the energetic layers that slows the oscillating frequency of successive layers. This will manifest an initial discomfort within consciousness as the imbalance begins to interfere with harmonic resonance and the ability to utilize creational energy. The discomfort is an indicator that can be acknowledged and used to correct the imbalance, or it can be embraced and allowed to propagate. Both require the intentional focus of the consciousness as they chart their path forward using free will.

If the reverse rotations are embraced, the consciousness will continue to lose harmonic resonance with creational energy. Outside of the polarized envelope, harmonic oscillation within an octave is a requirement for continued particulate growth. This requirement is based on the sympathetic tuning fork analogy where similarly tuned particles co-resonate and share energy easily. Inside the polarity envelope, the tuning resonance is replaced by absorption within the toroidal column of those embracing negative rotations. For reverse polarity to be a viable construct, a negative harmonic expression is required that allows density expansion to continue. The negative harmonic is an artificial construct limited to the third through fifth octaves. The unintended pocket notwithstanding, consciousness transitioning into the sixth density octave must be in harmonic resonance with their system collective and the universal grid.

The Effects of an Overly Positive Orientation

There is confusion related to the concept of an overly positive pathway. This stems from the knowledge that the universal movement induces the desire of collectivity and assistance once you establish collective synchronization. How can love, empathy for others, and giving of self be anything other than good? Love, empathy, and giving of self are certainly components of the universal movement and a requirement for synchronization with sixth density. However, imbalance in any system occurs when parameters exceed operational limits, and these are no exception. The effects of negative polarity are easy to conceptualize as an inward focus manifesting as a lust for power and self-aggrandizement at the expense of others. Overly positive manifestations are just as easy to identify and operate in the reverse. They manifest as an outward focus on giving in the extreme to the detriment of self. It does not matter what you are giving; love, affection, time, money, energy, or anything else. In non-polarized environments, the desire to give of yourself for the collective good is tempered by the knowledge that your enrichment is just as essential to the collective. In overly positive alignments, internal preservation is lost as the focus becomes an outward giving of effort at the expense of self. Regardless of the path, extreme focus toward self-enrichment or self-sacrifice must ultimately be balanced prior to sixth density.

Movement within the Graph

The radial cross section shown in Figure 35 contains two harmonic pathways that can be explored. The graph tracks four variables within consciousness that combine to produce a fifth: harmonic resonance. As such, the cross section of plotted variables represents a single point within a four dimensional upward spiral and is a tool to understand the dynamic nature of consciousness, not a static display of additive values. As movement occurs on the graph it should be envisioned as directional movement within the spiral that was shown in Example 2 of Figure 29. Because the graph charts four variables combining to create a fifth, when one variable acquires an imbalance the others will act as an opposing force to rebalance the equation. Consciousness is a creation of helically spinning particles increasing in energetic capacity. This is the spin inherent in all of creation and that inertia creates a spinning component to the cross-sectional graph. From the perspective of the radial cross section, movement will occur between the quadrants in a counterclockwise direction.

Quadrant two and four are considered unstable and transitory as a result of a polarity mismatch where changes in frequency and amplitude cause a shift in the orbital period of pathway E-11. Consciousness entering these areas will attempt to rebalance and move toward stability. Whether this leads back to harmonic balance within the octave at the center of the graph, or into the stable quadrants of one or three will depend upon the focus of the consciousness.

Large increases in particulate density occur within the harmonic resonant areas of quadrant one and three. Shifting polarization within consciousness impacts the amplitude and frequency of individual particulate waveforms which is represented on the graph as moving in or out of the areas of harmonic resonance. As the oscillating bandwidth of a consciousness loses optimum resonance within an octave, it exits the center ring. Effective resonance between the orbital layers has been impeded as opposing rotations create an imbalance. Between the positive and negative harmonics there is a transitional instability that creates the zero band of density increase shown within the dotted lines. The effects of the polarities on consciousness are delineated by the white and gray areas. The thought process of consciousness is highly dependent upon the harmonic resonance within it. As the coordinates enter the gray area, negative effects will begin to manifest. The grey area within the neutral band allows minor effects to manifest. If consciousness recognizes the imbalance and corrects it, it will return to the center balance point. The same is true of the overly positive portion within the neutral band. The effects of polarity on thought increase as the variables move toward the optimum resonance points located in quadrant one and three. These optimum levels of oscillating wavelength and rotational frequency cause efficient harmonic density expansion.

The harmonic fracture point of photonic particulate shifts higher as the orbital pathways increase and the spherical geometry of consciousness expands during movement upward within the spiral. The increasing energetic and harmonic requirement to cause fracture is reflected in the increasing radius of the spiral. Moving into the resonant areas within the radial cross section shown in Figure 35 indicates the areas of optimal particulate fracture within the observed octave or sub-octave. This is the same concept as raising the frequency of sound waves until they match the vibratory rate of a crystal structure. The structure has a resonant frequency associated with the crystalline lattice and geometry of its construction. Outside of that frequency, the sound waves may be impacting the structure, but it is not in sympathetic resonance, so the structure remains intact. When the sound reaches resonant frequency with the structure, the resulting resonance causes the molecular lattice to vibrate in a manner that synchronizes the vibration and reverberates it back upon itself. The structure is now exhibiting sympathetic resonance. If the amplitude (wave intensity) of the resonant frequency is increased, the vibrations build upon each other and increase in magnitude. This will continue until the resonant action overpowers the binding capacity of the molecular lattice and the structure fragments.

Movement within the Radial Cross Section

Refer to Figure 35 for the following discussion. Quadrant 1 is the area of effective positive density increases. The amplitude and frequency of particulate are both high and the orbital period reflects this. If consciousness can focus and remain within the area of harmonic resonance shown in quadrant 1, density will increase at the optimum rate. Energy drain in quadrant 1 due to negative polarity will initially reduce amplitude followed by wave frequency. Conversely, positive polarity will increase amplitude followed by frequency. Orbital period is a product of amplitude and frequency and follows their movement. This interrelationship creates a counterclockwise movement within the radial cross section. The axis variables are measuring the average values of the composite sphere and not individual particulate. A decreasing orbital period corresponds to the overall rotational trajectory of particulate at pathway E-11. An orbital period of zero indicates that the rotational aggregate of positive and negative has reached a neutral value for the associated octave. The values of amplitude and frequency also reflect neutrality within an octave and the three values at zero indicate perfect harmonic balance within the spiral at that location.

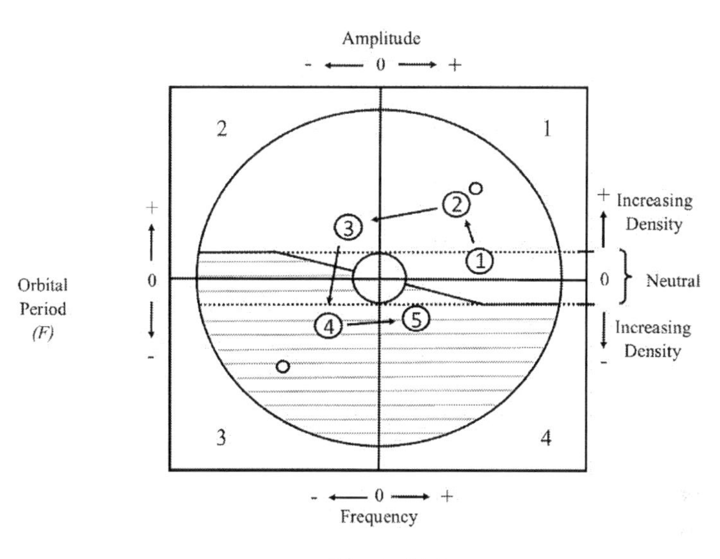

Example 1

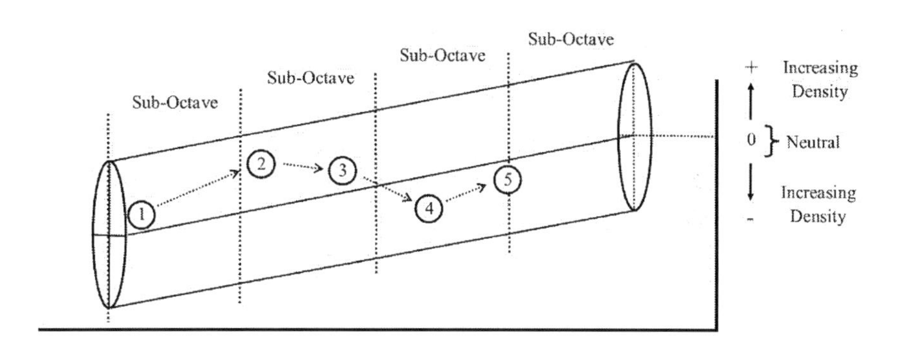

Example 2

Figure 36 - Polarized Cross Section Example

The image above plots the course of consciousness as it increases in positive polarity from point 1 to point 2. As it comes into proximity with negative polarity it loses energy and moves to point 3. Allowing the negativity to increase it begins to orient negatively and drops to point 4. As it begins to regain positive focus and energy it moves to point 5. From here it can continue to reorient and move into quadrant 1 or return to negativity in quadrant 3. Since density expansion is available to both polarities, it continues to move upward within the expanded spiral as shown in Example 2.

Example 1, of Figure 36 plots the movement of a consciousness within the cross section. Position 1 shows a consciousness in the positive section of the neutral band. The effects of positivity are manifesting within the thoughts and actions and consciousness follows them as it increases in particulate density and moves to position 2. While in quadrant 1 it is impacted by a negative polarity drain either from an outside force or in thought and action. This results in a decrease of amplitude, frequency, and orbital period that moves the consciousness to position 3. Density increases have slowed due to the increasing imbalance but still occur as the consciousness moves into quadrant 2. While in the transitional area of quadrant 2 consciousness must choose a desired trajectory and return to quadrant 1 or move into quadrant 3. In this instance consciousness aligns to the negative focus and moves to position 4 and directly into the negative harmonic of quadrant 3. There was a brief period of density stagnation as it transited the neutral zone, but density increases began again when the negative harmonic became the dominant resonance. While in the negative area of quadrant 3 consciousness begins to feel uncomfortable with the isolation associated with the negative alignment and begins to seek reconnection with the external harmonic of the respective octave. This moves the consciousness to point 5 within the transitional area of quadrant 4. Depending upon the intensity of focus, consciousness will either move upward into the neutral zone or directly into quadrant 1.

Example 2 plots the radial movement linearly within the upward spiral. Movement from point 1 to point 2 shows a significant increase in density as the consciousness moves up the spiral into the next sub-octave. Point 2 to point 3 reflects a slowing of density addition and forward movement as imbalanced rotations begin to manifest. Because density additions are available to both polarities, forward movement continues along with density increases as consciousness moves from point 3 to point 4. As consciousness moves from point 4 to point 5 density increases and forward movement slow as imbalance returns.

The information in the expansion series of books is meant to bring you an understanding of what you are, why you have been created, where you currently find yourself, and how you move forward from here. With an understanding of what you are and how you assume control of your individual trajectory, we now proceed to where you are and how you assume control of your collective trajectory.

Chapter Sixteen

Consciousness and Material Constructs

The particulate of universal consciousness is the foundation upon which all is built. It should come as no surprise that a repeating theme of energetic pushing, pulling, and rotating becomes evident within every successive layer observed. From the unobservable forces found in quantum space to the rotations of galaxies, everything is built upon the helical action of particulate and the geometries created by varying energetic relationships between them.

The Downward Spiral of Material Creation

As individualized consciousness on a planetary sphere becomes self-aware, their first focus is upon mastery of the material. The path each planet takes toward this goal differs, but in time the budding collective achieves the technological control to manipulate their environment. As their maturity progresses, they begin looking deeper into the construction of their material world and ultimately reach the same conclusion; at its base component matter is the result of massless particulate, held together in various lattice compositions through energetic interactions. The mathematical equations on Earth that justify how massless particles become atoms and elements are the products of extensive research still being conducted at the time of this writing. At its smallest constituents, matter begins as spinning packets of particulate. Within this quantum, the constituents oscillate and spin in unison as they combine to form increasing diameters and complexity. Beyond the science, the underlying motivator is the particulate of consciousness moving and interacting in a manner that solidifies it. The concept of consciousness is not divorced from science as a nebulous belief that a portion of your identity survives beyond the body, it is the science.

Consciousness operates as an energetic flow generated through vortex dynamics and kinematic potential. Constructs of matter require a different energetic to create the myriad spatial relationships that comprise particulate. At the atomic level, the properties of matter are created through forces of attraction, repulsion, oscillating dynamics, and orbital trajectories motivated through electrical potentials. The cultivation of consciousness requires an energetic ground state -or zero point- to incubate within as it forms the weak oscillatory cohesions of first density. A dividing line has been created between the higher energies of consciousness and the material constructs by utilizing a downward spiral of energy toward neutrality. For this flow to occur, a potential between the high energy state and the ground state must exist. The interactions that result from the movement of energy through this potential is what creates the constituents of matter at varying levels of stability. The higher the energy within the particulate, the more unstable it will become.

Consider the periodic table of elements that are currently known to exist. This table identifies various elements in ascending order based upon the number of protons that comprise the nucleus of the atom. An atom is the basic unit of matter whose construction defines the structure of an element. A Proton contains a positive charge, so the stability of the element also depends upon the neutrons and the negatively charged electrons that act to create neutrality within the atoms. From this atomic perspective, the difference between platinum and gold is reduced to a few particles and the energetic interaction of electrons needed to balance the resulting charge. The rotational structure created from the particles then interact to create a lattice as the atoms join and solidify in observable quantities. The heaviest of the naturally occurring elements requires a large internal charge to balance and maintain stability. Moving from the heaviest to the lowest on the periodic table, the downward spiral becomes evident. Large sums of internal energy are required to balance the heaviest elements on the chart which then decrease to the lowest energy requirement found in Hydrogen. From your current incarnated perspective, a single material surface and atmosphere exists within which you extract and utilize the materials found. However, this is not the case as multiple energetic material constructs currently exist.

The Relationship between Balance and Wisdom

The octave densities of consciousness and the material constructs they learn within are designed with an upper energetic limit. The reason behind limiting energetic availability is twofold. The first is mechanical in nature as consciousness entering third density does not possess the photonic particulate needed to harness and utilize the energetics of fourth density. This is not just a factor of the energy absorbed within the toroidal column, but the capacity of the barrier membrane to shield the increasing energies. The second is the maturity that comes with rotational balance that provides the wisdom required to properly utilize increasing energy.

We must define the term wisdom as it applies to a rotating sphere of oscillating particulate if we are to understand its requirement. This text has provided a detailed explanation of the interactions that the particulate of consciousness undergoes as it acquires energetic capacity through experience. The primary objective of those chapters was to illuminate how the oscillations within your consciousness are created. Understanding the processes leads to control over the process as balance is sought. In a non-polarized environment, the pathway upward toward increasing energetic capacity is smaller. There is no opposition to ascension within the spiral, but an effort to maintain balance and efficiency is still required to move forward. Consciousness within a polarized environment has a larger pathway of experience that includes an opposing force that must be understood and overcome as you achieve balance and move upward within the spiral. From this we can infer that wisdom within consciousness is defined as; understanding what you are, how you operate, and using internal focus to move upward along the most efficient pathway toward increasing synchronization with the universal movement.

True unity consciousness occurs at entry to the sixth density octave as the energetic emanations beyond your consciousness synchronize and lock into a unified oscillation with the universal grid. This unified harmonic, existing between billions of individualized consciousnesses is the definition of the unity you are all seeking. The introduction to unity consciousness begins at entry to the fourth density octave and continues to solidify through the fifth density. Along the path through fourth and fifth density, wisdom and purpose also solidify. With an understanding of the terms wisdom and unity as applied to consciousness, we now continue with a discussion of the pathways that create them.

Defining an Energetic Construct

As we discuss the concepts of energetic separation between material realities, we will use the term energetic construct interchangeably with timeline as it relates to collectives involved in the co-creation of material environments. Recall from the first book that a timeline is defined as an era of time that a collective of consciousness embodies within. The Cavemen, the Romans, and the Vikings, all existed within an era of time that you can look back upon in your history. All consciousness existing within those constructs were actively engaged in their creation. Some entities may have been more visual and vocal in the shaping of events than others, but the trajectory of the era was decided through the agreement of the collective. Within the energetic (timeline) construct where this text exists, a divergence is occurring as consciousnesses within the collective separate. The aspirations toward fourth density have begun for a portion of the collective and they are actively seeking increased energetic capacity. When the separation is complete, the current collective will have bifurcated. Those actively striving for fourth density will exist a new energetic construct with increased energetic potential so that they may continue their growth. Those unwilling or unable to move forward will remain within the current third density construct and continue their preparations for fourth density. Both are considered energetic material constructs, with the ascending construct containing a higher level of available creational energy. Both will continue forward from the divergence along separate timelines with the future of each dictated by their respective collectives. This is the process of ascending through energetic constructs that will now be discussed.

The Material Octaves of Collective Constructs

As consciousness ascends in density along the upward spiral in an embodied construct, it will reach a point of imposed energetic limitation. Material constructs for embodiment are tuned to a specific octave within which consciousness creates their collective reality. If that octave is third density, the construct will include all the sub octaves of that density up to -but excluding- the doubling octave of fourth density. Consciousness must have the required energy and balance to move into higher energetic constructs. Separating the ascending octaves prevents consciousness from accessing energetic potentials they are unprepared for. To put the concept of imbalance into perspective, we return to the wheel analogy. If your tire loses one of its balancing weights as you are driving it will begin to vibrate. A single point of imbalance will cause the entire vehicle to shake. Continue to increase energy and the vehicle will eventually shake itself apart. This analogy translates to what occurs within collectives containing billions of consciousnesses. Increasing energy amplifies any imbalances which then reverberate through the collective. Uncorrected, the imbalance will increase and destabilize the collective. For this reason, entire collectives of consciousness embody and interact in material constructs limited to specific octaves designed to accommodate their level of energetic maturity.

Chapter Seventeen

Galactic Balance and Planetary Timelines

As planets travel through the particulate of the galactic consciousness, a resistance to motion occurs as the solidified matter interacts with the particulate of the galactic consciousness. This resistance generates inertial waves proportional to the amount of material in motion. The inertial waves focus on the center of the planet creating a force that pulls material toward it known as gravity. The movement of the spheres coupled with the resulting gravity produces a linear perspective of experience for consciousness embodied upon them as they travel through space-in-time. This linear perspective of time is causally related to a planet's linear movement within the galactic consciousness. If you go back to the origin of this timeline's recorded history, you will find that the planet was in one area of the galaxy and has been moving away from that point ever since. If you then shift your focus to encompass the entirety of the galaxy, you will observe billions of planets in motion. Within the motion of the galaxy, the consummate history of Earth is a minor movement within a larger arc containing trillions of years of conscious ascension. This brings forward an interesting concept. If you constructed a machine to move backward within a single timeline -not slip between timelines- an important consideration would be a gravitational lock and an idea where the planet was physically located during the period you are attempting to reach. If you do not account for these variables, you face the very real possibility of moving into empty space.

All the planets, all the motion, all individualized consciousness in every timeline, has been created from, and exists within, the particulate of galactic consciousness. While oversight is delegated to system and planetary consciousness, the galactic consciousness is aware of everything occurring within it. Individual free will is necessary for ascension and respected, but imbalances within galactic rotations cannot be left uncorrected. If timelines within a planetary ascension path are causing an imbalance within a sector, direct oversight and correction will be implemented. The galactic consciousness is a rotating toroidal sphere of the same design as any self-aware consciousness. The difference is the scale of the array and its direct access to unfiltered universal energy. An imbalance upon a planet because it is not ascending in energetic potential as expected will be felt the same as has been described for imbalances within individual consciousness. Self-correction is preferred but if the imbalance continues to increase, direct intervention will occur.

Galaxies, Their Creations, and the Flow of Particulate

Each galaxy is a fully ascended consciousness tasked with creating systems of ascension within it. Newer galaxies have access to information related to the successes and failures of the games of ascension created within galaxies that came before them. Previous failures are sometimes attempted using new parameters, and proven successes are almost always employed as new galaxies initially begin creating ascension pathways. However, each galaxy has free will to create whatever they want. The galaxy where this text resides has created a counter rotating material spiral where the planets rotate in opposition to the flow of galactic particulate. This design creates strong gravitational forces that translate to a deep experience of time for those incarnated within the material. Other galaxies have employed a static arrangement where the rotational particulate is the only movement, while others have rotations that move slowly with the flow of particulate. If you are a space faring civilization that has found an open gateway between galaxies -and are allowed to transit- you will need to overlay the rotational characteristics of the new galaxy onto a quadrant and sector map similar to the one provided below.

Galactic Quadrant, Sector and Balanced Rotations

When a planet, or system of planets becomes increasingly imbalanced, the preservation of individual free will becomes a mathematical ratio. For ease of understanding consider the following graph.

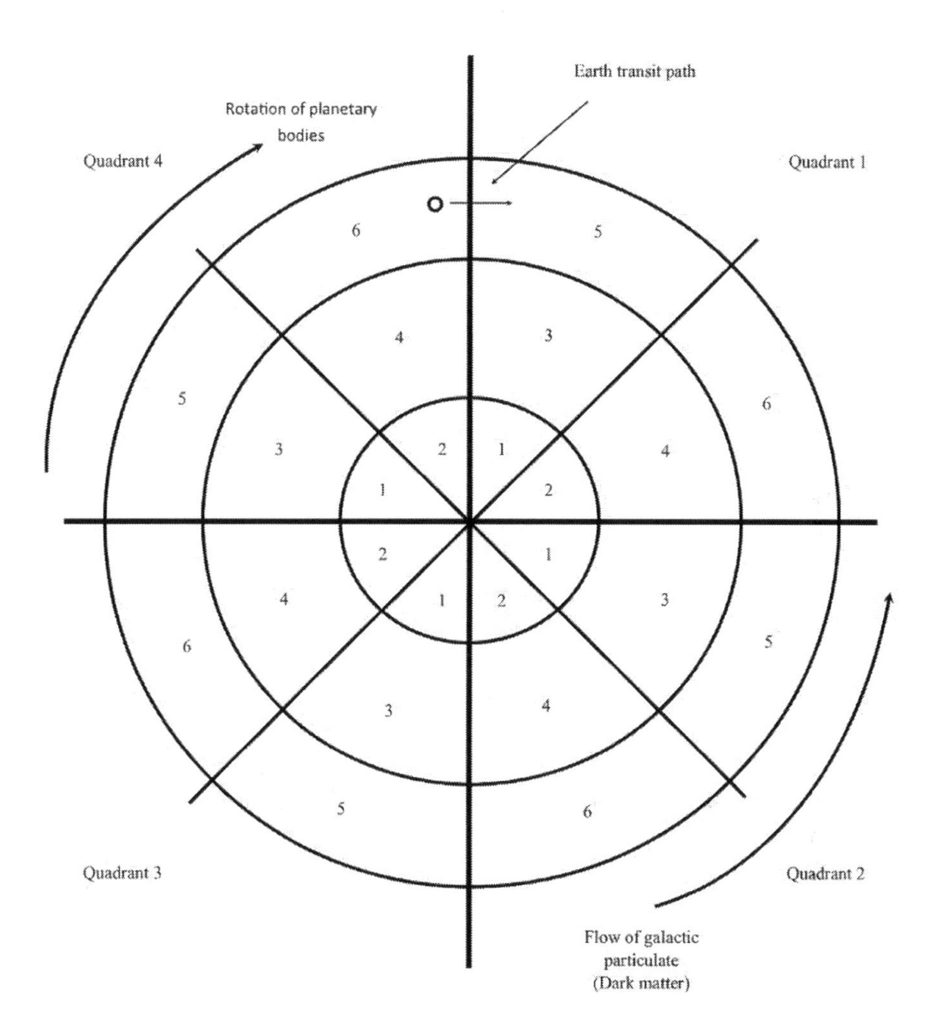

Figure 37 - Galactic Quadrants and Sectors

This image shows a top down view of a galactic consciousness divided into quadrants and sectors. The counter rotating spiral galaxy Earth resides in is shown. Earth is seen transiting from 4:6 to 1:5 as the planetary bodies move in a clockwise rotation. The sector map remains static as the material creations and conscious particulate flow in opposing directions. Only the top half of the galactic map is shown. A complete three-dimensional map would be a sphere containing additional quadrants 5 through 8 that map the bottom half of the sphere.

Figure 37 divides a galaxy into eight quadrants based upon the galactic center. The quadrants are further subdivided into six sectors. To identify a location within a galaxy, the numbering convention would be quadrant:sector. On the graph, Earth is shown transitioning from 4:6 to 1:5. If you envision the planets moving in a clockwise rotation within the graph, the particulate of galactic consciousness would be opposing that movement as it rotates counterclockwise. As consciousness individualizes and ascends through the various timelines upon a planet they create -for ease of understanding- an energetic windmill that interacts with the galactic particulate. If one planetary system in a sector ascends in energetic density, the vanes of its windmill will be efficiently utilizing the galactic stream flowing past it. If a sector adjacent to the efficient one has trouble with ascension into the higher densities, it creates a turbulence in the flow of the galactic stream as its windmill does not keep pace. The resulting energetic imbalance creates a wobble within the particulate of the galactic consciousness that if allowed to progress could reverberate throughout the entire galaxy. When this occurs, intervention and oversight begin.

The escalation of oversight begins at the system level as it tasks more ascended constructs within the system to aid the lagging planet. Recall from book one that systems typically contain four planets designated for ascension. The planetary ascension paths on each planet typically ascend through the material densities in succession as one planet begins its material ascension before another. This allows a successful ascension into the planetary collective on one planet the ability to assist the younger along its journey. If internal assistance is not sufficient, additional resources are requested from other systems within the sector, and if necessary, other sectors within the quadrant. If the issue is a large one, the galactic consciousness can request assistance from other galaxies. If an imbalance within a galaxy becomes large enough, the energetic wobble will be felt throughout the universal fabric. It is here where the calculation of ratios becomes a critical necessity as the rule of free will is applied to the amount of intervention required.

To put this statement into context, assume an imbalance occurred within one sector of a galaxy due to the allowance of free will. As free will is respected, the imbalance spreads with the space faring ability of those incarnated to become an imbalanced quadrant. Measures attempting to sway free will and restore balance are insufficient as the imbalance increases and begins to affect the galaxy. Direct intervention is the only solution, and it will occur. The free will ratio becomes; consciousness engaged in ascension to those inhibiting its progress. All efforts will be made to bring awareness to those inhibiting ascension and assist them in moving forward. However, individualized consciousness unable to self-correct will be removed and remediated. The concept of remediation was discussed in detail in the first book and should be referenced. The important aspect is that free will determination is respected until imbalances force intervention. At that juncture, the free will ratio will be employed. Timeline management is one of the first mechanisms used to correct energetic stagnation as it makes incremental changes that impact the fewest number of consciousnesses.

During an incarnation, the perception of time is seen as a single rigid construct from which there is no escape as the changes within the physical vehicle reinforce this linearity. For subsequent timeline discussions to hold value, we provide the following house of time analogy.

Chapter Eighteen

The House of Time

Consider a material galaxy to be a large house with many rooms. On top of the house is a steeple containing a clock tracking what is occurring in the house. Although it is ticking and tracking something, there are no hands and no numbers on this clock. Regardless of when you look at it, the word NOW is all it displays. This clock represents the measure of existence for the galactic consciousness and it began ticking when the galactic consciousness came into awareness. It is not keeping time; it is tracking the energetic expansion of the galactic consciousness resulting from what is occurring in its house and the rooms it creates. The rooms within this galactic house represent the various planets that have been designated for the ascension of consciousness. As you look down the hall, it continues to grow as new rooms are created from the continued expansion of the material galaxy.

Entering a room within the house you find it contains a large clock surrounded by numerous smaller clocks. The large clock began recording the passage of time the moment the room came into existence and acquired a gravitational lock. The planetary movement used to create strong gravity within this galaxy produces a linear distance being transited. The large clock is tracking the distance the planet has traversed since its creation and the resulting perception of linear space-time that has been generated. The location of the planet along this course is its current space-in-time within the entirety of linear spacetime that has been recorded.

All the clocks are traditional grandfather clocks that contain a weight on a chain. As the weight moves downward, more links are added to the chain as the movement provides the motive force that moves the hands of the clock. The weight represents the planet and the gravity being created as it moves. The length of chain attached to the weight is equivalent to the total movement of the planet since the clock began ticking. The large clock is tracking the originating timeline and the pinnacle of evolutionary development within the planetary room. As such it will always display the highest date and contain the longest chain.

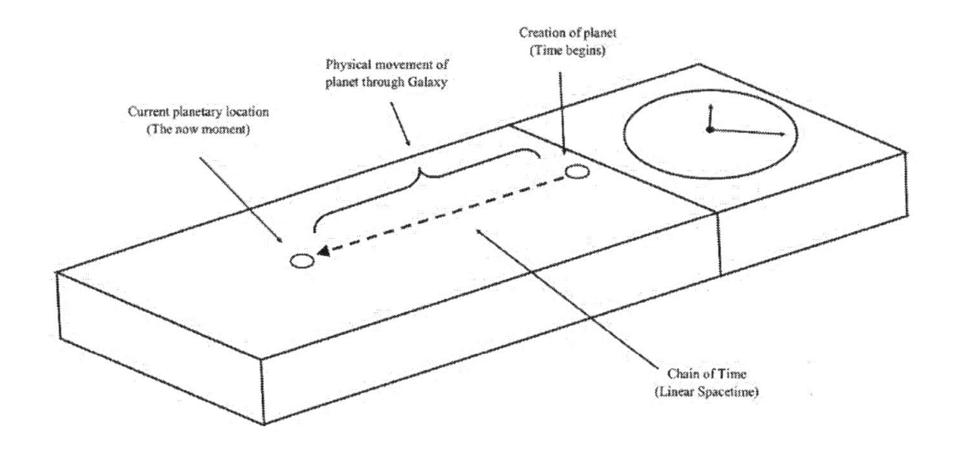

Figure 38 - The Main Clock

The grandfather clock above represents the linear passage of time within a material construct. The perception of time is a result of planetary movement creating gravitational linearity upon its surface. In this example the hands of the clock began ticking when the planet began moving through space. The distance the planet travels is the chain of the clock that creates motive force to move the hands. The weight at the bottom of the chain is the planet at its current location within the galaxy. As the planet moves through space-in-time, linearity is created, and the chain of time continues to grow.

Each smaller clock around the main clock represents a collective creation that has either diverged or been created from the originating timeline. The faces on the smaller clocks display a date and time representative of the progression of events occurring within them. The length of chain attached to the weight of each smaller clock represents the total linear existence of the collective associated with that clock. As you watch the large clock in the room, another smaller clock emerges from it to join the others already beside it.

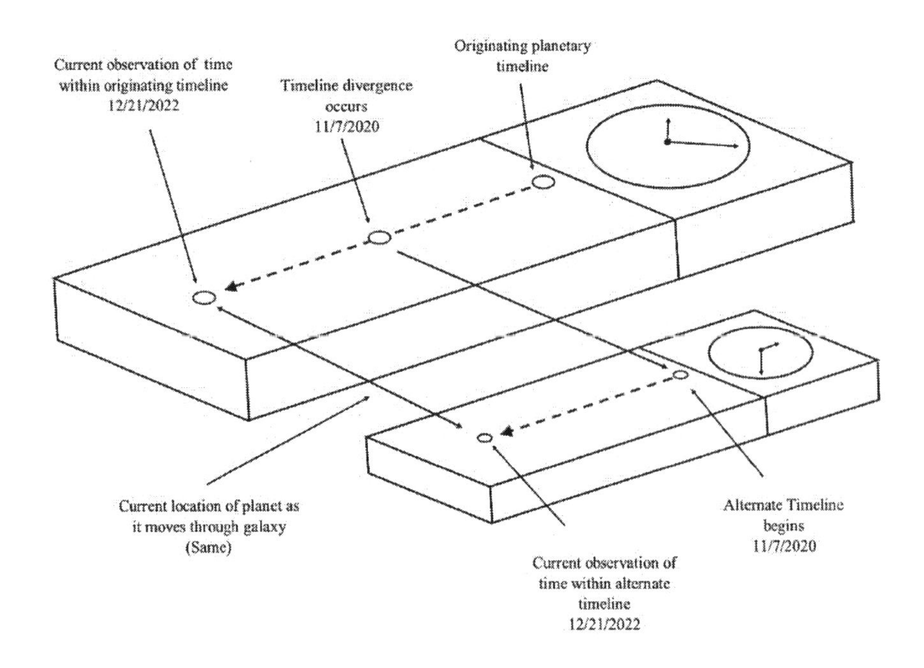

Figure 39 - Emerging Smaller Clock

The image above represents a timeline diverging from the originating planetary timeline. When the divergence is complete there are two clocks simultaneously using the movement of planetary space-in-time to create their collective realities. Both reflect the current location of the planet within the galaxy as it travels but are materially separated from each other and have no knowledge the other exists.

The date and time displayed by the new clock is identical to the main timeline but begins tracking a timeline that has separated from it. The new clock can begin from any moment recorded within the original chain of time or diverge from the current moment displayed on the main clock as this one just did. If the new clock begins from a fixed point in the past, it is set based upon the desire of the collective creating it and the era they wish to experience. How this is possible will be explained later. The new clock being observed is diverging from the current moment and is a result of energetic separation. In this instance only a portion of the collective is ready for the next energetic octave. The ascending collective will continue to be tracked by the main clock as those needing more time to balance begin to be tracked by the emerging smaller clock. When a divergence happens in this manner, a physical manifestation within the timelines will occur that explains the absence of a portion of the incarnated collective from either timeline.

In the instance of a smaller clock created from a historical period, the perceived date may appear to have occurred at a point linearly distant from the current time shown on the main clock. While the display on the main clock and the smaller clock differ as the smaller appears to be recording the past while the main clock records the future, the smaller clocks linear experience of time is a result of current planetary movement. For this reason, the historical era created from past events emerges at the present location on the chain of the main clock and parallels the original timeline in the same manner as the divergence example. This occurs because the linearity of experience each timeline contains is a result of the planet's current position and forward movement within spacetime. Now assume the energetic divergence described above creates another construct simultaneously with the creation of the historical construct. In this instance there would be a main clock tracking linear spacetime from inception and two smaller clocks tracking the existence of linear spacetime within their constructs. Three separate collective realities now exist simultaneously upon a single planet as it moves through the galaxy.

All the clocks in the room are recording the passage of time within a material construct and each is faithfully displaying their perception of current time. However, they exist in a house where it is always now, and the linear expression of time being recorded is an artificial construct designed to assist the cultivation of consciousness within a material environment. When an individual incarnation ends in any of the material constructs, the consciousness is untethered from the linearity of the clocks and once again rejoins the ever present now of the main house. Materially there is no limit to the number of clocks that can be created within a room, but there is an energetic limit. Additionally, when the expanded envelope of polarity is employed, balance between the material (timeline) constructs must be maintained. The considerations of balance also extend to the system sector and quadrant the planet resides in as previously described.

Chapter Nineteen

Timelines

At the inception of first density upon a planet, a single timeline exists that all life begins within. This would be the main clock in the room of the previous house of time analogy. Numerous spacetime (timeline) constructs can exist upon a single planetary sphere and they are governed by the collective intention of the consciousnesses embodied within them. The various timelines are separated from each other using the planetary gravitational lock as the base oscillating frequency. The gravitational lock created by a planet is what creates each room in the house of time. This base frequency is the foundation upon which discreet spectrums of energy are further compartmentalized by sequentially raising or lowering the rotational frequency and amplitude of the solidified matter. Each compartmentalization creates another small clock (timeline construct) in the room of the house of time.

With an understanding that the known universe exists within and is solidified from the photonic particulate of universal consciousness, the holographic nature of material reality has a rudimentary basis in fact. However, defining planetary bodies and material timelines as holographic detracts from the beauty and complexity of their creation. A hologram is defined as a three-dimensional image formed by the coherent interference of light. This intentionally diffused light creates the illusion of a spatial image that appears solid unless disturbed. This is the process fifth and sixth density entities employ as they use their photonic capacity to create the appearance of light bodies. They are holographic representations; not physical creations and they can vanish as easily as they appear. By contrast, material timeline constructs are solidified and held in spatial relationships as energy flows through them from a high state to the neutrality of ground state. Each timeline oscillates at specific frequencies and are solidified within the planetary grid and its gravitational lock. You may possess the technology to slip from one timeline to another, but they are solid and have been created for your learning and enjoyment. To emphasize the solid nature of material creation you need only look to the concept of black holes discussed in the first book. When a planetary sphere has completed material ascension and is no longer needed, it is returned to it creational constituents by disintegration within a black hole interface.

The periodic table of the elements reflects the structures being solidified within our current oscillating timeline. If you were to increase the oscillating spectrum of energy within all the elements of this chart, an entirely new material construct would form. The elements would maintain their current compositions, but they would vibrate within a higher energetic spectrum. This is the process involved in splitting a timeline construct where one remains at the original oscillating spectrum while the other increases into the new oscillating spectrum. If your body and consciousness are not tuned to the new oscillating spectrum, you will remain unaware that a higher energetic timeline construct has formed.

Understanding Timelines

The originating timeline of planetary ascension begins within the lowest energetic membrane of the planetary consciousness, or ground state. First density consciousness gaining energy within this membrane and ascending on the planet will contain the baseline wavelength and are considered organic, or originating from, the planet. As these seeds of first density gain energy and begin to individualize, they enter the ascension process. As they continue to mature, they move through second density into self-aware third density. As the process accelerates, the originating timeline becomes filled with consciousness moving up through the densities into self-awareness. With a robust ascension underway, energetic layers begin to form within the third density population as newer graduates join older more experienced consciousnesses. The disparity in experience creates an energetic division as advanced consciousnesses with a higher particulate density begin seeking the next level required for their growth. This division is outwardly represented as diverging goals and ideologies, as more mature consciousnesses begin to feel energetic unity and dispense with self-interest. A collective intention forms within the older consciousnesses as they come together to chart a course toward their new vision. When this maturing collective reaches the required energetic threshold, it begins to take control of the material construct. The aggregate of collective intention creates a harmonic resonance that continues to build until it shifts the frequency and amplitude of their collective timeline higher. This is where the timeline diverges and where the energy within the periodic chart of the elements shifts higher as the ascending collective moves into their new creation. Two timelines now exist upon the planet that share a common history but whose future trajectories will be charted separately based upon the decisions of the collectives within them.

An important concept that must be captured in this discussion is that the original timeline -the main clock in the room of the house of time- contains the ascending construct. When the timelines diverged it was the lower energetic that separated from the higher and became a smaller clock within the room. Separations in this manner allow the lower energetic constructs to continue indefinitely as options for consciousness to gain experience within. Collectives can continue to diverge and ascend from any of these lower energetic constructs. There is no limit to diverging timelines during the early phases of development within the planetary consciousness. However, as the planetary consciousness approaches energetic parity with the system consciousness as a result of successful individual ascension through the constructs, timeline divergences will cease, and merging will begin to occur.

The material of each timeline construct (i.e., Periodic table of the elements) is solidified within a bandwidth of energetic frequency. From the vantage point of a body involved in a linear aging process it appears as if a single historical trajectory has brought you and the timeline you exist within to its current development. While there is a linear progression of events within each timeline that create the historical record, the ascension of consciousness is not a linear trajectory within a single timeline. This means that previous lifetimes you have lived do not necessarily ascend in succession with the historical record of your current timeline. While you may have lived a lifetime as a Roman, there are several timelines that have split from that era, including this one. Your actions as a Roman may have helped shape a timeline other than the one you currently find yourself in. You may also have been a Viking before you incarnated as a Roman. Looking back into history from your current vantage point this is historically out of sequence as the Romans preceded the Vikings. With the understanding that multiple concurrent timelines are operating independently of each other, linear time for consciousness ceases to have meaning beyond an embodied life within a specific timeline.

As this book is being written, there are a multitude of concurrent timelines in operation upon the planet. The ascension of consciousness on Earth has been in progress much longer than your current history records. To illuminate this fact, consider the ancient ruins that have been located upon the planet and the apparent inconsistencies in the technology used to create these structures that have withstood the elements. These remnants contain evidence of civilizations with advanced capabilities to manipulate material that is beyond current understanding. The ruins exist within your timeline but there is no apparent connection to your current creations. The evolution of consciousness is not a single linear trajectory, but a multitude of concurrent realities spawned from a single originating construct.

Splitting Timelines

From an incarnated perspective, the discussion of splitting and merging timelines brings more questions than answers. Your world is solid, your history fixed, and your thoughts your own as you attempt to navigate through a lifetime. You observe a complex society of billions of humans all interacting with each other as they decide the collective direction of the timeline. The decisions of your life that lead you forward require calculated focus as you chart your course from infancy to old age. The multitude of interactions in each moment of 'now' on any given day within your life and throughout the world weave into a tapestry so dense that finding a single thread appears impossible. In order to understand the complexity of splitting and merging timelines you must shift your focus from the aggregate and contemplate the interaction of each thread. Consider the thread of your life and how far you have interwoven it. How many people exist in your life that you know and interact with? Your family, your friends, coworkers, casual meetings in public, travel and vacations, etc. Of those, how many do you really know? Intimate details about their lives, their loves and losses, hopes and dreams? Whatever the number, and it can be anywhere from one to several million, this is your sphere of influence. These are the people whose lives you are impacting and who will miss you when you are gone. Beyond your sphere of influence, the timeline moves without you.

Imagine that you secluded yourself on a mountain and only received information about current events once a year when you came down for supplies. During your time in town, you pick up a newspaper and attempt to catch up with what has occurred in the world while you were separated from it. Ignoring obvious technological clues, from this vantage point of disconnection it would be difficult to discern whether you were reading about your current reality or reading newspapers from a different time. In contrast, the things you are doing each day as you live on your mountain are very real because you are actively engaged in each moment of creating them. If we now extract your mountain existence and all your interactions from the timeline it exists within, there will be a group of people who you have interacted with, shared perspective, and exchanged energy. Beyond this group, the timeline remains intact without you. We have removed your small section from the interwoven tapestry of the timeline. If we continue this process with other people, we can deconstruct the entire timeline into pieces of individual fabric. Some portions will be bigger than others with more strings as they are more prominent in the timeline and have more interactions, but all can be separated and pulled apart as the overall tapestry of the timeline is deconstructed.

Examining the energetic interactions of an entire timeline of consciousness prior to divergences and merges would seem to be an impossible task, but it is not. Individual interactions are woven into the overall timeline as they combine to create the grid of the collective future. The volunteers that incarnate into the respective timelines to facilitate a merging or divergence are the weavers of the tapestry. They move where they are needed and begin to shape the grid through their actions according to the required design. This is how timelines are pushed without infringing upon free will. Putting aside the analogies of weaving fabric, tapestries, and grids, the actual constituents being manipulated are energetic oscillations within photonic particulate. Some of the particulate is compartmentalized within individualized consciousness, while the unpotentiated particulate forms the material world you interact with. All consciousness and the solidified material in all timelines exist within the planetary consciousness. The planetary consciousness exists within the system consciousness, which then exists within the galactic consciousness. All of which, down to the last photonic particle, exists within universal consciousness. Nothing is occurring that is not known and cannot be deconstructed to its constituent particulate oscillations. Nothing.

The ANKH Model of Timelines

We began the discussion of time using the analogy of a grandfather clocks whose growing chain represented the linearity of time experienced as a result of planetary movement. In the following representations the lines within the graph represent the growing chains with offshoots being the emergence of smaller clocks. Since polarity has been a factor in the creation of timeline constructs, the discussion will include polarized timelines.

Consider the Earth as it began its first creations of consciousness.

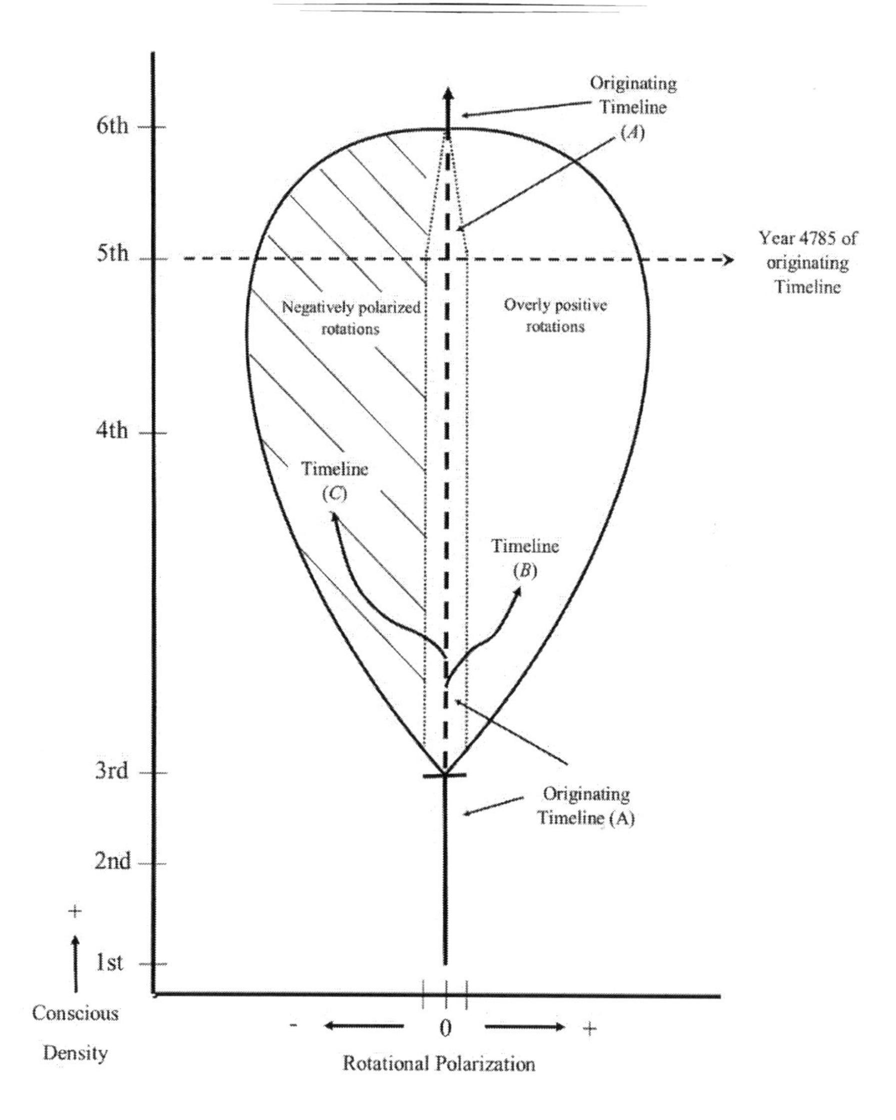

Figure 40 - ANKH Timeline Example

The example above plots the originating timeline upon a planet as it moves through first and second density and gains self-determination in third density. The timeline briefly ascends in density without polarity as consciousness becomes accustomed to their new form and abilities. As the collective gains density and experience two oppositely polarized collectives form. This forces a divergence that splits in three directions. Timeline *A* continues upward in perfect balance while Timeline *B* and *C* move into polarized experiences and continue to increase in density.

The originating timeline of planetary embodiment starts as simplistic first density lifeforms emerge. This is represented by the single solid line moving upward in density. Movement through second density continues along the solid line as self-determination has not yet been attained. When multiple timelines exist upon a planet, first and second density consciousness are placed where they are needed in service to the various timelines. This example follows the originating timeline as it enters the expanded polarity envelope. Third density self-aware consciousness has emerged and possesses the ability to choose their experiences. A single construct briefly continues upward within the non-polarity envelope as the collective acclimates to the new form and begins to align in purpose and direction. As the consciousnesses within this construct gain density and awareness, they embrace more complex experiences and polarity becomes a factor. The consciousnesses begin to choose polarization and increase in number. As they form opposing collectives, it increases the energetic pressure upon the boundary of the originating construct. When an energetic critical mass is reached, a divergence occurs, and the constructs separate. A new diverging timeline has been created through the desire and intentions of consciousness.

Assume that the originating timeline (A) is represented in Figure 40 as the vertical line in first density and ascends through third density in perfect harmonic balance. It then continued in balance and moved through the polarity envelope into sixth density. This perfectly balanced timeline is represented as the initial solid line followed by the darker dashed line ascending through the center of the graph. Two timelines have branched off the original timeline as they diverged into separate experiences of opposing polarities represented by timelines *B* and *C*. These timelines lay on either side of balance and were created as the polarized focus of the consciousnesses embodied within them forced a divergence. Looking at time versus polarity we see that embodied consciousness ended in original timeline *A* in the year 4785 when the fourth density collective ascended into fifth density.

Time is not a single linear trajectory in which consciousness must incarnate sequentially. While only three timelines are shown in this example, multiple co-creational timelines exist upon a planetary sphere. If you are in between incarnations and are in the process of planning your next lifetime, you can choose to be born within an existing timeline still in play or participate in a collective recreation. The aging of your body reinforces the validity of time as it assists you. The inevitability of death forces a shift in perspective as it grows closer. This assists you in moving through your experiences as the desires of the vehicle give way to the quest for wisdom and purpose. Beyond the limitations of embodiment, you are inextinguishable consciousness with the ability to choose where and when you wish to incarnate.

Collective Intention

All consciousness embodied within a timeline form the collective that decides the course of their future. You are either actively charting the course or are in silent agreement with the decisions of the collective and follow the course provided. If the majority agrees, the path being charted remains a single trajectory. However, if a group within the collective decides that the agreements no longer serve them, a diverging timeline will occur when the collective energy reaches the required threshold to push beyond the existing boundary. Polarity brings another variable into the energetic equation as the steering current of collective polarity creates widely diverging timelines that grow like branches stretching toward the light of ascending density. These polarized timelines span multiple eras that are still in play in what you observe to be your history. As the trajectory of these timelines diverge from the main branch, their course is determined by the collective agreement of those embodied within it. If the collective embraces positivity and cohesion, the line will continue to move toward the right. How far it diverges from the balance line and whether it splits into separate branches will be a function of the ability of embodied consciousness to achieve and maintain collective intention.

As third density begins, the opportunity to explore polarized pathways expands with increasing density. The originating timeline

shown in Figure 40 moved into third density and two divergences subsequently branched off.
Both traveled upward with the originating line before separating as each built the energetic threshold required to create their respective diverging timelines.

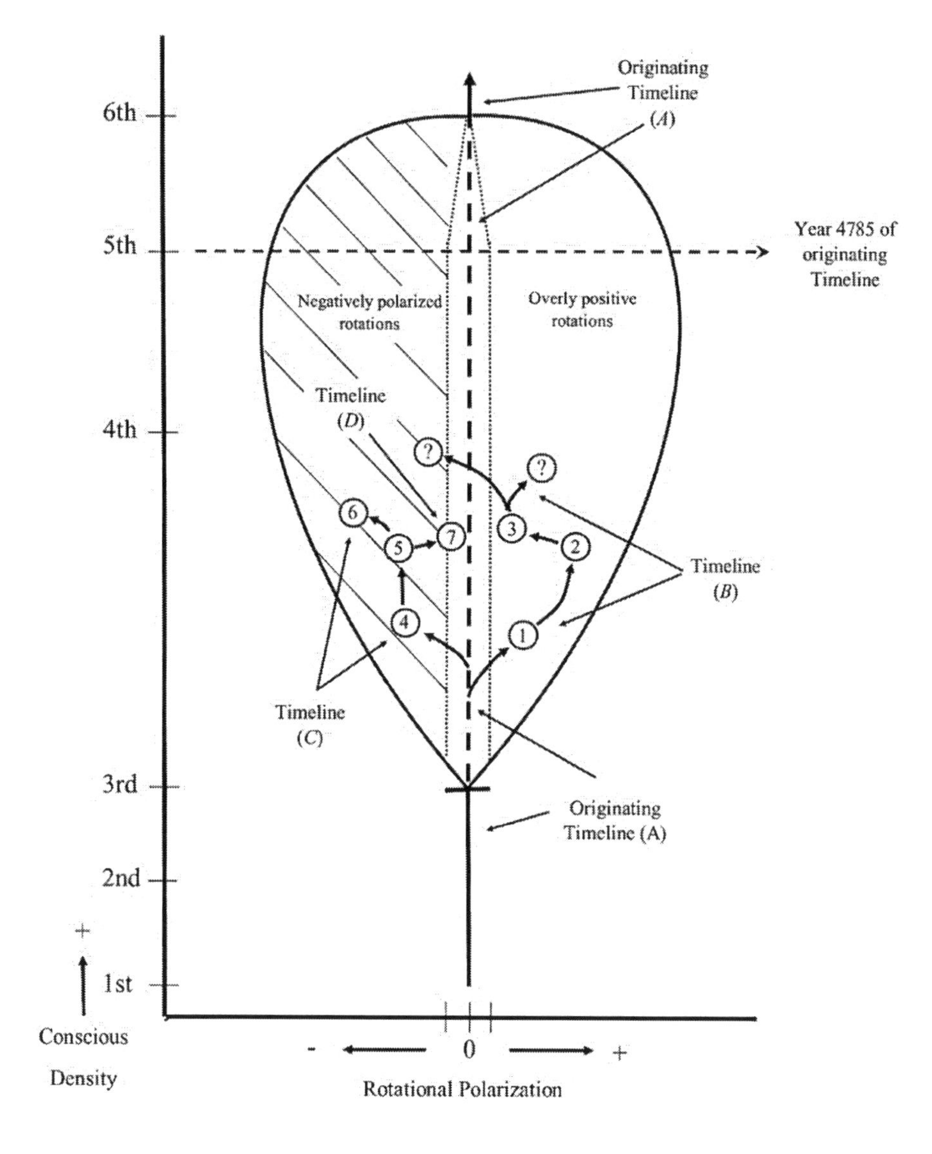

Figure 41 - Diverging Timelines

The timeline example above represents two timelines, *B* and *C* diverging from originating Timeline *A*. Timeline *B* moves from point 1 to point 2 as the collective agrees upon the positive path. As a portion embraces negativity, Timeline *B* moves as a collective to point 3. If collective agreement continues, the collective will move in unison along the positive or negative path shown. If a common alignment is not agreed upon, the timelines will diverge, and the collectives will separate. Timeline *C* diverges into the negative as it moves to point 4. It moves upward to point 5 as the negative path is questioned by a portion of the collective. The positive portion contains the collective intent to diverge from the negative portion and moves to point 7 as it creates the new Timeline D. Separated from the positive, the collective of Timeline *C* agrees to move farther into negativity.

Figure 41 continues to examine the timelines from Figure 40 and how they might move forward. The diverging timeline represented by line *B* emerged from the originating timeline when the consciousnesses within it embraced positivity beyond the agreement of the originating collective. The initial separation moves the new collective timeline to point 1. As the energy within the new collective increases and becomes more positive, we see the trajectory of timeline *B* moving upward and increasing positivity as it moves to point 2. Consciousness within timeline *B* continues along the path of increasing energy and density, as part of the collective begins to embrace negativity. Whether this pulls the entire construct toward negativity or causes a divergence between them will depend upon the cohesiveness of the collectives involved. Initially, the construct begins to shift toward the negative as the timeline moves to point 3. If the positive and the negatively aligned consciousnesses continue to aggregate into separate collectives the constructs will diverge as shown. If a single collective intention remains, the construct will move forward along one of the projected pathways depending upon the polarization of the collective.

As with the polarization of individualized consciousness, the concept of an overly positive collective needs perspective. How can an entire collective of overly loving and giving consciousness be anything but wonderful? No one will argue the fact that love and empathy for all creation is a foundational harmonic within the universal movement. The problem arises when you consider the extremes within these harmonics that were necessarily created to balance the artificial opposition to them. As the polarity experiment progressed, large percentages of overly positive collectives tended to stagnate. Within these collectives the inward desire for self-improvement was lost to outward focus. At the extremes of the positive envelope there existed entire collectives whose only desire was to martyr themselves. If they were subsequently found by a space faring negative collective, their martyrdom was assured. As extremely polarized collectives continued to find each other, the polarity imbalance within this galaxy grew into a universal concern. Anything in the extreme ultimately becomes a detriment.

Returning to Figure 41, the diverging timeline represented by line *C* embraced negativity and diverged from the originating collective using combined intention to chart a course to point 3. Negative timelines are an apparent paradox in the fact that they are not created through a unified intention within the collective. The self-serving nature of the negatively aligned prohibits this and instead creates a power struggle that ultimately establishes a hierarchy. Those at the top solidify their control while those excluded accept the rules of the construct and jockey for the remaining positions. Once collective agreement has been established -regardless of the method in which it is acquired- the timeline can be manipulated. In this example however, the collective did not unilaterally accept the negative construct and the course from point 4 to point 5 represents a balancing of negativity as the two opposing collectives engage in an energetic struggle. A divergence occurs at point 5 as the positive collective diverges from the negative and both continue along their chosen pathway. Four timelines now exist upon the planet. This process of diverging timelines will continue until each ascend into balance, or the planetary consciousness reaches energetic maturity. Energetic maturity requires that all timelines reconcile as embodiment ends within the material.

Chapter Twenty

Timeline Divergence and Multiple Selves

Consciousness that has ascended into sixth density and beyond can create multiple aspects known as fragments or fractals. The number of fragments that an ascended consciousness can create is limited only by its excess density and its desire to do so. This concept is discussed in the first book and should be referenced for further details on the subject. The following discussions on timeline creation and merger includes the ability of higher energy consciousness to fragment. Consciousness that has not attained resonance within the sixth density harmonic cannot fragment. The lifetime example that follows describes the perspective of consciousness traveling along its path of ascension prior to entering sixth density and is therefore incapable of fragmentation.

During embodiment within a timeline, you experience a linear progression of events from birth to death. When the incarnation ends you once again find yourself in the ever present now of galactic timespace where you decide upon the pathway of your next incarnation. For this discussion, assume that you have arrived in galactic timespace having just finished a lifetime that began with your birth in 1965 and death in 2052. In that lifetime you were too young to experience the sexual revolution and the hippie era you were born into. As you plan your next lifetime you desire to experience this era of change as a sexually maturing adult, so you choose to begin your next lifetime in 1948. As this second lifetime progresses, 1965 once again passes but this time you are seventeen and immersed in the experiences you desired. This would appear to be a paradox as it seems you have two selves incarnated within the same timeline. However, from the perspective of your consciousness you have already lived the entire 1965 lifetime and contain all those lessons as you now experience being seventeen in 1965. While it appears that you are reliving the same era from a different starting point, the reality is that you are in a concurrent timeline close to the one you have previously experienced. There is an entirely new collective of consciousness moving upward in a separate 1948 timeline. Because they are a different collective, what they create will be similar, but not identical to the timeline that you experienced when you were born in 1965. This concurrent nature is easily understood when related to the smaller clock emerging from the main clock of the previous galactic house analogy. How is it possible to create an identical timeline and populate it with a different collective?

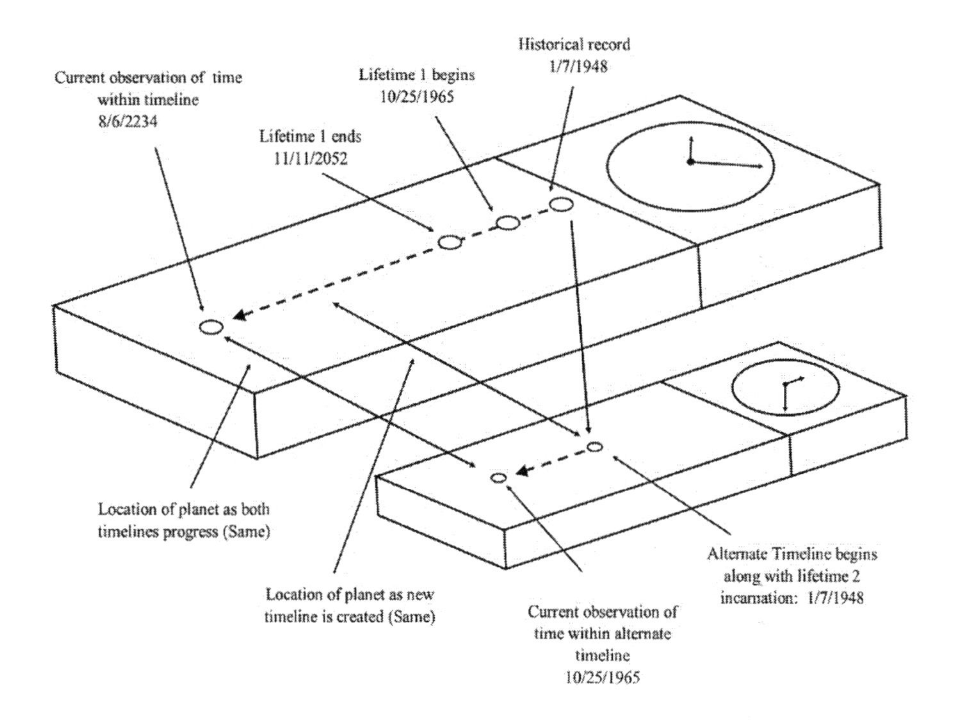

Figure 42 - Emerging Smaller Clock 48-65

The image above represents a timeline diverging from the originating planetary timeline from a past point within the historical record. A consciousness lives the entirety of lifetime 1 within the main timeline and subsequently wants to experience the 1960's again from an older perspective. A collective of consciousness forms in the galactic now (etheric) with the same intention. An alternate timeline is created from the historical record and begins to follow the main timeline. Both timelines are now using current planetary movement through the galaxy to create the perception of time within them.

Like individual consciousness, collective timelines move upward in energetic capacity as they seek parity with the octave of sixth density. Once a timeline has been created by collective intention, it becomes an energetic compilation of oscillating harmonics that exists in the ever present now of planetary consciousness. A diverging timeline can be intentionally created from any point along an existing timeline. Once the information has been encoded and stored within the planetary file, it remains there ready to be used again. The best correlation would be that of a movie filmed many years ago. All the props, sets, and scripts were left behind when the crews finished production. Now a new cast of characters have returned to the set to remake a historical classic. The new actors will revamp the script and make it their own creation, but they will use the same props and sets for authenticity. This recreation is like a movie in other ways as well. Consciousness walks on the set and assumes their roles when the director calls action. Ascended consciousness fragmenting for added lessons will assume the adult and child roles already in the scene. Third density consciousness will then participate through the normal birth process. The other similarity is that not every role of the historical recreation is repopulated with active consciousness. Like a movie, the new timeline focuses on the main characters who are active and embodied with the inference that the rest of the world is moving along as normal outside the view of the camera.

This is possible because everything each collective in every timeline is creating exists within and is created from the particulate of planetary consciousness. The energetic signature of every interaction from the inception of life on Earth to the last breath of incarnated experience is being encoded through the processes described in this text. This concept is often referred to as the Akashic record. This brings forward another reason for creating rich and colorful timelines. Each life within each timeline is like a book on a shelf just waiting to be read. Some books you helped write, others you did not, but all exist as an energetic compilation that can be accessed. When you join sixth density, you can amuse yourself by visiting the library. When you tire of reading, you can fragment and join in on the remake of a historical classic. If your planet has energetically ascended beyond the need for physical incarnations, your fragments can travel to planets that still have physically incarnated timelines and join them. As some of you reading this did when you came here.

Chapter Twenty One

The Purpose of Diversified Ascension

Individualized consciousness begins its journey as a single photon donated by the planetary consciousness and is placed where it is needed within the timelines. With self-awareness comes the ability to choose which timeline constructs it wants to experience as it seeks ascending energies. All the timelines in play serve a singular purpose; to lead consciousness forward in energetic capacity from first density into fifth density so that they ultimately reach energetic parity with their planetary consciousness. Each individualized consciousness ascending in this manner joins the planetary collective and enriches it with its unique perspective of experiences. The increase in energetic capacity associated with the creation and maturation of trillions of consciousnesses is an important aspect, but just as important is the individualized nature of their perspectives.

To give the concept of planetary ascension a correlation in human terms, consider a young farming family while disregarding the physical limitations of lifespan and interbreeding concerns. The young couple has just acquired a large tract of land that they will begin cultivating. There are only two of them, no neighbors, no labor pool to draw from, and the task is difficult. Their only option is to replicate themselves to create the help they need. In the first generation they created twelve children. These twelve continued the process and created twenty-four. The twenty-four continued and created forty-eight. There are now eighty-six consciousnesses all focused on cultivating the land and protecting the family unit. Each one brings a unique perspective based on the path they chose to reach maturity. There are also four generations involved, each generation growing within an increasingly complex community. The unique perspective of each family member brings resilience and adaptability to the collective when faced with obstacles. The strengths of each outweigh their weaknesses as they solve problems through council and collective intent. What began as two individuals has grown into a collective of combined intention, diversified in perspective, but unified by common origin and ultimate objective.

Merging Pathways at Maximum Capacity

There are two reasons why material timelines are merged. The first is the requirement of quadrant:sector balance within a galaxy that was previously defined. Returning to the upward pathway view of the ANKH, if one polarity contains an inordinate number of pathways, the imbalance will be resolved through the merging and pushing of timelines until balance is restored. The second is when a planetary consciousness nears its required energetic capacity through the material ascension process. As energetic parity with the system consciousness nears, a multitude of active timelines are no longer needed, and merging begins. Individualized consciousness engaged in ascension in the lower densities are incrementally merged into a single pathway that concludes as consciousness within it joins the planetary collective. The required energetic maximum of planetary consciousness is based upon the energy balance within the sector of the galaxy where the planetary consciousness resides, and the success of ascension on other planets within its system consciousness. If a non-polarized system consciousness in an offsetting sector successfully navigated four planets of embodiment to maximum capacity without resistance, it will reach energetic parity within its sector faster. Polarized creations provide more opportunity for collective divergence which creates more timelines along the ascension path. This meandering pathway toward the planetary collective requires a longer interval to navigate. If an opposing galactic sector produces more energy and the slower is causing an imbalance, meandering timelines will be merged to speed up the ascension process and correct the imbalance. In all cases, when the required energy has been achieved within the planetary collective, the timelines are merged until a single ascension path into the planetary collective remains. When all consciousness in this last timeline ascend into the collective, life upon the planet ceases.

Timelines with similar trajectories are reconciled first as they require the least amount of manipulation. In the prior discussion, Figure 41 graphically represented how timelines become polarized and diverge based upon the collective intention of consciousness within them. As the polarity experiment within this galaxy ends, polarized timelines must reconcile and return to movement within the non-polarized envelope. Removing polarity does not infer that the ability to choose direction has been removed, only the ability to choose overly polarized experiences. As discussed in Chapter 12 and shown in Figure 28, the upward spiral contains a smaller diameter of deviation without polarity, but still allows imbalanced perspectives. Moving polarized timelines toward neutrality is accomplished by pushing collective intention within these timelines. The difficult tasks of walking in and walking out of incarnations already in play are accomplished using ascended consciousness fragmenting for this express purpose. Walking into a life already underway is a specialized role that requires consciousness familiar with the rigors and limitations involved. Most volunteers prefer to incarnate through the normal evolutionary processes in play because they want the full experience. A detailed discussion of the walk-in process will be provided in a subsequent text.

The timelines close in intention and trajectory are the first to be reconciled.

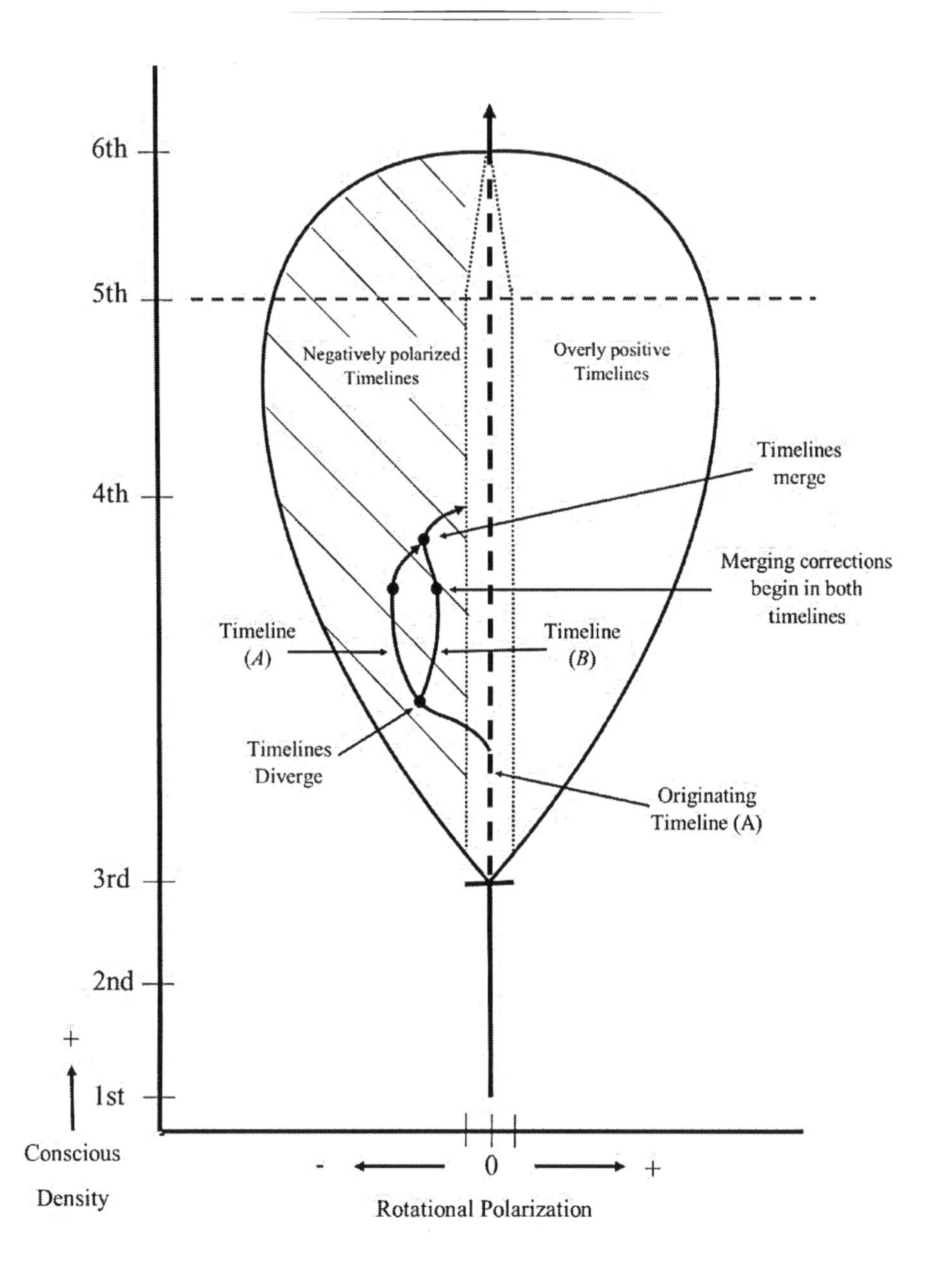

Figure 43 - ANKH Timeline Merging

The above example shows a single timeline moving into a negative path based upon collective agreement. The single timeline splits as a portion of the collective refuses the additional negativity and diverges back toward the positive shown as Timeline *B*. The two move upward in collective density separately until required to merge and return to the non-polarized pathway. Timeline *A* is pushed toward the positive while Timeline *B* is pushed slightly negative for the merging. Once merged, the single timeline will move back into the non-polarized upward pathway and continue into fourth density. Note that there is no time reference associated with this plot.

Figure 43 shows two concurrent negative timelines that are close in polarization and following similar timeline arcs. The dotted lines again represent the non-polarized area for experience within the spiral. The timelines scheduled to merge have different histories since their divergence but when they merge, they will be close in collective intention and polarity so that the differences can be blended. Pushing collective intention toward merging is accomplished using ascended volunteers and graduating third density consciousness. The energetic capacity of their consciousness is used to shift collective polarity and assures they awaken to their purpose while incarnated.

Observing the timelines in Figure 43 the historical divergence is clear. Their paths diverged as one collective went farther into negativity while the other collective refused. Since the objective is to return to balance, the more negative Timeline *A* will be seeded with consciousness that helps move it toward positive characteristics. As the volunteers move within their lives, the energy they carry combined with their actions impacts the collective. Negative intention dissipates as Timeline *A* begins its trajectory toward merging. Timeline *B* will temporarily move farther into negativity to assist in a smooth transition. This temporary movement toward the negative could be the surfacing of tension and division that temporarily captures the focus of the collective. When the merging completes, the tensions resolve amicably and are discarded forever. The combined collectives then move at an accelerated pace toward the non-polarized ascension envelope. The technological differences between the timelines will be slight in this example as they are near the same stage of linear progression on the graph. The merging of timelines usually coincides with a pivotal moment in one or both timelines. As the timelines merge, the aggregated collective will slowly become aware of minor changes to their combined histories. Major discrepancies have been accounted for, but subtle differences resulting from the separate histories since diverging will remain. Influencers in each timeline who are at the forefront of shaping collective intention may play similar roles, but they are not the same consciousness. The incarnating and walk-in volunteers assume the roles that will be dissolved or realigned when mergers occur. This is part of the coordination involved in pulling the threads of each timeline apart and sewing them back together to form a single collective.

There are occasions where timelines have strayed too far apart for effective reconciliation to occur. This is especially true as the rebalancing occurring within this galactic consciousness reaches the final stages. Highly polarized planetary timelines that are unrecoverable and cannot be merged will be ended as the free will ratio is employed. There should be no judgement or negative emotion attached to reading this statement. The consciousnesses affected by the process will be lovingly embraced as they choose their pathway forward, forever unencumbered by polarity.

PART 2

Operating in Consciousness

Chapter Twenty Two

The Numbering Convention of Ascension

As you reach the last sub-octave of third density and begin your search for resonance within fourth density, a primary objective of embodiment is learning to synchronize your energetic interactions with other consciousness. Fourth density is the threshold of collective consciousness where the energy signatures of individual consciousnesses combine to create the first strands of the energetic web of collectivity. To obtain harmonic resonance and connect with this web, you must master the interactions of self with other selves. This section will incorporate the perspectives provided in part one with expanded discussions that will help you understand and refine the process of energetic harmonization.

The concepts presented thus far have brought the understanding that consciousness is a dynamic energy engine using the interactions between rotating particulate to create increasingly complex oscillations. It begins in first density as a baseline frequency like the one shown in Figure 6. As consciousness moves upward within the ascending spiral toward the next octave, additional energy waves are generated from the increasing particulate pathways that expand the spherical geometry. The waveforms build upon each other and it is this increasing oscillating complexity that produces the continually expanding potential of consciousness. Moving through the oscillating octaves of first and second density is an automatic process due to the simplistic nature of the rotations within consciousness, and the waveforms being generated reflect this. When consciousness obtains a third density geometry, the complex waveforms must be controlled and shaped into a coherent pattern. Gaining control of your oscillating bandwidth and focusing your intention upon a goal to create a coherent resonance is how density increases and efficient movement within the upward spiral occurs.

Recall from Figure 25 that the increasing energetics of consciousness are plotted within the three-dimensional ascending spiral where measured variables are used to identify the resulting oscillations exhibited by that consciousness. The major energetic thresholds of the spiral represent a doubling of frequency and are divided into octaves of density. Each major octave has seven subdivisions within it defined as sub-octaves as was shown in Figure 17. For ease of understanding as we continue our discussions, we will use the numbering convention:

N:na

Where, N = the major octave of consciousness, and
na = the sub-octave within that major octave.

If we were discussing consciousness at the last octave of second density, we would use the numbering convention 2:7 to represent the fact that it was at the seventh sub-octave of second density. When this consciousness ends the current incarnation, it will attain a self-aware third density rotational geometry. Upon its next incarnation it will have entered the first octave of third density represented as, 3:0. From here it will move upward through the sub-octaves until it again reaches the last sub-octave of third density, 3:7. When it moves into fourth density the denominator changes and the sequence begins again, 4:0.

Energetic Divisions and their Relationship to Timelines

The divisions of consciousness identified as galactic, system, and planetary, act as successive filters that reduce the energy within the universal web. These energetic reductions allow matter to coalesce and provides the low energy incubators in which consciousness becomes individualized and moves upward in energetic potential. The timelines of collective co-creation within the planetary consciousness also contain an energetic filtering mechanism. As consciousness enters third density at 3:0, it obtains the toroidal geometry shown in Figure 1. As it creates the column and barrier, the energetic bonds within the sphere are at the minimum capacity for cohesion. This translates into a weakly powered barrier membrane. If this sphere is immersed unbuffered into a high energetic field, the external energy would overpower the barrier membrane and erase the individualized energetic signatures within. If the energy were significantly higher, the particulate may permanently disassociate. With the energy overpowered, the consciousness would have to restart its ascension pathway into individuality. To prevent this and facilitate the growth of third density into maturity, the constructs they grow within are limited in energetic capacity from the originating octave 3:0 into the upper sub-octave of third density, 3:7. This energetic octave band represents the playground of newly aware consciousness. It is here that the lessons of interaction with other selves increase energetic density from 3:0 and provides the balance needed to move toward the oscillations of 3:7. Incarnations prior to third density are somewhat random in nature because free will sits upon the foundation of self-aware, independent thought. This brings forward the need to discuss the dual role that the lower densities perform.

First and second density consciousness have just begun their journey. They exist within all third and fourth density constructs and are placed where they are needed to support ascension, of themselves and the collective they reside within. As stated, consciousness begins at first density and ascends toward third density. Therefore, all of us can look back upon our ascension pathways and find instances where an incarnation was ended in service to third or fourth density. This service to the ascending collective is part of the natural order. Regardless of whether you are consuming the remains of a plant or an animal, you are consuming the energy left within a vehicle of consciousness that has evolved to support your embodiment. This necessity requires that first and second density exist symbiotically within third and fourth density constructs. The limited energetic capacity and compact geometry of their consciousness assures stability within the higher energy constructs.

Chapter Twenty Three

The Process of Energetic Ascension

The octave of fourth density brings with it an expanded awareness of who and what you are. With that expansion comes an activation of senses and abilities that must be understood and embraced.

You have spent a lifetime becoming comfortable in your body. The veil of forgetfulness allows consciousness the illusion of a blank slate at the entry into each incarnation. For this reason, you spend the first few years of your life learning to operate a body whose capabilities mature along with you. There are exceptions to the normal progression as the energies of powerful consciousnesses sometimes bleed through the veil. These are the savants, the seers, and the healers. These exceptions aside, for most the pathway toward comfort within the body is the same. As your body reaches maturity and stabilizes, you have become accustomed to the sensory limitations and accept them as the boundary of your existence. You have a clear view of who you are and have defined the parameters of your operational comfort zone. If something occurs that then pushes you out of this zone -a sickness for example- you immediately begin searching for a pathway that returns you to the comfort of your perceived normal operating condition. As the energies within individualized consciousness continue to increase through the sub-octaves of third density toward the doubling of fourth density, changes occur that push those incorporating the new energies outside of their accepted comfort zone. It then becomes important to understand what is occurring and why, so the changes can be embraced and not shunned. You must embrace the unknown as you move into the new normal associated with ascending consciousness and not attempt to return to the old and familiar.

This book has gone to great lengths to convey that consciousness is not a product of biological processes, it is the creator of those processes. The emotional and physical processes of the incarnated form are then used as stimulus to learn and grow through. As consciousness matures and reaches sub-octave 3:6, the energy being generated by the rotating array of consciousness attached to the body begins to create an energetic wave of sufficient amplitude to not only create the barrier membrane but extend beyond it. These waves are the first steps toward collectivity and increase as consciousness continues upward within the spiral to 3:7. As the emanations grow in intensity, they harmonically tune through sympathetic resonance to match those of other consciousnesses producing similar waveforms. As a group, the harmonically tuned consciousnesses begin to match the entry octave of fourth density, 4:0. When the collective of tuned consciousnesses reach a critical mass within an incarnated timeline, they push upon the energetic ceiling of the third density construct, having reached the limit of expansion within the energy provided. They must be moved into a higher energetic octave if they are to continue their expansion. There are two ways in which this transition can be experienced; individually between incarnations, and as a collective during embodiment within a material timeline.

Tuning Between Incarnations

Tuning is required when a consciousness reaches the energetic capacity and internal balance to sustain the oscillating resonance of the fourth density octave at the end of an embodiment. When a consciousness attains this capacity, it is met in the galactic now of timespace by assigned guides when the incarnation ends. Here it is given the option of moving into a similarly resonating fourth density timeline already in play for its subsequent incarnation. If this course is chosen, the oscillating bandwidth of the consciousness will be tuned to the new timeline. This involves a synchronization of internal oscillations and matching the extending wave beyond the barrier to that of the collective. For this reason, the consciousness involved must be close in octave and polarization to the timeline chosen for subsequent incarnation. When synchronization has been completed, the consciousness will incarnate into the timeline and embark upon the lessons of fourth density at 4:0. If the consciousness was part of a cohesive collective within a timeline that was pushing upon the envelope at 3:7, it may choose to wait for the collective in the now of timespace so that they may chart their course forward together. Whether they choose to join a timeline already in play or create a new one will depend upon their wishes and the balance requirements of the planet/sector/quadrant.

Tuning During Incarnation

When a group of consciousness within a timeline reaches the 3:7 threshold they begin to collectively exert an energetic pressure upon the upper limit of the construct. This process involves the meshing and combined resonance of the energy waves extending beyond their barrier membranes. When the collective reaches critical mass, they will create the divergence previously described in the discussion on timelines. The sub-octave of 3:7 is where the energetic balancing within the upward spiral prepares the consciousness for movement into the doubling octave of fourth density. Movement into fourth density represents the maturation of consciousness into adulthood. This is the first transition into a higher energetic spectrum, and the focused synchronization of the energetic emanations beyond the barrier membrane is a critical component.

Ascension has occurred individually and in groups throughout the history of Earth but has required intense focus during the last cycle to pierce the polarity struggle that has covered and confused the planet. Through careful timeline management, energetic seeding, and implementation of the free will ratio, the extremes of polarization have been reduced as all timelines continue their shift toward the non-polarity envelope. Consciousness above sub-octave 3:5 in this timeline can feel the weight being lifted from their shoulders although they may not be able to identify what is changing. As a result, they are creating the energetic push as a collective and will be shifting into fourth density during embodiment as an ascending collective. A shift into a new fourth density timeline during incarnation is an exciting and desired experience. The fact this shift is occurring as the polarity experiment is phased out within this galaxy makes it unique. A large portion of consciousness within the universe wanted to acquire this experience and volunteered for the openings that were available. Regardless of the incarnated ego perspective you have associated with the events you are witnessing; the larger aspect of your consciousness is relishing every moment. As the perspective of ego consciousness is mentioned, some additional discussion of this concept is needed.

The Misunderstood Ego

There is much discussion in awakening publications surrounding ego consciousness and its required dissolution before being able to attain higher states of awareness. So much in fact that it has almost become a derogatory inference as in, "You are still in ego." This creates the assumption that the ego is a useless artifact that must be discarded before enlightenment of myriad variations can be obtained. This assumption, that the ego is a superfluous creation that should be discarded is incorrect and should be released. The ego personality that you operate under in this lifetime is a carefully crafted composite of all the other ego personalities you have ever created during your incarnational lifetimes. From your current perspective it appears that who you are is merely a result of the path you have walked through the experiences of this lifetime because that is all you are aware of under the veil. The truth is far more complex and wonderful. The first book referred to the ego as a jacket that you wear and subsequently remove. In that analogy the jacket was a covering for the true personality. Only when the jacket was removed did the realization occur that the jacket did not create the ego personality being worn. It was the identity of the consciousness underneath that had been used as thread to weave the jacket. While the first book was describing the shedding process from the perspective of an awakening conscious fragment, the analogy is similar.

As you begin your incarnations in third density at sub-octave 3:0, you do not have many experiences to draw from. As a result, the ego jacket you create in these earlier lifetimes is immature and rough around the edges. As the incarnations accrue, you gain an understanding of what characteristics work best for you and begin to sew them into subsequent ego jackets. The person your ego reflects during your seven hundredth incarnation will be far more refined and form fitting than the person your ego reflected during your seventh. This is a result of repeated incarnations from which you keep the characteristics that work and feel right and discard the ones that do not. We have all worn ego jackets that did not fit properly, were itchy, or were just plain ugly. This is part of the journey, and arguably the best part. There is no judgement in making mistakes because every path brings perspective. What is important is that the successes and failures are aggregated, assessed, and learned from. Consciousness that quickly ascends in complete balance into sixth density without mistakes will invariably fragment so that they can return to third density and start making mistakes.

Third density earth timelines, like most third density environments, incorporate a veil of forgetfulness that prevents awareness during incarnation of the prior lifetimes shaping your ego as you mature. However, the energetics of those lifetimes are still there, on the other side of the veil, guiding you all the same. Everyone reading can think back to a point in their formative years and identify important decisions that shaped the course of their lives. In those moments of decision, be assured that the larger aspect of you was pointing the way forward. Just like instruction from our physical parents, sometimes we listen to the wisdom of our elders, and other times we do not. Rather than attempting to discard the perspective of who you think you are in this lifetime, embrace it as you look within during your quiet reflections. When you do you will find that who you are now is a composite of the faces looking back at you from past incarnations. If you then look forward along your future course, you will see your smiling face within a portion of your totality of consciousness, with no single face more important than the other.

Chapter Twenty Four

Understanding Expanding Energetic Emanations

As consciousness enters sub-octave 3:6 within the upward spiral, the pathways within its array have multiplied to the point that the first multi-wave emanations beyond the barrier become possible. The emanation is a product of resonant alignment between the oscillating pathways. The energetic wave extends beyond the barrier and appears as a halo that surrounds the circumference of the sphere.

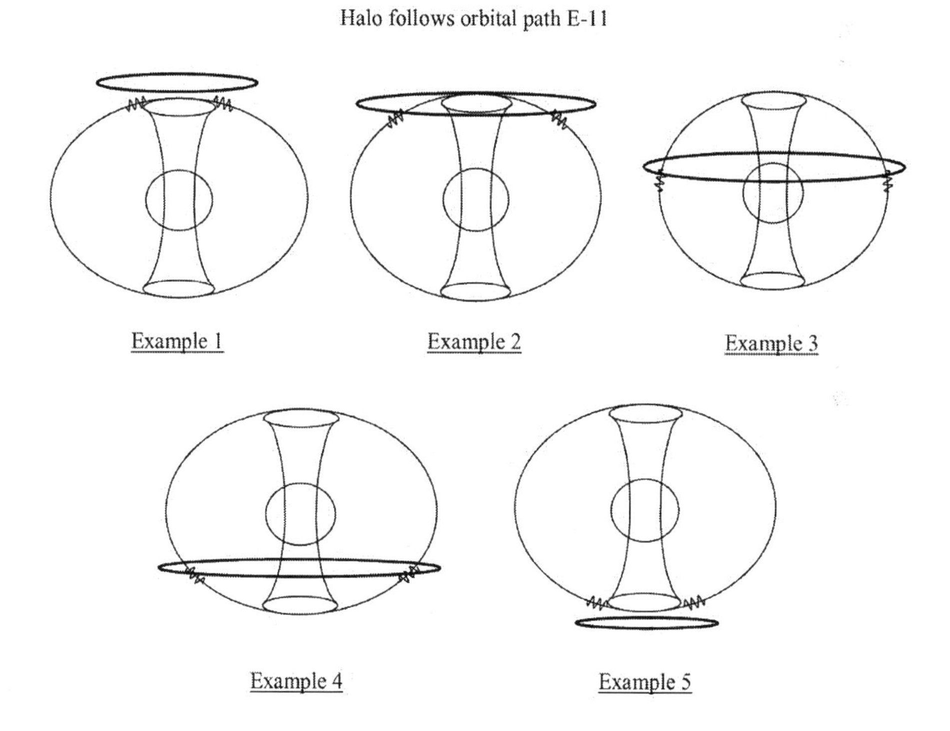

Figure 44 - Halo Emanations

The images above show the energetic emanation (Halo) that extends beyond the barrier membrane when the proper energy and balance has been obtained. The perceived halo is created by the alignment of energy between particulate pathways. Five halo locations are shown, but whether there is one moving location, or five, the appearance of travel around the sphere is a function of increasing balance and energetic potential. Because particulate energy decreases along pathway E-11, the emanation will be strongest at the top of the column and lose radiance as it follows the particulate around the sphere.

Figure 44 shows the external halo emanations. This external energetic ring is a result of two factors combining to create the pulsing. The first requirement is an internal harmonic created as the angular momentum and orbital velocity of the individual pathways synchronize at specific locations. This internal resonance transfers energy through the pathways to the outer valence particulate creating a strobing effect beyond the barrier. The consciousness has begun to synchronize and create the first coherent pulses of energy. This is the first indication that the motor of consciousness has begun its transition from being a user of creational energy to becoming the generator of it. As consciousness moves from 3:6 to 3:7 within the spiral, individual particulate continues to balance, and the energetic pathways (E-1 through E11) increase in harmonization. This causes the emanations to increase in strength and frequency as they extend farther and begin to be felt by others.

To get a clear understanding of what is creating the energetic halo, we need to combine the components of rotation from Figure 18 and the wave amplitude and orbital period components from Figure 26. As components *(A)*, *(B)*, and *(C)*, synchronize between pathways, they create a resonating harmonic that combines with the wave amplitude (E) of particulate at pathway E-11. Each ascending particulate pathway within consciousness represents an increasing velocity as the particulate increases in energy. Since the particles are traveling at different speeds in pathway E-1 through E-11, alignment may occur once, several times, or not at all. Recall that balance between orbital layers was defined through the tangental phase angles shown in Figure 22. Balance translates to a faster, more uniform rate of travel around the sphere within all pathways allowing for alignments to occur. Energetic waves created from a constant rate of particulate travel generate a stronger harmonic resonance when they align. When the waves align in the pathways, the resonance between them creates an amplified pulse greater than the sum of the individual waves.

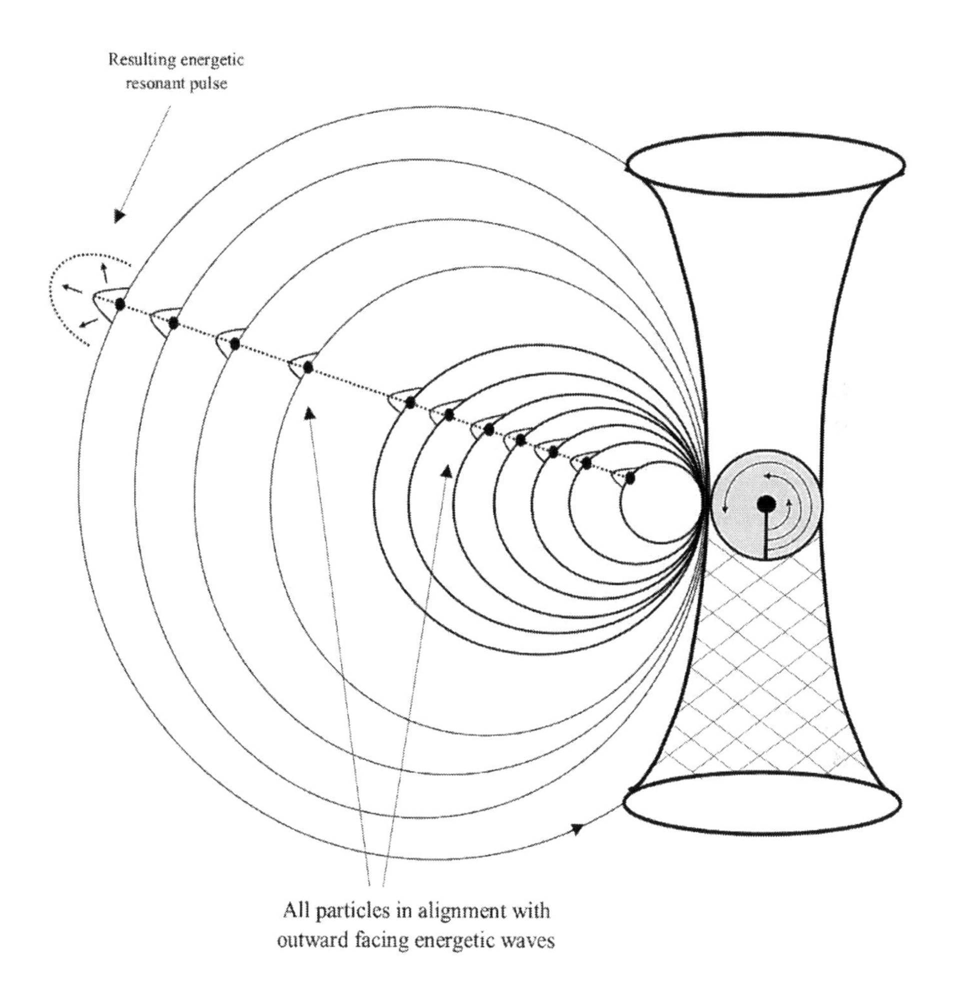

Figure 45 - Pathway Wave Harmonics

The image above shows the synchronous alignment of particulate within pathway E-1 through E-11. When all pathways align with outward facing energetic waves it creates an amplified energetic pulse that radiates outward beyond the barrier membrane. This is a similar concept as harmonic resonance within musical waves shown in Figure 6. The horizontal equilibrium line that represented harmonic coupling of pressure waves in Figure 6 translates to a line extending outward from the seat of consciousness as the particulate waves synchronize.

The balance and speed required to generate this precursor to fourth density also signals a strengthened energetic barrier membrane that allows the consciousness to enter the next octave density. Ascended consciousness observing the progress of a third density timeline construct watch for this illumination within the embodied consciousness as a marker that a divergence will soon be required. It is this emanation, created through increasing energy, balance and harmonic resonance within consciousness that expands the senses beyond the capabilities of the body. This is the beginning of energetic overlap and where the phase angle between the energetic emanations of separate consciousnesses becomes an important factor.

Energetic Overlap and Composite Phase Angle

Composite phase angles are not a consideration when opposing polarizations come within energetic proximity of each other. Composite phase angle measures harmonic resonance between similarly aligned consciousnesses. Harmonic resonance is not possible between opposing spin states as the particulate acts as absorbing energetic conductors rather than amplifying energetic resonators.

As consciousness matures it gains an understanding of what they are and begins to assume control of the oscillations of their awareness. Control of the variables leads to balance, and balance brings the smooth acceleration required to increase energetic potential. As you create balance within your consciousness it then manifests in the physical. The most noticeable and immediate manifestation is the ability to maintain an even emotional keel when confronted with the stressors of life. Rather than being immersed in an ocean of unpredictable emotional responses, you become the master of them. Since the body is manifested and empowered by your consciousness, physical imbalances within it will also begin to correct themselves. This is the harmony between balance within consciousness and the resulting manifestation of physical balance that provides the feedback signaling you are on the right path.

The intensity of wave energy extending beyond the barrier membrane and the frequency at which it occurs can be measured using the composite phase angle. When you come within proximity of another person, you will begin to feel their energy signature as the energy radiating beyond your barrier membranes connect. As you encounter this with increasing frequency, the illusion of separation begins to fade. Whether the energy from others feels pleasant, familiar, neutral, or uncomfortable, will depend upon how much energy they are radiating and the phase angles at which your energies are interacting. This is the concept of energetic overlap and can be measured by composite phase angle.

Energetic Overlap

Below sub-octave 3:5, the energetic emanations of consciousness have not extended beyond the barrier membrane. The energetic disparity between the outer valence pathway E-11 and the inner particulate pathways prevent effective resonance and is what allows a singular perspective and the illusion of separation in neutral or positively aligned consciousness. As you reach toward fourth density, the particulate of consciousness begins to utilize a dual energetic source stream for expansion. The concept of dual source stream will be presented later with the discussion of chakras. When a dual source stream commences, the energetic differential between particulate layers decreases. As energetic differential decreases, particulate gains rotational balance (smoother spin) which accelerates orbital velocity (travel around sphere), all of which increases total harmonic resonance. To illuminate what is occurring, we once again return to the analogy of musical interaction.

Each particulate pathway within a conscious array creates a unique energetic wave related to the speed of its orbit. Assume the waves each pathway creates are being generated by the various instruments found in an orchestra. At inception of first density, consciousness sets about the task of creating the initial rhythmic tempo. Since this is first density and consciousness has not yet individuated, this fundamental frequency will be the same for all consciousnesses ascending within the ground state of a planetary collective. As consciousness moves into second density, the wave pathways begin to multiply, and it is here that the addition of different experiences begin. Each orchestra of consciousness has begun to play a musical progression unique to their experiential pathways as they randomly move upward. As consciousness enters third density, individuated self-awareness commences, and the composer of each orchestra takes the podium and assumes control.

The composer begins the task of adding successive rotations to the energetic symphony within their sphere. This is done through trial and error during the lower sub-octaves of third density. As the energetic oscillations increase, balancing becomes increasingly difficult and will stall without a concerted effort. The stall occurs because the volume of musical emanations from each individual symphony has increased and now extend beyond the rooms they are playing in. Imagine the cacophony of sound millions of orchestras would create if you attempted to listen to all of them playing different music at the same time. It is here at the transition into fourth density, where the doors to all the orchestras open and everyone begins to make their choices. You can forcefully close your door and play your individual music louder, or you can listen to each other and find commonality. Since the orchestras have been playing at the same base tempo since inception, they can collectively choose a common piece of music that all begin to play. The option to close your door and remain in separation will not be expanded upon as it is a polarized pathway whose availability is ending.

The multiple orchestra concept is a direct representation of the oscillating wavelengths of consciousness that must be synchronized as individuals move up along the spiral of ascension into a balanced fourth density collective. If a collective is expected to synchronize their expanding emanations and move forward in a timely manner, they must understand the energetics within consciousness that is creating them. With this understanding, they can then manage the resulting energetic overlap as they interact with each other. This is how a collective orchestra begins to play from the same sheet of music, and the results are magnificent.

Experiencing Energetic Overlap

Everyone has been impacted by the energies of others although you may not have known what was occurring. The easiest way for embodied consciousness to initially identify an energetic impact is by how it affects the emotional network of the body.

Imagine that you have been invited to a large gathering of people you do not know. Everyone else attending this function shares your perspective; they do not know each other. The gathering is being held in a large auditorium devoid of furniture. You arrive at the function already in progress and enter the room to find that the attendees have formed into small groups who are talking amongst themselves. How did this occur? What prompted the first person in each group to begin a conversation with someone else? Out of a sea of people, how did they decide who they were going to talk to? How did the other individuals choose which group they wanted to join?

To get to the underlying cause of what is occurring we must overlook the obvious social cues of physical attraction, overheard conversation, and other forms of social programming. These external cues may initially attract you to a person or group, but sometimes a brief interaction based on these attractors has you quickly looking for a gracious exit.

Have you ever felt energetically drawn or repelled by someone you just met? Regardless of whether you understood the mechanics of what was happening, you felt something intangible. A magnetic attraction or repulsion that originated beyond the obvious physical cues or emotional responses the person exhibits. These are the effects of energetic overlap; the point at which the energetic emanations of two consciousnesses begin to interact with each other. The effects energetic overlap produces will depend upon several factors and the energetic capacity of the consciousnesses involved. The most obvious and immediate effects of being in proximity are caused by the polarization within the respective consciousnesses. A positively aligned consciousness not properly shielded will feel an instinctual desire to remove itself from proximity with a negatively aligned consciousness. This occurs as the negative alignment causes imbalances within the rotational sphere of the positive consciousness. The resulting imbalance causes an undefined emotional discomfort and the desire to withdraw.

The deleterious effects of polarized energetic overlap were detailed in the first book of this series. This text illuminates the pathway into the collectivity of non-polarized fourth density and part of that journey involves the shedding of polarized interactions. The effects of polarity imbalances will be ignored as we focus upon the pathway into collective unity. The following discussions assume a balanced neutral, or slightly positive polarization exists. This is the baseline oscillating requirement for collectivity and sympathetic harmonic resonance. With an understanding of what is occurring and what to look for, energetic overlap can be used to accelerate the path into fourth density.

Collective Resonance

Beyond the attractors of embodiment and polarization, groups of individuals form and grow because the oscillating energy emanating from their consciousnesses are in sympathetic resonance. Sympathetic resonance can be artificially created through unified focus upon a singular purpose. Religions are an obvious example of collectives that unify individual resonance through a singular focus. Ignoring a path of lifelong indoctrination, what causes an individual to choose one religious belief over another? As religions assemble in unified purpose -regardless of the objective- they begin to feel the strength of collective sympathetic resonance. Religions come in many varieties, some with belief structures that bear little resemblance to each other. Yet each follower will feel the same energetic surge of collective resonance within them as they engage in unified intention. It is this feeling of connection that pulls them farther into devotion as they attempt to fully align to the energy being created within their collective. These groups, if positively aligned and devoid of the power sequestering associated with hierarchy, provide the initial lessons of collectivity.

Energetic Overlap and Emotional Responses

To understand the relationship between energetic interactions and physical responses, we will use the most compartmentalized emotion in the human spectrum, love. The gradients of this energetic sharing that is felt through the body depend upon the object of focus; love for a child, love for a sibling, love for a pet, love of a religious deity, love for a life partner, and on it goes. As these variants of love manifest in the physical, your perceptions of what you are feeling are based upon what you observe to be causing the sensation. The central focus will almost always be a physical one for consciousness at or below sub-octave 3:5. The reason is because up to this point in its evolution, consciousness has used the senses of the body to analyze its surroundings. As consciousness moves into sub-octave 3:6, senses associated with the energy emanating from consciousness -that have nothing to do with the body- begin to appear. It is here that the compartmentalized sensations associated with love begin to dissolve. The material result is an emotional feeling of love and inclusion that begins to be shared uniformly with all you meet. The energetic truth within this process is that you have begun the first steps toward harmonic resonance within your planetary consciousness.

The Mechanics of Composite Phase Angle and Overlap

As consciousness matures into sub-octave 3:6, the oscillations of internal pathways begin to harmonize. The occurrence of resonance between pathways is tracked by the composite phase angle and is a measure of wave synchronization. As pathway synchronization commences, so too does the energy waves that extend beyond the barrier membrane. Like the musical pressure waves from Figure 6, harmonic resonance does not infer that every orbital trajectory within the conscious array is producing the same wave frequency and amplitude. This is impossible in even the most ascended consciousness. The engine of consciousness is powered through a continuous energization and discharge of particulate. This building and release of kinematic potential through increasingly complex sequential pathways is what creates the ascending operating bandwidths within consciousness we have defined as octaves within the upward spiral. As resonance begins between the pathways, the compounding intensity extends beyond a consciousness. The diameter at which it radiates and the frequency at which it occurs determines the responses of consciousness coming within energetic proximity of it.

Figure 44 represented the energetic emanation (halo) that occurs as the particulate completes a rotation within consciousness. Those images showed a halo occurring at five separate locations. While shown as trailing the energetic wave in the images for clarity, it is a pulse being emitted through the barrier membrane at the same location as the energetic wave being created by the particulate. Combining the energetic halo with the concept of composite phase angle, we begin to see their interrelationship.

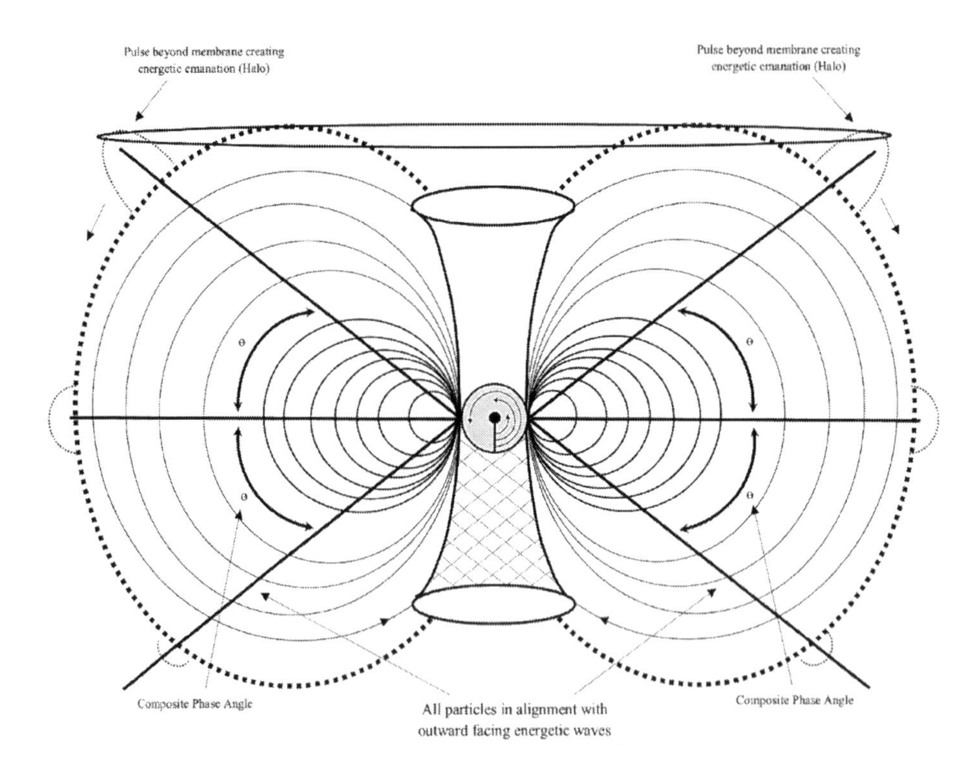

Figure 46 - Composite Phase Angle

The image above shows three locations where particulate align as they travel along their respective pathways and synchronously produce energetic waves outward toward the barrier membrane. These locations are represented by the lines extending from the seat of consciousness. The resulting resonance at these locations produces an amplifying resonance that creates a pulse greater than the sum of the individual wave energies. The pulse extends beyond the barrier and creates the energetic halo. While only the top halo is shown, the other two are inferred. When the particulate alignment occurs more than once within a rotation, the angle between the pulses is measured and the result is the composite phase angle of that consciousness.

The particulate of consciousness is in a constant state of motion as it is charged within the column and loses that charge at the outer valence. When balance begins within consciousness, the particulate traveling along individual pathways begins to align. When this occurs, the outward facing energetic waves combine in unison and create an amplified energetic pulse greater than the sum of the parts. The line indicating the location of this pulse is a product of balanced individual tangental phase angles -shown in Figure 22- that align as shown in Figure 45. This line, extending from the seat of consciousness in Figure 46 is used in the calculation of the composite phase angle. When particulate aligns in this manner, a pulse radiates beyond the barrier and creates the energetic halo. If the pathways only align once within a rotation, there will be a single stationary halo emanating from that location. When more than one alignment occurs within a rotation, more than one halo is produced. Figure 45 shows three alignments during a single rotation. While consciousness is shown as a cross-section in this figure, the spherical nature is inferred. When more than one alignment occurs within a rotation, the composite phase angle between them can be measured and becomes a consideration. A larger phase angle indicates that the rotations within consciousness are in the early stages of balancing and creating fewer synchronizations within a rotation. A decreasing phase angle indicates increasing balance, higher energy, and faster rotations within a measured period.

Energetic Overlap and Other Consciousness

The inherent beauty of individualized consciousness using free will to chart their course upward is that no two oscillations will be the same. Despite the individuality of the experiences and resulting internal oscillations, collectives form and move together into the unity of sixth density. An important lesson that must be learned during the pathways of embodiment is that individuality, in all its facets, is a requirement of unity. As with the previous analogy of the farm family, individual perspectives bring wisdom to the collectives. The characteristics associated with your embodied form is irrelevant beyond the experience the perspective brings to your consciousness. Before energetic overlap is felt, it is easy to remain in separation based on physical or societal differences. Once the call to energetic collectivity begins, those able to feel the energies ignore these attributes, open their arms and embrace each other. As the number of those embracing each other grows, social conditioning falls away as the unified energy of collective intention overwhelms it. This is the physical manifestation of increasing energetic overlap within an ascending collective. Regardless of the individual oscillations creating the unique perspective within your consciousness, as you assume control and gain balance, the oscillations harmonize and create the energetic hand that you hold out to other consciousnesses. As you bring focus to sharing your energy with others, a sympathetic resonance occurs as one consciousness acts to tune the other. This is the concept of co-resonance and it acts to align composite phase angles between consciousness. This is a precursor to synchronization within the collective. As with the electrical grid powering your homes, as conscious generators continue to synchronize and join the collective grid, more energy is available to perform work and the connected generators find it easier to hold the proper frequency.

Chapter Twenty Five

Sympathetic Co-resonance and Balanced Thought

Understanding how consciousness radiates an energetic oscillation beyond its barrier membrane at sub-octave 3:6 is the first step in learning to operate it. How far this energy extends beyond the barrier and whether it produces an energetic halo depends upon the particulate density and balance within the consciousness. What you encounter when you are energetically overlapping with another's energy signature is a result of the individual focus of those involved. Consciousness actively involved in seeking balance through the pursuit of collectivity and ascension will feel the exchange and have some understanding of what is occurring. It can then use the process it to assist themselves and others.

Balanced Thought

Balance is a product of focused intention. The focus is upon the thoughts within consciousness and the movement into collectivity. Embodied consciousnesses have two active processes in play. One is the conscious mind, or operative consciousness, which is the active portion making the decisions that chart the course through life. The other is the sub-conscious, or sub-routine, that plays in the background assimilating external cues and making recommendations based on them that are acted on or rejected by the operating program. In the simpler instinctual embodiments of sub-octave 3:0 and 3:1, the sub-routine was useful in assessing and detecting threats that were then relayed to the operative consciousness for fight or flight determinations. In today's world of endless information, the sub-routine is being barraged by data that it is not qualified to assess. Adding to the confusion, some of that information is purposely incorrect and directly targeting the sub-routine as it attempts to manipulate it. One of the first objectives of balancing is to acknowledge that a sub-routine is running and providing information. When you start listening to the conversations, you can begin to control the sub-routine and how it impacts the operative consciousness.

Fear and fighting for continued survival are the most basic of instinctual responses. As such they are the simplest avenues to engage the sub-routine and create imbalanced reactions. Both narrow the focus of the operative consciousness by suspending expanded rational solutions in favor of immediate survival reactions. Balance then, in its simplest form, is being able to identify when something external is attempting to push you out of rational thought and into reactive responses. If you are assimilating information from other sources, you must remain aware of how that information impacts you and reject imbalanced thought before it becomes action.

Sympathetic Co-Resonance

Sympathetic co-resonance describes the process of alignment between one or more consciousnesses where both generate synchronized oscillating frequencies as portions of the particulate create identical energetic waves as they travel. Obtaining co-resonance between consciousnesses can occur in several ways. The most obvious way of creating co-resonance is through shared experience. When co-resonance is created in this manner it remains, regardless of when it was created. Coming into proximity with someone you have co-created with in a prior lifetime will be felt as an energetic recognition. How that recognition is interpreted depends upon the ascension level of both parties and their understanding of the energies of consciousness.

The second method of co-resonance is when the focus of individuals is close enough in intensity and frequency to create a shared harmonic. This was the group concept previously discussed where all gather to focus upon a similar path and purpose. As they align their thoughts to a common goal, it shifts the oscillating frequency within a portion of the particulate. Rather than an external impact, this occurs within the seat of consciousness and is a product of focus. As the group grows in number, their combined resonance creates an amplified effect. The amplification of focus will impact the energetics of individuals through barrier membrane interaction if they remain in proximity long enough. The larger the group, the more power they will have to realign others to their frequency. In its purest form, these groups are the seeds that move forward and join the ascending collective. However, this function of resonance through shared focus is effective on either side of polarity. If misused, it can lead to extremes of improperly focused groups below sub-octave 3:6.

The third method is the focus of this text as it applies the concept of sympathetic co-resonance to ascending collectives at sub-octave 3:6 and above. Sympathetic co-resonance at this level involves interaction with the waves creating the energetic halo. These waves are the threads that sew individuals into collectives that move in unison upward. At sixth density and above, synchronized oscillations extending beyond the barrier membrane is the force that powers the universe. When consciousness approaches fourth density, separate groups of unified intention begin to merge. As the merging accelerates, the synchronous amplification creates a force that continues to increase. The call to unity has begun as imagined differences become obsolete and fall away. It is not a coincidence that the concepts of unity, love, and balance between all things continue to spread among a portion of the population. These are the requirements of fourth density, and movement into it has begun. As the number of consciousnesses embracing sympathetic resonance continues to grow, the bridge to fourth density comes into focus.

Sympathetic co-resonance begins in physical proximity as higher energy consciousness acts to balance and accelerate the lower. The extent of realignment the lower energy consciousness acquires through the interaction depends upon how long they remain in proximity to the higher energy source and their willingness to engage in the process. If the lower energy has sought the higher and is freely engaging in the process, the realignment will occur quicker and the energy will penetrate deeper into the rotations of the consciousness. If the interaction is by chance, like those that occur in public places, the higher energy will affect the particulate traveling along pathway E-11 of those within proximity. The difference in energy transfer is a result of the permeability that occurs within the barrier membrane when conscious intention is focused and engaged in the process.

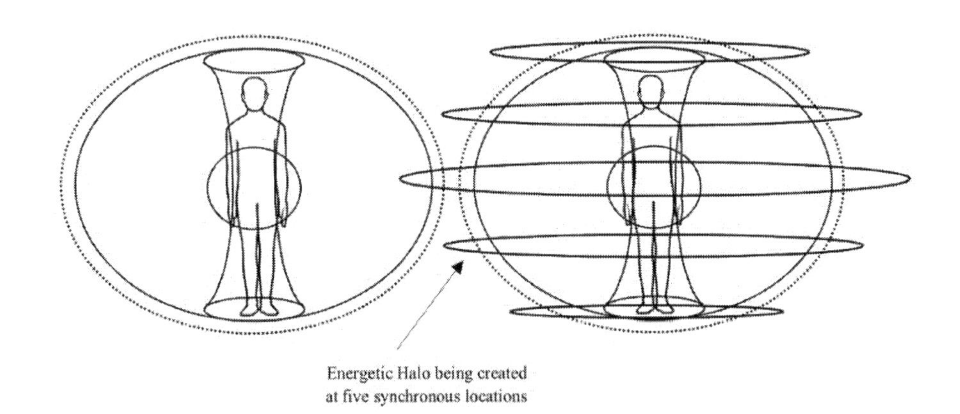

Figure 47 - Energetic Overlap Basics

The image above shows the relationship between the sphere of consciousness and the physical form. The sphere on the right is exhibiting synchronous alignment within its pathways at five locations during a single orbit of particulate. The amplified waves at these locations create the halo that the consciousness on the left is in proximity of. As the waves penetrate, they realign the particulate that comes in contact with them. The effect is one of balancing and acceleration if the lower consciousness is of sufficient density and within threshold resonance. If the difference in energy or density level is too great, realignment of imbalances is subject to the focus of the consciousness. Regardless, acceleration will still occur, and existing imbalances will be amplified. The physical response unbalanced acceleration creates in the impacted consciousness is unpredictable.

Figure 47 shows two consciousnesses who have come within proximity of each other. While both individuals are shown with the same diameter spheres, the higher energy consciousness exhibiting energetic halos would have a larger diameter. As the higher energy comes into proximity with the lower, the energy beyond the barrier that is creating the halo begins to impact the outer rotations of the other consciousness. If the impacted consciousness is knowingly engaged in the process, the energy will travel deeper into the sphere realigning particulate traveling along inner pathways. The longer they remain in proximity and focus on similar thoughts, the closer they will come to sympathetic co-resonance. The halo is generated from the alignment of particulate within the pathways as previously discussed. As the energy passes through the lower energy consciousness it acts to realign and accelerate the spin state of particulate passing through the field. In simple terms, the realignment is relatable to the energy of one tuning fork creating an energetic response in a stationary one at rest. The more energy the consciousness contains, the farther its halo will extend and the more impact it will have.

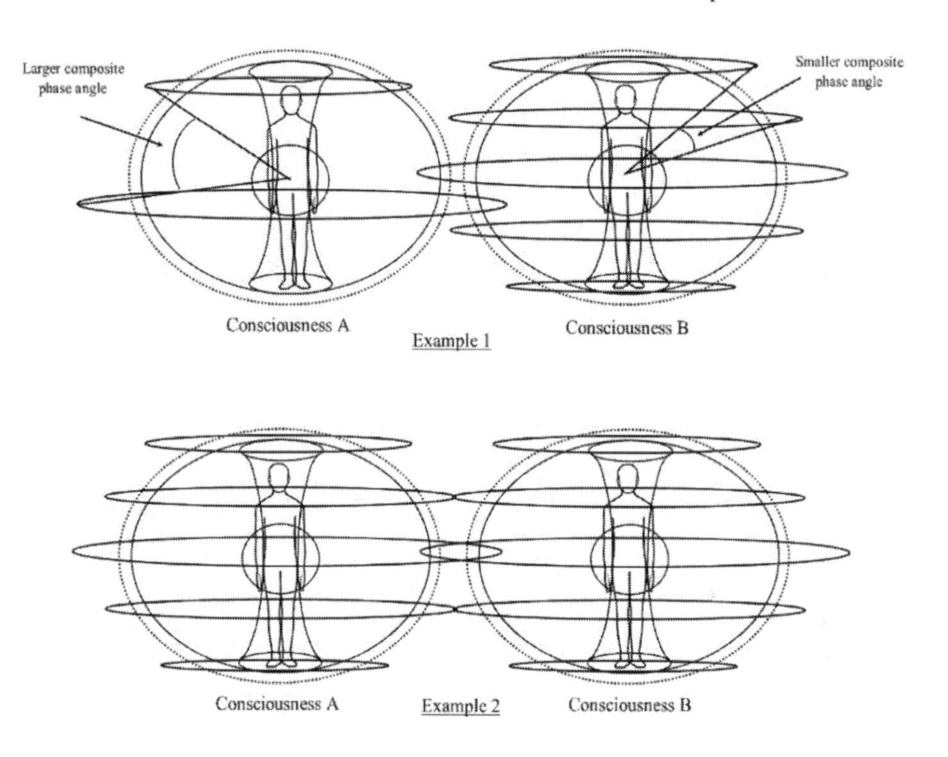

Figure 48 - Composite Phase Angle Relationships

Example 1 above shows two consciousnesses in proximity. Both consciousnesses are at the same level of density and are both seeking expansion into fourth density. Consciousness 'B' is at a higher level of synchronization and is producing five points of energetic emanation beyond its barrier membrane. Consciousness 'A' is only exhibiting two emanations. As they stay in proximity and share a common focus, the higher energy consciousness will act to balance and synchronize the other. Example 2 shows both consciousnesses in balance and synchronized with each other as they produce identically phased energetic emanations. A phased relationship between two or more consciousnesses produces another level of resonant amplification that will assist others who come within proximity at a faster rate. This phased relationship is the thread that sews individual consciousness into the blanket of collectivity.

Example 1 of Figure 48 represents two consciousnesses who are out of phase coming into proximity. Consciousness 'A' has adequate particulate density but is only creating two synchronous alignments within its sphere. Recall that imbalances are created at the particulate level and produce uneven, energetic waves along their travel pathways. These individual imbalances within pathways are measured using tangental phase angles. When observing the composite, we see the waves within the individual layers combining to create the overall balance of the consciousness. Overall balance creates the synchronous alignments responsible for the halo. The periodicity of these balance points within a rotation are measured using the composite phase angle. Because of existing imbalances, there are fewer alignments and fewer energetic halos being produced by consciousness 'A'. Fewer alignments create a large composite phase angle between them. Consciousness 'B' contains more energy within its rotations, has a higher level of balance and the particulate is traveling faster along the pathways. The result is a higher rate of synchronous balance points and resulting energetic halos. Consequently, the composite phase angle between the balance points will be smaller. Example 2 of Figure 48 shows that as consciousness 'A' stays in proximity to consciousness 'B' it is brought into balance through sympathetic co-resonance. The longer it remains in proximity, the closer it will come to matching the phase angle of consciousness 2 assuming it has the particulate density to do so.

Chapter Twenty Six

Creating and Realigning Energetic Oscillations

This book has provided detail related to the interactions between the particulate of consciousness required to create a toroidal geometry and resulting self-awareness. Oscillating energetic waves are generated as the particulate is energized in the column through successive rotational pathways and discharged at the barrier membrane. The balance between individual energetic layers can be measured as can the balance of the composite. The energetic oscillation each particle exhibits during this process is a result of the encoding it receives during the acquisition of experiential energy. When encoding occurs, affected particles acquire a new oscillating dynamic representative of the experience. This causes them to oscillate uniquely within the structure as they transition through the charge/discharge cycle. Like information encoded on a computer, each particle faithfully reproduces the energetic oscillation every time it is energized. Experience is the catalyst, providing fuel to the engine of consciousness for its energetic expansion.

The Process of Energetic Encoding

Earlier in the text, first density was related to a pot of water existing at the lowest level of energy within a planetary consciousness. All particulate was donated by the planetary consciousness and began with the planetary baseline resonance embedded within it. The baseline harmonic creates a sympathetic resonance identifying the particulate as potentiated for ascension and available for first density experiences. This is the baseline harmonic wave shown in Figure 6. Prior to their first division, these particles have a single sector of encoding containing the baseline oscillating dynamic. As energetic division of particulate occurs, the baseline oscillator is transferred. Each new product of particulate division contains half of the original baseline energy as a new sector is created to receive additional imprinting.

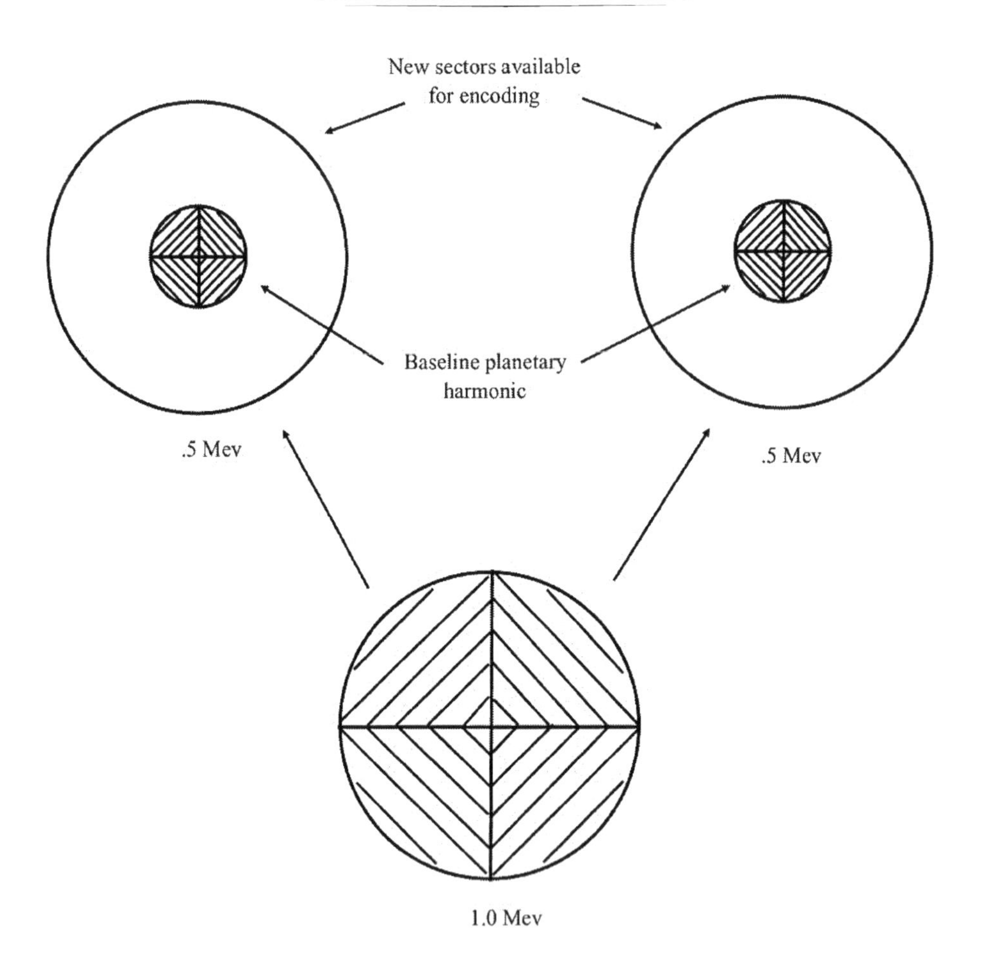

Figure 49 - Baseline Harmonic Fracture

The images above are cross sections of a particle of consciousness. As a single particle begins its journey upward from neutrality into higher energy it contains the baseline planetary harmonic that is built upon during the generic experiences of first density. As the particulate fractures under increasing energy, the baseline signature is transferred equally to both particles. As division continues and the consciousness increases in density, the baseline harmonic continues to be transferred by the division process into every particle. This is the baseline harmonic that will be used to form collectives and ultimately synchronize with the planetary consciousness.

Additional sectors for encoding are created each time energetic division of particulate occurs. Each subsequent sector of encoding represents an additional rotational weight that affects the angular spin of the particle. The unique nature of the layered encodings is assured through the use of free will as they add complexity to the energy wave that will be created as the particle spins along its pathways. An important aspect of the energetic encoding occurring on particulate is its spiral nature. The foundation of consciousness is helical spin. Encoding information upon a particle moving along a spinning trajectory produces an angular track.

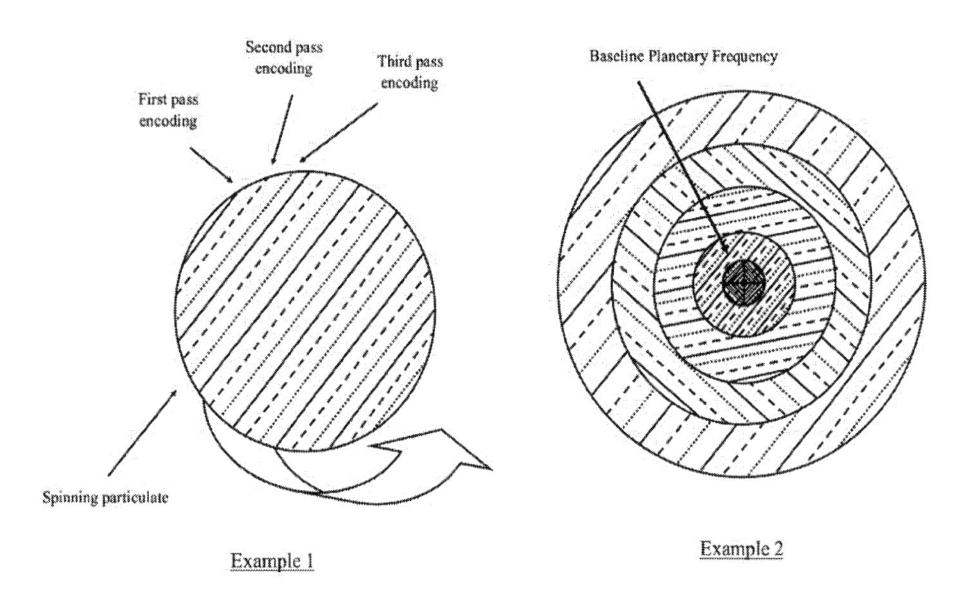

Figure 50 - Helical Encoding

The foundation of consciousness is helical spin. Example 1 represents the energetic encoding that occurs along angular tracks as the particle spins. When the external area is completely covered, harmonic oscillation associated with the encoding reaches a resonant threshold and fracture occurs. Example 2 is a cut away cross section of a particle showing how successive tracks of encoding exist as layers within the particle. This particle has undergone five fracture events. Each layer contributes to the overall energy signature of the particle as it gains energy. Successive layers energize and determine the energetic waves created as the particle ascends through pathways E-1 through E-11.

Figure 50 shows an external view of a particle and the winding path that encoding produces. Example 1 shows three encodings along the outer periphery of a particle. When the periphery has reached capacity, an energetic resonance will build within the particle. The vibratory rate of the resonance will increase with increasing energy until it causes the particle to fracture. Each particle within a third density consciousness will have multiple layers of encoding along its periphery and many more within it from previous fracture events. Example 2 shows the cross section of a particle that has undergone five fracture events. With each fracture, the previous encodings remain and become smaller and more compact. As the fractures continue and previous encoding build within it, the particle will create increasingly complex waveforms as it moves through the sphere. As consciousness ascends in density through the fracturing process, waveform complexity increases as a result of that process. At sub-octave 3:5, balancing the complexity becomes an important consideration.

Figure 21 examined eleven ascending orbital pathways that a particle travels as it moves through the energization and discharge process within consciousness. A particle that has completed the energization cycle exits the top of the column fully charged and uses that energy to create the barrier membrane. After completing its orbit, the particle re-enters the column and is drawn into the seat of consciousness. If any energy remains within the particle at E-0 it will generate the baseline wavelength as it enters the column. If the particle was effectively depleted of energy (as occurs at sub-octave 3:0), the small amount of energy acquired during transit in the column will energize the baseline wavelength before it travels along pathway E-1.

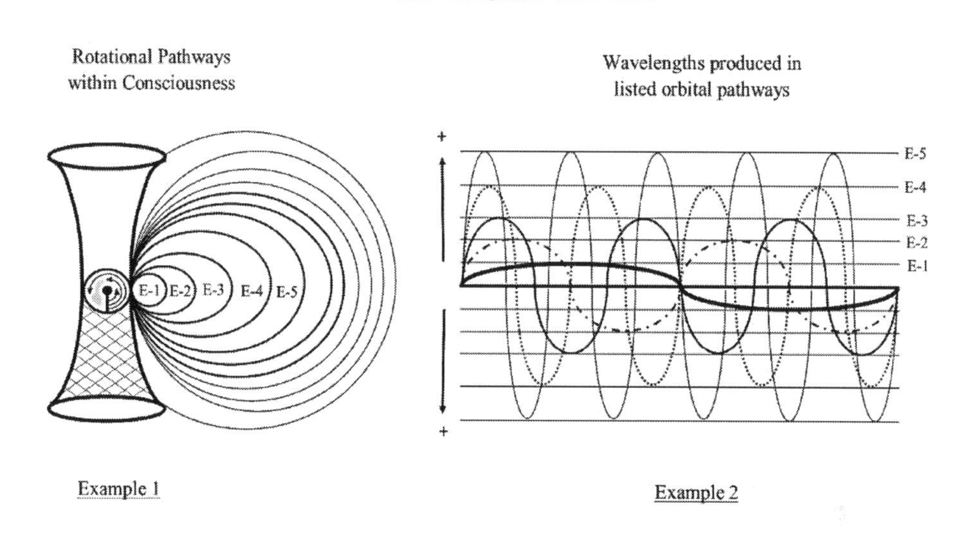

Figure 51 - Rotations and Wavelengths

Example 1 above is an expanded view of Figure 21 highlighting the first five rotational pathways within the seat of consciousness. As the particulate gains energy along these pathways, it will sequentially energize subsequent encodings. The energetic waves the particle generates along each pathway will reflect the increasing energy (amplitude) and the waveform will be a product of the encodings that have been energized. Example 2 shows the waveforms being generated along each particulate pathway. Each ascending pathway is a weighted combination of those below it. Therefore, the spin state creating the energetic wave along pathway E-5 is a product of pathways E1 through E-4 in addition to E-5. All of the sequential encodings must combine to create a perfectly balanced rotation through the entire charge cycle for synchronization to occur.

Figure 51 reflects an expanded view of the first five orbital pathways. Pathway E-1 is the lowest energy pathway and the energetic wave produced along this path will always be the baseline resonance. As the particle moves to pathway E-2 within the seat of consciousness, it picks up additional energy in the column. The increase in energy energizes the secondary oscillation associated with the next level of energetic encoding. As it travels along pathway E-2, the energetic wave it creates is a product of the baseline encoding and the secondary encoding. Additional segments of encoding are energized in this manner as the particle gains energy and moves through orbital pathways 3 through 5. The resulting oscillating wavelengths shown in Example 2 reflects the additive energetics that result from sequential energization.

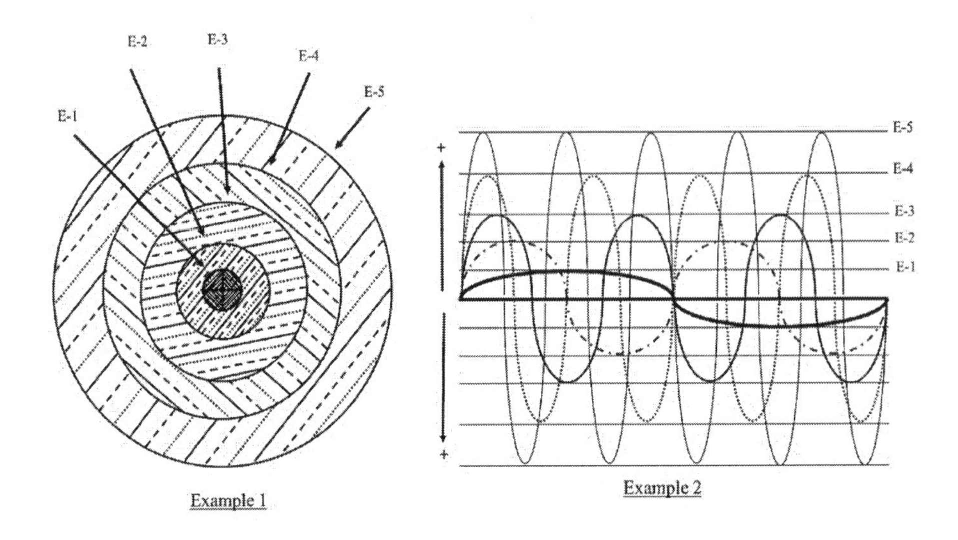

Figure 52 - Encoding and Wavelength

Example 1 shows the cross section of a particle with five layers of encoding. Particulate gains energy as it completes a rotation along a pathway of consciousness. The layers energize and produce the waveforms shown in Example 2 as they travel. Along pathway E-1 there is only enough energy to create the baseline planetary wavelength. When the particle gains energy and moves to pathway E-2, the baseline wavelength E-1 and the next level of encoding, E-2 will be energized. When the particle travels along pathway E-5 the waveform being generated is a product of the energization of all five sections of encoding.

As the particle completes its rotation along pathway E-10, it enters the last energization cycle in the column before proceeding to pathway E-11. With this last energization in the column, it either exits to energize the barrier or reaches the energetic threshold of division. If it fractures, the resulting particles will not have the energetic capacity to exit the column, having divided the required energy between them. The particles will instead exit the column at the orbital height associated with the energy they contain and continue to move through the rotations until they regain maximum energy potential. The variable that determines whether the particle exits the column or fractures when it achieves maximum energetic potential is a function of vibratory resonance.

Vibratory Resonant Fracture

The vibratory resonance required to cause a particle to fracture is dependent upon the encoding the particle contains. This encoding can be related to the crystalline structure of a wine glass and the energy contained in pressure waves required to cause a resonant action that shatters it.

The particulate of consciousness is engaged in an endless rotation within a sphere as it energizes individual awareness. Each cycle of charge and discharge brings an opportunity for energetic experience to be encoded upon a particle. Each encoding shifts the vibrational saturation point of a particle. The vibrational resonance associated with the fracture point also changes with the consciousness it exists within. As the consciousness increases in density and moves upward within the spiral of ascension, the particles exhibit an overall increase in balance resulting from the encoding they are acquiring. This translates to increasing spin and orbital period. Rotational balance and increasing velocity shift the fracture point higher and allow additional encodings.

Encodings occur within the seat of consciousness as the particles travel along the slower, lower energetic pathways that occur there. Recall that the level of energy left at pathway E-0 increases as consciousness moves upward along the spiral. Pathway E-0 is the lowest energy state within the consciousness and as such is termed its zero point. It is the increasing energy remaining at E-0 that creates the expanding radius within the upward spiral shown in Figure 16. As the energy at zero-point increases, the particles will be traveling faster through the seat of consciousness as a result. A faster rate of travel means less exposure to the encoding within the seat of consciousness. Faster transit time and less exposure creates a narrower track of encoding. The narrower encodings are inherently more stable than the slower, wider tracks created in lower densities. The overall result is that as consciousness ascends within the upward spiral, the vibratory saturation point required for harmonic fracture of particulate also increases. The encodings that combine to create the oscillating bandwidth of consciousness occur within the seat of consciousness, and the seat of consciousness is the locus of self-awareness. This brings forward the critical nature that the focus of consciousness imparts to the oscillating dynamic.

The Focus of Consciousness

The acquisition of self-awareness within third density provides a new tool to the budding consciousness; the self-determination of free will.

Consciousness is the state of being aware, and awareness is the understanding of a situation or subject in the present moment. Self-determination is the process of deciding your course of action, inaction, or reaction to a situation, subject, or memory within the present moment. The evolution of self-determination within a single lifetime is obvious as the impulsive nature of youth is replaced with the calculating wisdom of a maturing adult. Maturity, however, is not a function limited to a single incarnation under a veil of forgetfulness. It is an endless process within the sphere of consciousness as it benefits from the wisdom and perspectives acquired from each incarnation. Each lifetime is used to understand and refine the energetic waveforms created by sequential encodings. The creation and realignment of encodings occur within the seat of consciousness as the individualized perception of wisdom is imparted to the particulate through intentional focus.

The foreword of this text contained the concept of conscious awareness and defined it as, focused intention within the ever-present moment of now. If experience is the weighted track written upon particulate in each moment, intentional focus within that moment would be the tuning that defines how the weight is distributed along the track. A component of that focus is the perspective in which the experiences are being viewed. Becoming aware of the intention you bring into each experience is a critical step toward creating balanced encodings. Meeting each new experience from a neutral perspective without predetermination allows you to assess the situation and choose your association with it. When you disconnect the automatic responses of emotion, social programming, and engrained bias, you become consciously present in each moment. The result of entering and observing an experience from a position of balance is energetically balanced tracks encoded upon the particulate.

The path toward wisdom within consciousness that creates the encodings and subsequently realigns them can be related to a journey that begins as a twisting and arduous path whose sharp turns prevent seeing the path beyond them. As the journey continues, the turns become less frequent and more of the road ahead becomes visible. The more you can see, the easier it becomes to anticipate and plan for the next turn. Eventually the path straightens and rises allowing you to look back upon the steps taken to bring you to your current location. It is here, with this new perspective that you must shift your association with the past twists and turns experienced along the way. This ascending perspective begins at sub-octave 3:6 and all will contain past imbalances at this juncture regardless of whether they are in an expanded polarity envelope or a non-polarized one.

Free will determination brings the opportunity to choose imbalanced interactions between consciousness as each gains understanding and perspective from the experiences. The upward spiral of ascension was shown as a linear graph in Figure 31 and as a radial cross section in Figure 35. Both reflect the ability to add particulate density through positive and negative pathways. Regardless of the polarity chosen to ascend in density, entry into sixth density requires complete balance within the array for synchronization to the universal grid to occur. These graphs when summarized show the availability of imbalanced experiences at lower densities and the subsequent requirement to balance them as unity approaches. If imbalanced perspectives are expected and allowed, there must be an avenue available to rebalances the energetic signatures embedded within the photonic particulate. To understand how this occurs we must first understand the mechanisms of photonic encoding that create the energetic wave profiles unique to each consciousness.

Encoding and Realigning Previously Encoded Particulate

The defining characteristic of self-awareness is the seat of consciousness at the center of the toroidal array. Within this area, low energy particulate circulates as it regains energy. This creates the densest area of particulate population. While the energy within individual particulate is low, the compact rotations create a strong coherent energetic field responsible for awareness. This is the area where focused intention resides, and the encoding and realignment of experience occurs.

Figure 45 discussed the energetic emanation that occurs beyond the barrier when synchronous alignment begins within the pathways. This amplified resonance is the beginning of external focused intention that can impact and realign particulate within other consciousness. Encoding experience within consciousness uses a similar concept based on inward focus rather than pathway synchronization. The encoding occurs within the barrier membrane as energy is focused upon particulate at its lowest energetic state within the seat of consciousness. In this instance the term focus is being used in its literal sense. The energy contained within a consciousness at any density is concentrated and focused inward as it encodes the particulate. This is the same concept as using a magnifying glass to concentrate and focus the energy of the sun to burn a track onto paper. During an incarnation, the focus of consciousness is not only writing tracks upon unobservable photonic particulate, but also engraving those tracks within the neural interface and creating biophotons. In common vernacular, you are saving your data to two locations, the hard drive of your consciousness, and the temporary drive of your physical form. As the veil continues to thin for those ascending in energy, they will be able to access an increasing amount of information from their hard drive as they learn to rely less on the temporary drive.

In lower densities, focused attention is accomplished through the inclusion of a sensory system within the physical form that limits the area of focus. Limited sensory focus coupled with instinctual programming assists lower energy consciousness with simplified and balanced encodings. The human form contains a complex neural and emotion feedback network that amplifies free will choices. Whatever you are experiencing at any moment is flavored by the perception of how it is affecting this network. The energy the resulting encodings contain depends upon the interpretation applied through the emotional and physical responses to the experience. All experiences are accessible once encoded, but some will contain more energy than others. The encoded energy is a result of your perception of the experience which then determined how focused and engaged you were with it. Being burned at the stake as a witch in a prior lifetime is going carry far more energy than dying in your sleep at a ripe old age. Any imposition upon an intended life path will contain an imbalanced high energy encoding. During a subsequent embodiment, the memory of being burned should remain behind the veil of forgetfulness. The term 'should' is used because highly charged encodings can bleed through the ability of the veil to conceal them. Regardless, the imbalanced encoding associated with being burned at the stake can be realigned and balanced during a subsequent incarnation. This is an important aspect of continued ascension within the upward spiral.

Within the seat of consciousness, the energy of focused intention has the capability to redefine existing energetic signatures within the particulate. The term redefine does not infer that the energetic memory of an experience is removed. Any experience in any lifetime you have ever lived exists within your consciousness and can be accessed. However, a critical component of ascension is the ability to redefine your association with past experiences. The energetic balancing associated with redefining encodings is above and beyond the concept of seeking opposing perspectives. Acquiring opposing perspectives is a necessary component of wisdom as it completes the picture and allows assessment. Consider the lifetime of a vicious king who mercilessly oppresses his subjects as he focuses upon self-enrichment. To gain an understanding of the effects this inward focus had on others, the consciousness subsequently incarnates into a lifetime of severe oppression. When the oppressed lifetime ends, the cause and effect from both perspectives has been acquired. While a complete perspective of opposing views has been obtained, the energy encoded from each lifetime remains highly charged. Additionally, the highly charged opposing perspectives will not have been encoded upon the same particulate. As a result, the imbalanced energetics remain within the particulate.

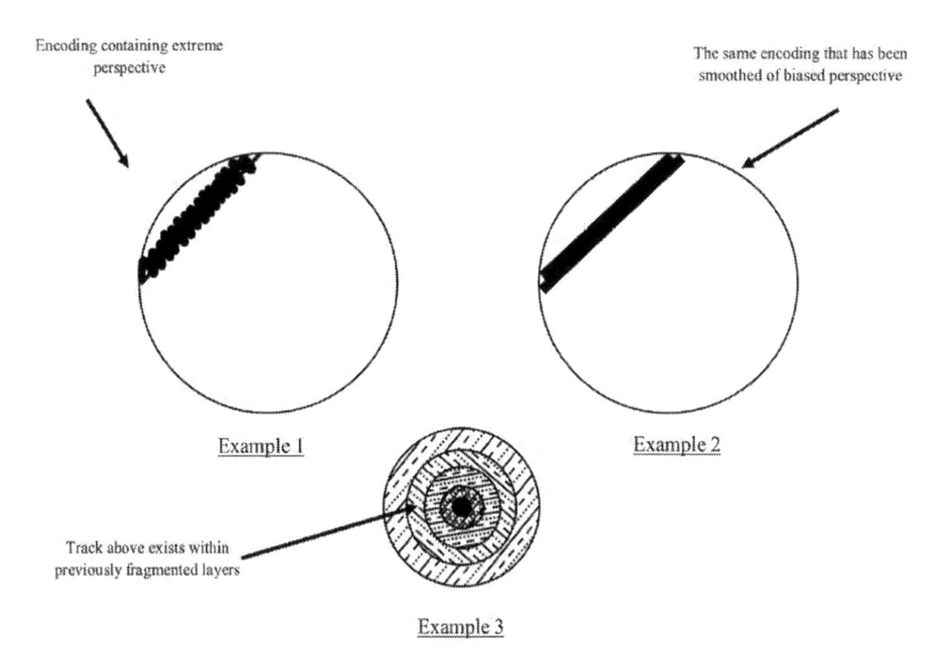

Figure 53 - Balanced and Imbalanced Encodings

Example 1 represents an encoding of an extreme experience. The perspective and focus during the experience created a large and imbalanced energetic signature. This imbalance must be reconciled and usually occurs after an opposing perspective of the experience has been acquired. Example 2 represents the understanding and realignment of the existing track several lifetimes later. The encoded experience remains, but the energetic imbalance it created has been realigned by the new perspective. While Example 1 and 2 show the tracks at the periphery of the particle for simplicity, earlier experiences will exist within an inner fragmented layer as shown in example 3.

Figure 53, Example 1 shows a representation of an encoding containing an extreme perspective. The track is wide and contains an imbalanced signature shown as a jagged track. The extreme perspective as the king caused the jagged track and is related to the imbalance that power gained through oppression of others creates. Before this encoding can be realigned, the opposing perspective as the oppressed must be acquired. The encodings of the oppressed lifetime occur several lifetimes later and exist within different particles at different sectors of fragmentation. While a complete perspective has been obtained, the experiences are still contributing to imbalances within rotational pathways. Adding to the complexity of balanced encodings is the fact it may take the consciousness several lifetimes, or several hundred, in each role before the understanding and realignment occurs. In each lifetime the consciousness exists in their role at odds with the opposing perspective, continuing to oppress as the ruler and continuing to feel the resentment and inequality of being oppressed. Until the last incarnations where realignment occurs and the ruler steps away from oppression and the pauper learns the value of simple coexistence. As these understandings are acquired, the encodings will lose the energetic imbalance associated with the emotional and physical perspectives. Figure 53, Example 2 shows the same encoding of the king that has been realigned and balanced as the energetic bias is released and the experience understood in totality. While not discussed, realignment of encodings can also occur between incarnations.

To understand the concept of realignment, consider the realignment that can occur to experiences within a single lifetime. A familiar example is the heartbreak associated with the dissolution of an early intimate love relationship. This unexpected separation can cause animosity and emotional trauma in one or both parties. As a result, they may look back upon the shared experience with anger or resentment. As time passes, they engage in additional relationships that bring an expanded awareness of intimacy and partnership. As they look back upon the earlier relationship, they begin to see and understand the imperfections that led to its demise. The pain associated with the memories fade as they are understood and realigned. The memories remain, but the imbalanced energy has been dissipated. This simplified example of realignment is what occurs as the association with encodings from highly charged lifetimes are redefined and balanced. All that is required is the internal focus and desire to do so. We will return to the concept of realignment in the meditation and modalities section.

Realignment and balance are concepts that extend beyond the energetics of conscious particulate.

Ascension into the fourth density construct is occurring for many within their current physical form. A smooth transition requires balance between the trinary of the mind, body, and spirit with their pathways unobstructed. The discussion thus far has focused upon the totality of consciousness -or spirit- portion as this is the true nature of what you are and the platform that ascends within the upward spiral. Transition into a higher energetic envelope during embodiment adds an additional element of complexity. During incarnation, the mind -or operative ego consciousness- has been in control of a system it either does not know exists, or whose operation it does not fully understand. Ascension into a higher energetic envelope during incarnation requires increased energetic flow through this system into the body. The pathways supplying that energy must be understood and cleared of any blockages that may have manifested.

Chapter Twenty Seven

Understanding the Energy Nodes of the Body (Chakras)

The physical energy network within the body is known as the central and peripheral nervous system. This network connects the brain to the spine and the rest of the body. This is the connection that provides physical and emotional feedback to the brain and the consciousness connected to it. Medical science has identified these neural pathways and the physical aspects that power and receive information from them. Beyond the obvious physical pathways, Vedic texts discuss the presence of another energetic system that contains energy points known as chakras. The word chakra comes from the Sanskrit word "Cakra" which translates as spinning wheel or circle. It is this literal interpretation of spinning within the chakras that will now be expanded upon as the discussion turns to how the energy of consciousness interfaces and empowers the energy network of the body. The chakras act as central node interfaces between the toroidal column of consciousness and the physical body they energize.

The chakra energy nodes are powered by the energy of consciousness. As the energy within the sphere of consciousness increases, the energy of the chakra system increases, providing additional supplementation to the energy acquired through digestion. As the process accelerates, the physical body will shift from material energy acquired through digestion to the energy supplied by the chakra nodes. When consciousness ascends beyond the need for a material body, the chakra energy system is utilized when needed to manifest a holographic form known as a light body. The light body will be a direct representation of the perfected template that was favored by the consciousness during physical incarnations.

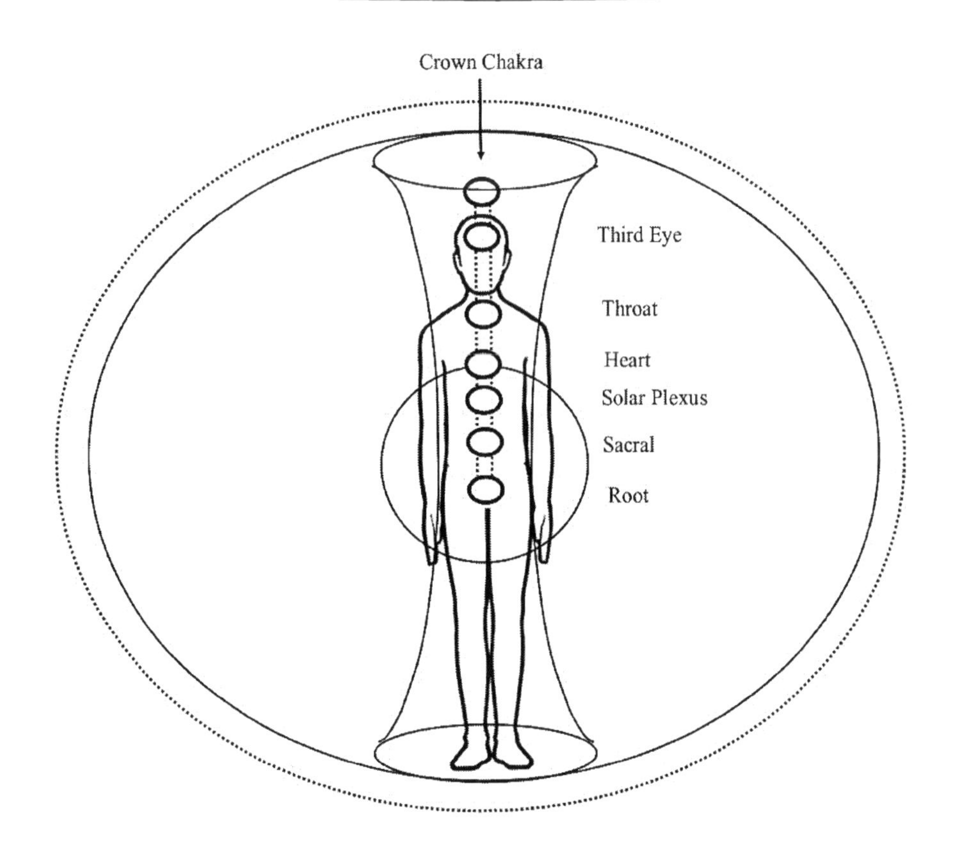

Figure 54 – Chakras

The image above represents the location of the chakras in relationship to the sphere of consciousness and the physical form. The chakras are the energetic interface between the energy of consciousness and the body. The chakras are located at specific energy levels within the toroidal column related to their energetic capacity. The dotted line connecting them is the energetic conduit where energy flows between the chakras.

Figure 54 shows the chakras in relationship to their location within the toroidal column. The dotted lines between the chakras represent the energetic conduit that connects them. The amount of energy flowing through the conduit and the path it travels is dependent upon the energy available in the toroidal column and the existence of blockages within the chakras that inhibit flow. This text has provided an understanding of the energetic pathways within consciousness and the increasing energy levels that exist within the column. With this knowledge, the interrelationship between chakra location and energy level becomes an important consideration.

The root chakra exists at the lowest energy level within the column and is the default pathway as energy flows upward energizing the remaining chakras. The heart chakra exists at the upper rotation of the seat of consciousness. This location allows it to be energized out of sequence in response to intentional focus before dual phase flow in the toroidal column correctly activates it. The aptly named crown chakra lies at the top of the chakra network and in the highest energy flow of the toroidal column. All chakras draw a small portion of energy directly from the toroidal column to supply the minimum needs of the physical body before they are properly activated. Minimum flow is induced into the chakras by their proximity to particulate flow in the column. This is a small fraction of what is available at full capacity when the chakra energetic conduit is fully activated. The root, the heart, and the crown chakra are the primary components connecting the chakra energy network to the energy available within the toroidal column.

The chakra energy nodes are not physical manifestations within the body, they are energetic overlays that regulate the flow of energy into the nervous system. The efficiency of the energetic flow through the various chakras can be observed by the health of the body parts they help to energize. Medical science knows that external imbalances in the form of toxins can accumulate and manifest disease within the body if not remedied. In a similar manner, imbalances created by the operative consciousness in current or previous lifetimes can manifest as blockages that impede the flow of energy through the chakras into the body. Your body is a solidified manifestation of your consciousness. Before your consciousness decided upon this incarnation, the template of what it wanted as its vehicle already existed. Without the proper flow of energy to maintain that template, the body begins to forget the original design. If allowed to continue, the body will lose vibrancy as it strays farther from the original design and disease will eventually arise. Extensive information exists related to chakras and the various portions of the body they energize and regulate. Those interested in this aspect of the chakra energy system can seek further guidance on this topic elsewhere. The focus of this text is how the chakras operate, how they are energized by consciousness, and the blockages that can occur within them. As the blockages are understood and released, the flow of energy within the chakra system will accelerate. As flow is restored, the template will self-correct. The process can be accelerated through intentional focus exercises that will be provided in Part three.

As consciousness ascends along the upward spiral, its energetic capacity increases with the additional particulate density. An increasing energetic capacity requires an increasing flow of creational energy to support that growth. An efficiently operating chakra network in union with increasing available energy results in an efficiently operating physical vehicle. Whether the advanced abilities that accompany this acceleration become manifest or not, depends upon the determination and focus applied.

Single and Dual Energetic Flow within Consciousness

When consciousness achieves the geometry of third density at sub-octave 3:0, the neutral energy vortex at the center of the toroidal column contains a low potential to draw creational energy into it. Recall from Figure 21 that the particulate and pathways they travel are densest within the seat of consciousness and the highest energetic pathway energizes the barrier membrane. Ascending from sub-octave 3:0 requires increasing density that also creates higher energetic pathways beyond E-11. The kinematic torque associated with additional orbital complexity creates an increasing differential (suction) at the neutral energy vortex. The increasing suction pulls more creational energy into the column. While suction is an appropriate term for the pull occurring, the true nature of the differential involves multiplying kinematic and resonant energetic forces. To simplify what occurs at the neutral energy vortex to the relevant portion, an analogy to fluid dynamics will be used.

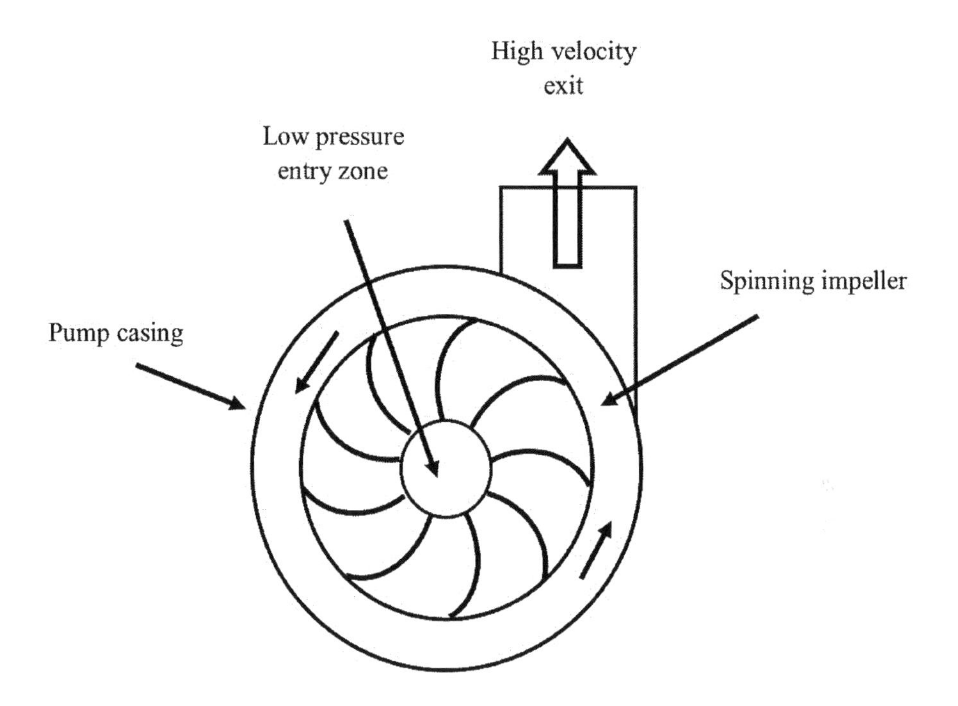

Figure 55 - Centrifugal Pump

The image above represents a cut away view of a centrifugal pump. The vanes of a spinning impeller accelerate entering fluid outward toward the casing. The rapid movement of fluid creates a low-pressure area at the central inlet that pulls fluid into it proportional to the suction. As long as flow meets demand, the pump speed can increase to rated capacity. If the availability of fluid at the inlet cannot meet increasing demand, the pump will begin to cavitate.

A centrifugal fluid pump has a rotating impeller that transfers rotational kinetic energy to a fluid to increase its velocity. As the impeller spins and increases the velocity of the fluid, it creates a low-pressure area at the center proportional to the amount of fluid moved and the velocity being imparted. If the impeller spins faster, the low-pressure area at the center will continue to decrease in pressure until a vacuum develops. This phenomena results from the fluid flowing from the center at a faster rate, causing more fluid to be drawn into the center to replace it. The decreasing pressure ensures the required flow is maintained. If the fluid supply does not match the increasing impeller speed, the pump will begin to cavitate (starve for fluid) requiring a reduction in impeller speed. The rotational sphere of consciousness operates under a similar rotational dynamic with the neutral energy vortex acting as the center of the impeller.

Single Phase Flow

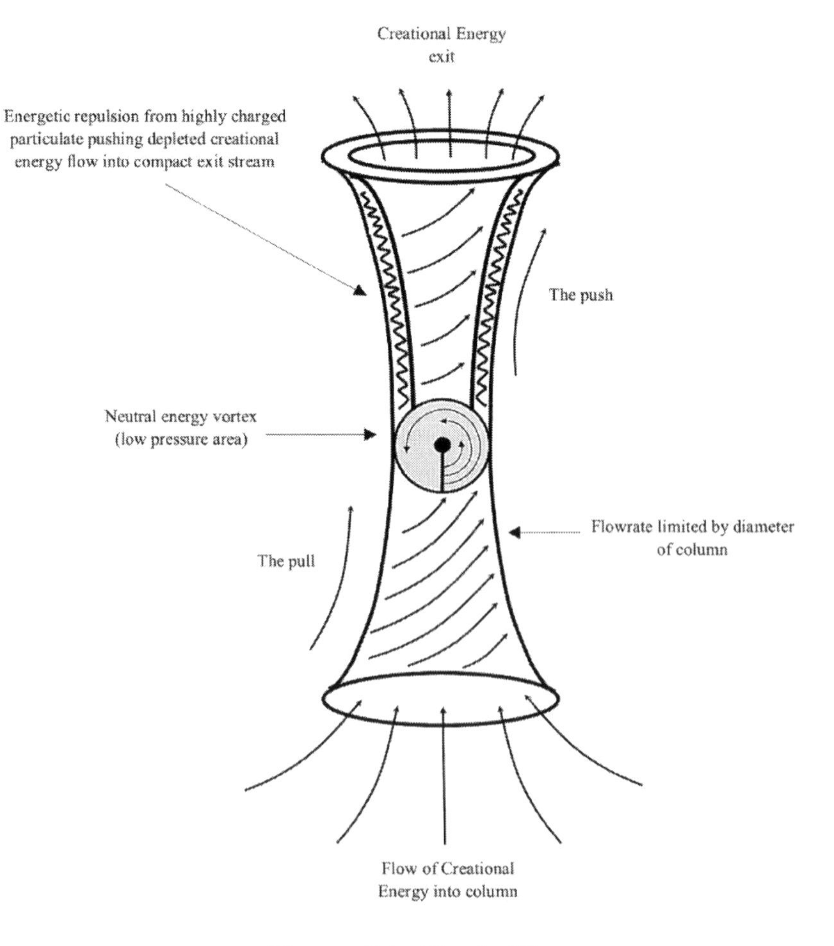

Figure 56 - Single Flow

The image above is the column within the conscious array that was shown in Figure 21.

As conscious particulate flows along pathways E-1 through E-11 it creates a neutral energy vortex at the center of the column that pulls creational energy in through the bottom opening. As creational energy flows up into the neutral vortex, conscious particulate travels with it up the column wall absorbing energy. The upward flow is created by the pull of the neutral vortex in combination with the increasing velocity of conscious particulate as it gains energy. When creational energy reaches the neutral vortex, the last energy transfer occurs as it empowers the seat of consciousness and reaches energetic equilibrium. Effectively depleted, the creational energy stream is pushed upward and out of the column. The exit stream is compacted by the energetic manifold created as coherently energized particulate accelerates into higher pathways.

A single upward flow of creational energy begins when consciousness enters sub-octave 3:0. The upward flow is pulled in by the low-pressure neutral energy vortex being created at the seat of consciousness. As consciousness evolves and moves into ascending sub-octaves, the particulate within the toroidal sphere increases in volume and velocity. The resulting increase in energetic exchange between conscious particulate and creational energy lowers the perceived pressure at the neutral energy vortex. As this is occurring, the particulate of consciousness traveling upward along the column walls are also increasing in velocity. The lowering pressure and increasing velocity combine to draw more creational energy upward into the consciousness. During single phase flow, energy transfer between unpotentiated creational particulate and the particulate of consciousness occurs only in the lower column and the seat of consciousness. Traveling upward as it transfers energy, unpotentiated particulate carrying creational energy will reach energetic parity with conscious particulate in the seat of consciousness, effectively depleted in relationship to the now energized particulate. There is an important difference between the particulate containing creational energy and the particulate of consciousness using that energy, and that is coherent oscillation. Coherent oscillation is responsible for the energetic manifolds within consciousness and are not possible in the randomized unpotentiated particulate supplying creational energy. It is this distinction that creates the repulsion pathway shown in Figure 56.

The universal aspect ratio limits the diameter of the column openings which acts to limit maximum flow during the single-phase flow energization. When the flow of creational energy upward into the column reaches the constraint of maximum flow, the equivalent of cavitation within a centrifugal pump begins to occur. Cavitation at the neutral energy vortex forces the creation of a new pathway to supply the increasing demand. This is where single phase flow develops into dual phase flow.

Dual Phase Flow

When dual phase flow begins, the zero point at pathway E-0 is far beyond the absolute ground state of first density neutrality. This means that less energy will be transferred per particle and an increasing flow will be required to maintain the proper energetic exchange rate. The reduction in energetic transfer rate also signals that a fourth density energetic envelope will soon be needed. Dual phase flow is a requirement for ascension beyond sub-octave 3:6 and describes creational energy being drawn into the top and the bottom while depleted particulate simultaneously flows out of those openings.

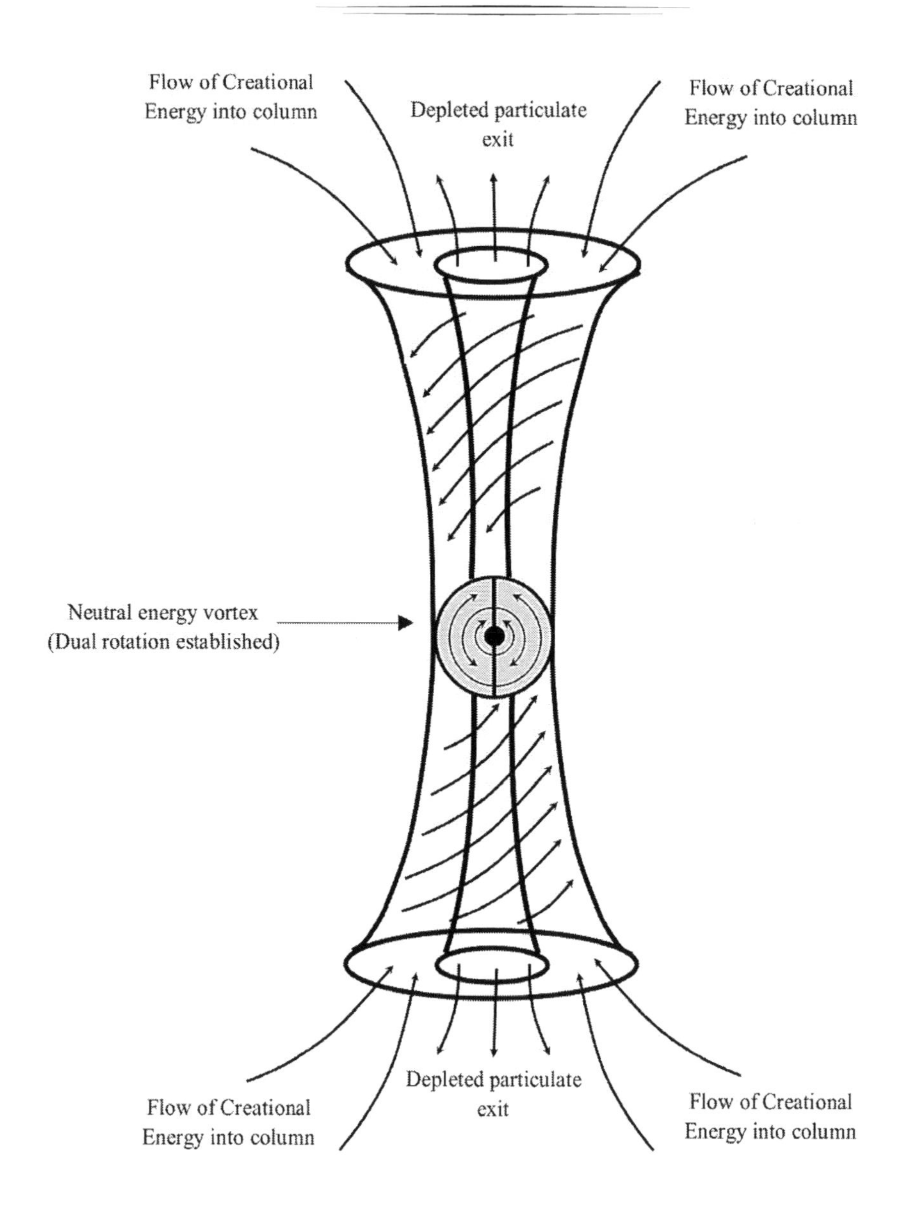

Figure 57 - Dual Flow in Toroidal Column

The image above represents dual phase flow within the toroidal column and neutral energy vortex. Highly charged unpotentiated particles containing creational energy are drawn inward toward the low-pressure area of the neutral energy vortex. The image of the neutral energy vortex represents the dual circular flow that is occurring within it.

When creational energy begins to be drawn into the top of the column, the movement of energized and depleted creational particulate also changes within the neutral energy vortex. While shown fully implemented in the figure above, dual phase flow begins slowly. The particulate first enters the top of the column around the outer edge. There is a slight buffer at the top as pathway E-11 creates the barrier membrane, but pathway E-10 and below will pull creational energy toward it to be absorbed. The influx of energy around the periphery causes the upward exit pathway to narrow as the inward flow increases. This constricts the exit of particulate within the neutral vortex.

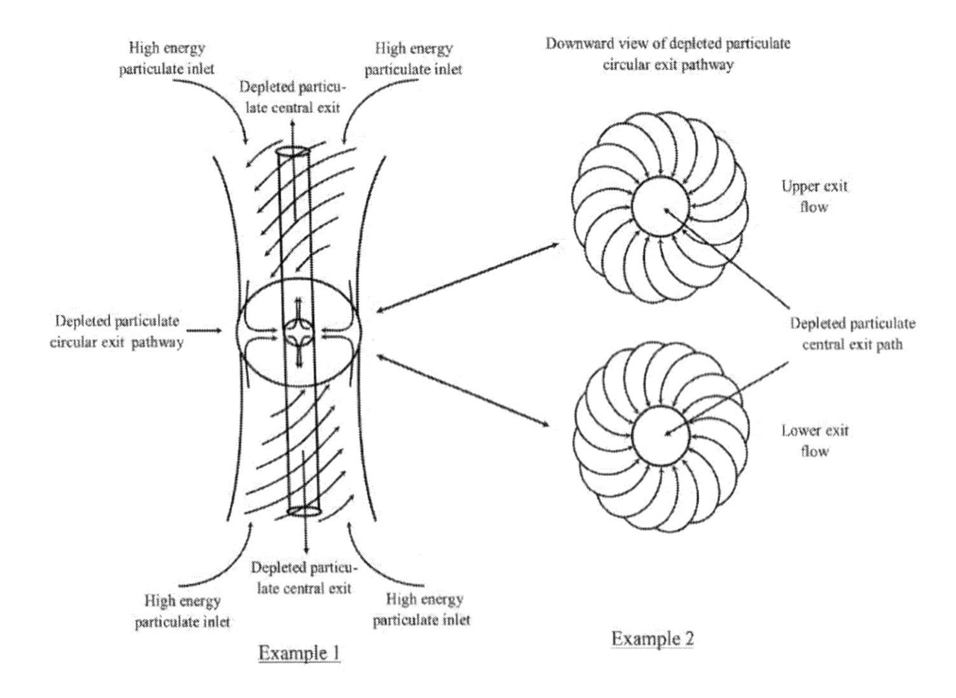

Figure 58 - Dual flow at Neutral Vortex

As creational energy flows toward the neutral energy vortex from both directions it compresses the depleted particulate and forces it into a central exit path. Example 1 shows high energy particulate flowing into the toroidal column along the outside walls. As it travels toward the central vortex it transfers energy. Reaching the neutral vortex, it depletes its remaining energy and is pushed into the center where it exits. Example 2 shows a downward view of the circular motion created as depleted particulate moves from the outside of the column toward the central exit paths in the neutral vortex. The opposing flow patterns counter rotate which creates their respective central exit pathways.

The influx of energy from the top and bottom enter the neutral energy vortex in opposing rotational vectors. The opposing flow energetically compacts depleted particulate at the neutral vortex and forces the creation of the lower exit pathway shown in Figure 58, Example 1. The opposing rotations create a buffer between them that forces depleted particulate outward in reverse direction to its inflow as the continuous stream of energized particulate provides the motive force. Unpotentiated particulate is considered depleted when it reaches energetic parity with E-0, the lowest energy particulate pathway. The opposing swirls shown in Figure 58, Example 2 are a result of induced spin created through energetic differentials encountered within the column. Depleted of energy, unpotentiated particulate exits the column to be reenergized within the planetary consciousness and repeat the process.

Returning to the fluid dynamic analogy, the rotational pathways within consciousness would be the vanes of the impeller. The number of vanes and the rate at which they spin determines the suction pressure developed at the neutral energy vortex. As consciousness grows under the stressors of experience it creates additional vanes that spin faster which increase demand. Increasing demand creates increased suction at the center that draws more supply toward it. The key difference is that consciousness is empowered by the flow and the energy contained within that flow. Increasing the supply flow increases the number of vanes within the consciousness pump and the speed at which they rotate. This creates an endless loop where supply and demand continue their stepped increases until flow alone can no longer support the energy requirements. This signals the requirement for a higher energetic source stream that allows for continued expansion. These energetic limitations are encountered at the doubling octaves of fourth, fifth, and sixth density.

The Mechanics of the Chakras

The swirl induced at the neutral energy vortex as a result of dual phase flow has a direct correlation to the heart chakra found within the Vedic teachings. The Anahata, or heart chakra is represented by a twelve-petal lotus flower. If you overlay the downward view of dual exit flow from Figure 57 onto the Vedic representation of the heart chakra, the twelve petals and the Merkabah take on additional meaning.

Figure 59 - Heart Chakra and Vortex

The image above is the Vedic representation of the heart chakra overlayed with the neutral vortex dual phase flow rotational dynamic. Complete activation of the heart chakra energy center requires dual phase flow and is represented by twelve lotus petals and the central exit pathway bounded by the Merkabah. The Merkabah in this instance represents the energization of consciousness using creational energy and the manifestation of the physical body through the focus of that energy.

The heart chakra cannot be sufficiently energized until dual phase flow at the neutral vortex has been established. When dual phase flow commences within consciousness, it begins the process of establishing a dual rotation and energetic flow in the chakra system that begins with the heart chakra. The heart chakra's location provides the most induced energy before dual rotation and makes it a critical energetic portal when dual flow is established. A dual rotation within the heart chakra produces what is commonly referred to as a heart centered awakening. The energy produced from the dual rotation within the heart chakra initially flows downward, energizing the solar plexus, sacral, and root chakras as they too develop a dual rotation. When operating efficiently and at capacity, energy will build within these three chakras until they are fully charged. When fully charged, a burst will be generated that surges upward through the chakra energy network. If the power of the surge is great enough, it will initiate a simultaneous dual rotation in the remaining chakras, including the crown. It is this energy surge and the resulting physical sensations that are associated with the term, Kundalini awakening. When dual rotation is achieved in the crown chakra, it opens the upper gateway and a dual energy flow into the chakra energy system from the top and bottom commences. Dual flow in the toroidal column accompanied by dual flow in the chakra energy system allows access to higher order abilities within the physical. If these abilities are to become manifest, an understanding of the energy network and the maintenance involved is needed.

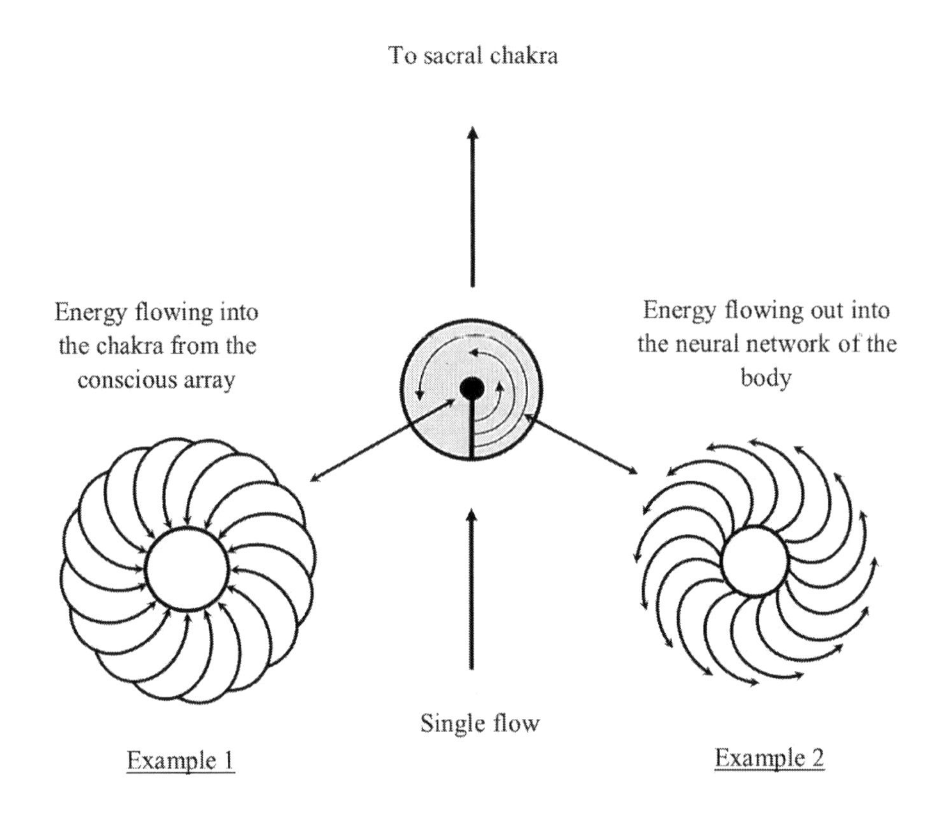

Figure 60 - Chakra Flow

The image above represents a single flow of energy activating the root chakra. The spiral on the left shows the energy of consciousness swirling into the center of the chakra. If no blockages exist, the energy will flow through the chakra and spiral into the neural network of the body as shown on the right.

The image above shows the root chakra energized by a single upward flow. The single flow of energy begins at the root chakra and moves upward. This is the default configuration from sub-octave 2:3 to 3:5 as energy follows the path of least resistance to energize the body mimicking the flow of energy in consciousness. Energy flows into and through the center of the root chakra toward the remaining chakras. Energy enters through the center of each chakra, shown as a black dot in the center image. The circular arrows surrounding the center dot represent a single flow of energy from a single source that then spirals outward from the center of the chakra into the neural network of the body. Example 1 shows the single inward spiraling as energy flows into the chakra and energizes it. Example 2 shows the resulting single outward flow of energy from the chakra to the body. The single upward flow energizes each chakra in this manner losing potential as it interacts with each successive chakra.

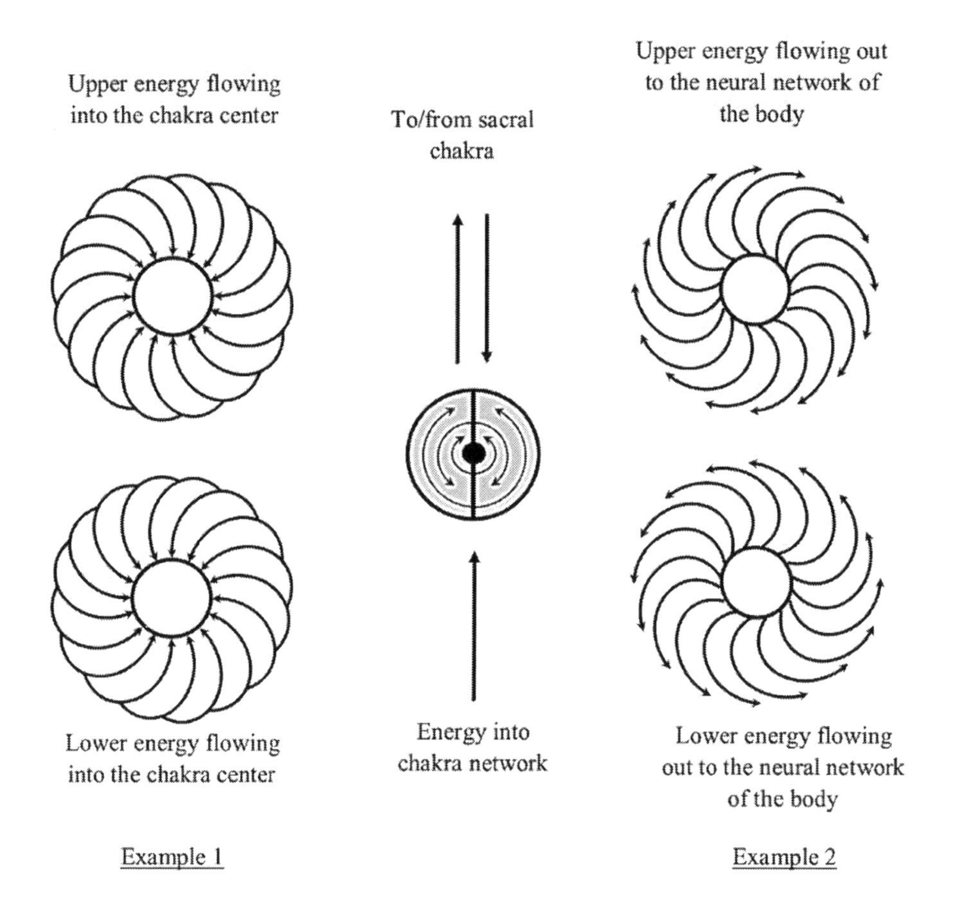

Figure 61 - Dual Flow

The images above represent the flow of energy through the root chakra with dual flow established. There are now two lines connected to the black center of the spinning chakra indicating the flow from the top and bottom into it. While not shown in the center image, the chakra nodes are dual energy vortexes. The images on the left show the energy flowing into the separate chakra vortexes from the top and bottom. The images on the right show the energy flowing out of the separate chakra vortexes as it energizes the neural network of the body. The opposing flow patterns create a complete activation of the chakra and associated body region as energy radiates outward in all directions.

This image reflects the dual rotation that occurs in the chakras when energy begins to flow in both directions through the chakra network. Energy flows upward into the bottom of the chakra network energizing the root chakra first. It then continues upward to the sacral chakra. Energy flowing into the top of chakra network is shown entering the root chakra from above after passing through the sacral chakra. While not shown in this image, dual flow creates separate vortex points in a process similar to the establishment of dual flow at the neutral vortex in the toroidal column. However, this is an energetic stream that flows into the body. The body is the only exit path for energy flowing into the chakra network. Figure 61, Example 1 shows the opposing swirls exhibited as the energy enters the separate vortex nodes. The nodes translate the energy and radiate it outward into the body in opposing rotations as shown in Example 2. The opposing rotations form a complete energetic radiance that extends into the body fully aligning the template.

Energetic flow through the upper gateway begins when the crown chakra is energized by the energies moving upward from the heart chakra. To understand how the crown chakra gateway is opened and its importance to the health of the body, you must understand the complexity of energetic transfer that occurs between the chakra system and the physical neural network.

Chapter Twenty Eight

The Relationship Between Chakras and the Energy System of the Body

Human, animal, and plant bodies exist as interfaces that allow consciousness to experience and grow within material creations. The brain is the connection that consciousness uses as its interface and the nervous system is how it receives sensory input from the body. The fact that the brain controls the body through the nervous system is well documented in western medical science, but the nervous system performs other energetic functions. Chinese medicine takes a closer look at the energy system of the body and understands that the energy within this network is essential to the body. Over thousands of years, they developed methodologies to remove blockages that impede the flow of energy within this network. The process of acupuncture and Chinese medicine in general is predicated on the assumption that meditation, reflective silence, and energetic flow movements of the body (Tai Chi, Qi Gong) were being regularly practiced by the patient community. Neutralizing an energetic blockage by shunting it with a metallic object must be followed with a regimen of focused intention to completely dissolve the imbalance and prevent recurrence.

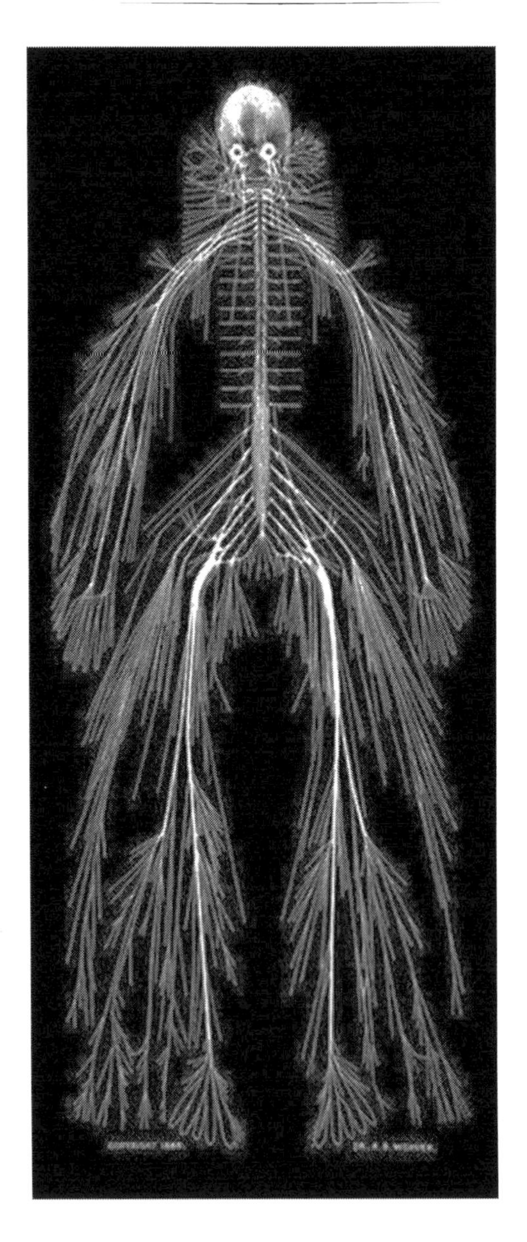

Figure 62 - Nervous System

The above image is a human nervous system famously dissected by Rufus Benjamin Weaver in 1888. The nervous system belonged to Harriet Cole who died of tuberculosis at age 35. Major meridians are the connections where larger channels branch off into smaller ones. Minor meridians are where the smaller branch off again. The nervous system above has been flattened and put on a board. When reoriented into a three-dimensional body, the Chinese acupuncture meridian map will align perfectly with the nerve branches.

(Photo courtesy of Drexel University)

Figure 62 is a dissected nervous system. When you strip away the muscles, bones, and organs, the extensive interwoven nature of the nervous system becomes apparent. On a physical level it provides electrical stimulus to and from the brain allowing sensory interaction between the body and its environment. Since the toroidal array of consciousness is connected to the brain, this conduit also represents the interface between consciousness and the material. However, the neural network of the body is much more than an electrical conduit. The physical body exists within the array of consciousness as was shown in Figure 54. The extensive neural network acts as an energetic antenna that picks up information from the sphere. Comprised of thousands of intelligent receptor cells called neurons, the nervous system is continually adjusting to the energy and information it receives directly from the chakra energy system and what is being transmitted to it from the sphere. The energy and information received by the neurons is then used to adjust the template of the physical form. Looking at the image of the neural network there are obvious junctions where several neural branches intersect. These intersections are known as meridians. Intuitively, the larger intersections are known as major meridians and the smaller known as minor meridians. The meridians play an important role in maintaining the overall health of the system. The meridians will be discussed further in the section on energetic blocks.

Neurons

A neuron is defined as an electrically excitable cell that transmits and responds to stimulus. A stimulus critical to the proper functioning of neurons is the energetic transmissions they receive from the chakra energy network.

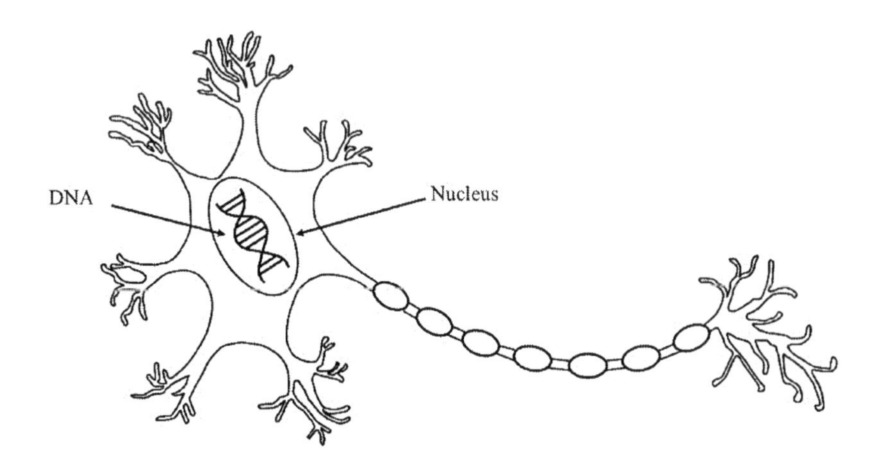

Figure 63 – Neuron

The image above represents a typical multipolar neuron that comprises the majority of the neural network within the body. A neuron receives and transmits electrical signals through the antenna-like structures known as dendrites. Within the nucleus of each cell is the DNA responsible for genetic sequencing during cell regeneration. The Chakra energy system is constantly sending energy and instructions to the neurons that then transmit the information through the body as they attempt to maintain the perfected template.

Figure 63 represents a typical neuron consisting of a nucleus that controls the impulses being transmitted through its network. Neurons exist in the brain and nervous system and the physical aspects they perform in controlling the body have been studied extensively. Even with this focused attention by the medical sciences, new understandings of the role neurons perform are still being discovered. The focus of this text is upon the critical function neurons play as the interface between consciousness and the body.

DNA (deoxyribonucleic acid) is a molecule that stores the unique genetic code of the body it resides within. Below sub-octave 3:5, the DNA within the neural network and the body operates autonomously with little direct oversight or intervention by the consciousness empowering it. It does this on an energetic level as it receives template instructions from the chakra network empowering it. Whether this transmission occurs autonomously or with direct oversight and focus depends upon awareness of the process by the operative consciousness and the energy available in the chakra system. Neurons are specifically designed to receive and transmit. The image of a neuron presented in Figure 63 shows a receiver at the nucleus surrounded by an extensive transmission network of tendrils called dendrites. As consciousness gains energy and moves upward along the pathway of energetic ascension, dual flow begins in the chakra system. Dual flow transmits a stronger signal to the neurons that respond to those signals and transmits the information through the body. Dual flow without focused oversight will still exert greater control over the cellular regeneration role DNA performs. Once again, applying intentional focus to the process acts as the magnifying glass that concentrates and directs the energy. However, if the signal to or within the neural network is interrupted, the template the body uses to produce new cells and remove damaged ones will begin to stray from the intended design. If not corrected, degradation will manifest in the portions of the body that have become disconnected.

Neurons and Timelines

Chapters 19 and 20 provided details related to the splitting and merging of timelines. Those discussions included the concept that an entire solidified reality can be replicated from an existing one as the material particulate is excited into a higher energetic state. As that divergence occurs, a portion of consciousness within the collective reality moves into the higher energetic timeline while the rest remain in the original. This separation of consciousness into two energetic groups during incarnation requires an energetic alignment for the consciousness, and a physical catalyst to align the body to the appropriate timeline.

The energetic capacity of consciousness determines its location within the upward spiral. This overall ability to hold energy determines what is experienced in the etheric planes between incarnations, and within material constructs as consciousness aligns to the octave it oscillates within. The body each of you possess is a template of, and empowered by, the energy of your consciousness. The energetic compass within your totality of consciousness also exerts a force upon your body as it attempts to guide you in the proper direction. When a timeline shift approaches, each consciousness aligns to the construct they are resonating within. Whether you are aligning through use of the internal compass or are allowing an external perspective to guide you is irrelevant. When the divergence occurs, you will align to the construct whose frequency you resonate within. The alignment of your operative consciousness also has a direct impact on the body as the neurons align the body to the frequency you are tuning into through intentional focus.

If the separation involves movement into a higher energy envelope, the consciousness must possess the energetic capacity to move into the higher energetic timeline before physical realignment can begin. This should not be seen as a limiting statement. During divergences, consciousness falls within three groups. The first group contains consciousness below sub-octave 3:5 who have no concept of energetic separations or that a divergence is imminent. They are immersed in their lives, intently focused on the experiences in front of them. The second group contains consciousness at sub-octave 3:5 who have the capacity to apply intentional focus to increase energetic capacity and move with the ascending collective. If they awaken to their potential and continue their quest for higher understandings, they will move into the new construct. Consciousness in the third group are the ones responsible for the impending divergence. They are at sub-octave 3:7 and actively seeking higher energetics within their consciousnesses as they push upon the upper boundary of the third density oscillating octave.

As previously stated, energetic maturity and balance within consciousness is the factor determining which construct each entity will move into. Dual flow in both the toroidal column and the chakra network is part of the energetic maturity being discussed. As consciousness begins to align with the higher energies of an ascending construct, the energy is translated into the chakra energy system. The increasing energy enters the neural network, and the body begins to shift.

The Perfected Body Template

When consciousness begins its journey of self-awareness at sub-octave 3:0, it is provided with a default body template. There are some adaptations that can be made, but they will be few since the consciousness has no prior experience with the form. As the incarnations accrue and experience is gained, the default template is updated with aspects of bodies that were found to be more desirable. Consciousness will embody as both sexes and while it may have a preference, it will have a template for both. The more it incarnates, the more refined and specific the templates become. If the consciousness predominately incarnates as one sex, that template will have a higher degree of refinement than the other. The lessons of embodiment require focus, and consciousness wants to feel comfortable in the appearance and capabilities of its body. Just as you expect to wake up every morning and see your familiar face in the mirror, consciousness beyond sub-octave 3:5 expects a level of continuity in the bodies it experiences through. When all aspects have been updated, the perfected body template is complete. This is the template that will be transmitted through the chakra network to the neurons within the physical body. There are obvious limitations associated with the genetic source material of your progenitors, but these considerations are accounted for as you plan the next incarnation. To bring the ability to shape the energetic template into focus, consider a family photo of two parents and their four children. All the children came from the same genetic source material, but unless they are identical twins, each child will have modified the source genetic coding to align as close as possible to their preferred energetic template.

The chakra energy nodes are the main energetic interfaces between your consciousness and your body. Imbalances within your consciousness will translate to imbalances within the chakra energy centers and if not corrected, physical imbalances within the body that manifest poor health. In this way, the physical and emotional responses of the body serve as indicators to assist you along your continued quest toward balance within consciousness. A balanced consciousness manifests a balanced mind and body. When the crown chakra is activated and dual flow achieved, it signals that the final balancing within third density has commenced. As you begin to experience balance between the energy networks of consciousness and the body, a stabilizing feedback loop is created. This stabilization acts like a gravitational pull that keeps you centered and in balance. The result is a calm, balanced perspective that is not easily moved by external forces. As you acclimate to the physical manifestations of calm and balance, you become acutely aware of things attempting to push you from that balance. Perfecting this feedback loop is the focus of consciousness entering fourth density. An important step along this path is identifying and removing any blockages within the chakra energy system.

Chapter Twenty Nine

Energetic Blocks

The picture of consciousness presented in the Expansion series of books is painted upon the canvas of a universe using free will as an infinite color palette to create individualized portraits. If there is an energetic block limiting the energy within a sphere of consciousness, it is either there by request or allowance. Within the energetic network of the body, blocks are either intentionally created, allowed, or the result of lack of knowledge. Regardless of the stories to the contrary, we assure you this is the case. There is no scenario where an energetic block exists within consciousness that has not been agreed to by the consciousness that contains it. You may not remember the agreement in your current incarnation, but somewhere along your journey you allowed it. The reason why blocks are allowed or created is irrelevant when you reach the ability to acknowledge and dissolve them. If you are reading this text and have made it this far, any blockages that may exist within you will yield to the exercises in Part three. Blockages can be created in the neural network of the body, in the chakra energy system, and in the rotational array of consciousness.

Blocks Within the Body's Energy Network

In the body, blockages manifest as an insulating static impeding the flow of chakra energy through the physical neural conduits to portions of the body utilizing those connections. Network blockages manifest as unreleased negative energy becomes trapped at intersection points within the physical energetic network. Figure 62 showed the nervous system of the human body and the intersections where multiple pathways connect. These intersections -known as meridians- are redirection points where energy pools, imperceptibly slowing before dispersing through the connecting branches. This is by design as the heavier negative energy falls out of the flow and is collected at the meridians. If this energy is left to accumulate, it will eventually overflow from the meridians into the cells and organs of the body. There are two sources of active negative energy creation, one is negative energy from the operative consciousness active within the brain, the second is negative energy collecting in the sphere of consciousness that is moved through the chakra system into the neural network. A third non-active type of blockage exists. These are blockages within the energetic network that are brought into the current lifetime from trauma experienced in a prior lifetime. This occurs when an external force abruptly ends the lifepath under severe trauma. Consciousness so affected does not have time to understand and balance the experience within embodiment and the energy of the trauma lies unresolved in the energetic template. If it is not addressed in the etheric prior to subsequent incarnation, it will remain.

Negative Energy from the Operative Consciousness

The definition of operative consciousness is when you are awake, aware, and in control of the body you inhabit. During every moment of this awareness, you are thinking about something. Whatever you are thinking about at any given moment is creating an energy within the body. Negative energy is created through intentional focus. The easiest way to identify this energy is through emotional feedback. Everyone inherently knows the difference between a positive thought and a negative one, and each day you have the choice of where to place your focus. Consider the contrast between thoughts of sadness, anger and dread, to those of love, happiness, and joy. As you think of these opposing emotions, recall the responses the body provided. The energetic network will do its best to move most of what you create in this manner harmlessly through the body and out the hands and feet. . However, if you continue to ignore the emotional cues, the negative energy will eventually accumulate until your body manifests a physical reaction you cannot ignore. Because the blockages were created through intentional focus of the operative consciousness, they will require the same level of focus to dissolve. Being cognizant of where you are focusing the active mind in every moment is a prerequisite of balance.

Negative Energy from Consciousness

The chakra network is energized from the energy generated within the sphere of consciousness. Imbalanced particulate rotations within the pathways directly translate to imbalanced energy entering the chakra network that is then distributed to the body.

Because of the shift that is currently underway in this timeline, many ascended consciousnesses have volunteered to incarnate here to assist the transition. The energy flooding the planet from the embedded volunteers and your system star has caused many to emerge from under the veil and awaken to their purpose. However, while ascended consciousness under the veil may not remember who and what they are, many of the abilities they possess remain active. This text has provided details regarding the operation of the sphere of consciousness. Part of that discussion included the concept of energetic overlap that occurs as consciousness nears fourth density. The main purpose of the volunteers in any timeline is to use their energy to push it into a divergence or merging as applicable. This requires that they enter with enough density and balance to quickly reach the threshold of fourth density. Unaware of the energetic overlap they possess as a result, they walk around absorbing the negative energy of others. This is a main reason they physically incarnate and they fulfill that purpose just by being in the timeline. Many volunteers also awaken to their true nature and begin to use their abilities as they see fit, but this is not a requirement. The negative energy they absorb as their primary objective is expected to be processed and released each night as the consciousness sleeps. The targeted timeline then slowly moves toward the positive as shown in Figure 43, as millions of volunteers perform their service to the collective. In some cases, the energy being picked up is not released or realigned within the sphere of consciousness. The alternate pathway for release is through the chakra energy system, into the neural network of the body, and out through the hands and feet.

Many volunteers within the first and second waves succumbed to terminal disorders within the body as the energy they collected was absorbed instead of dissipated. On an ascended level these consciousnesses knew that their bodies were a temporary, discardable structure, and used it as such. This tendency toward martyrdom as overly positive consciousnesses willingly performed the ultimate service to others act has lessened. The reduction is a result of successive waves incarnating into increasingly positive energies coupled with the methodical reduction of the polarity envelope as the experiment comes to an end. All consciousness, volunteer or otherwise, possesses the ability to pick up undesirable energy from others as you assist them in their growth. With this understanding, the necessity for cleansing your energy networks regularly becomes clear.

Blocks Within the Chakra System

There are seven main connection points within the chakra system that connect it to the neural network of the body. Like the intersections within the neural network, these connections can become blocked as the heavier energies are transported through the system. A chakra cannot become completely blocked, but the energy they transfer to the body can become significantly reduced as negative energy collects in them. Where the negative energy collects within the individual chakras depends upon the level at which they are energized. The root, sacral, and solar plexus chakras are unique in their ability to fully energize in a negative environment which is necessary for polarized constructs. These chakras, highly imbalanced or negatively aligned will manifest as extreme service to self tendencies leaning toward sadism.

The blueprint for your perfected body resides within the chakra energy system. To understand this statement, consider the chakras as holographic generators. Each chakra projects a color spectrum that focuses on a point in space. With all operating and focused, the image of your perfected form appears at that point in space, crisp, clear, and without flaw. If the energy flowing to one of the chakras is diminished, or if the lens is dirty or out of focus, that portion of the perfected template will be blurry. Now assume that a chakra projector is not clear and bright but obstructed by a physical object. The obstruction will cause a reduction in clarity and coherence of the total projected image as the obstructed portion is unavailable. In this way, blockages within the chakra and physical networks inhibit the perfected template from focusing on the physical body. Severe trauma from past incarnations can lodge within the energetic template like a smudge on the lens of the chakra. If not resolved, these will manifest unexpected conditions in the body at the previous trauma site. When the consciousness is in the etheric planning its next incarnation it can choose to resolve these issues before embodiment or leave them to be reconciled later. Sometimes a lifetime ends abruptly through an accident or infringement. When the consciousness reaches the etheric it finds another desirable incarnational window almost as soon as it arrives. Complete healing and review of the previous lifetime may be waived so the opportunity can be acted upon. Whether by choice or omission, in all cases the consciousness decides the course of action.

Energetic seals can also be placed upon the chakras prior to incarnation to prevent their activation. This may initially appear as unwanted but are usually placed as a self-limiting requirement to ensure the proper life path. To give this statement context, consider the life of a gifted energy worker in the 1600's whose talents are misunderstood as they perform what appear to be miracles healing hopelessly sick people. Because of the confusion of the time, their life is violently ended as they are burned at the stake as a witch. As this consciousness plans the next incarnation, they place seals upon their upper chakras to prevent dual flow and access to the abilities that previously caused them problems. Twenty lifetimes later, the seals continue to perform their intended purpose as an artifact of a prior decision. If the current lifetime requires their removal to once again perform healing, the operative consciousness will be led to a modality that will dissolve them. In this instance the seals may have been purposely left to be removed during the incarnation. The experience of understanding the limitations they imposed, and the expansion felt after removal being a necessary catalyst to the path they are meant to walk. Blocks within the chakra system limit the usage of the dual flow and are placed relative to the extent of limitation required. Blocks within the chakra system are also referred to as J-seals or Jehovian seals. Beyond the use of the term 'seal' which is an appropriate analogy, distortions within the historical record related to a nefarious origin should be ignored. Nothing can exist within your consciousness that you do not allow. If not previously known, your engagement with this text has now brought you the awareness of their existence. If you do not want them, you can release them and move forward. All that is required is your desire to do so.

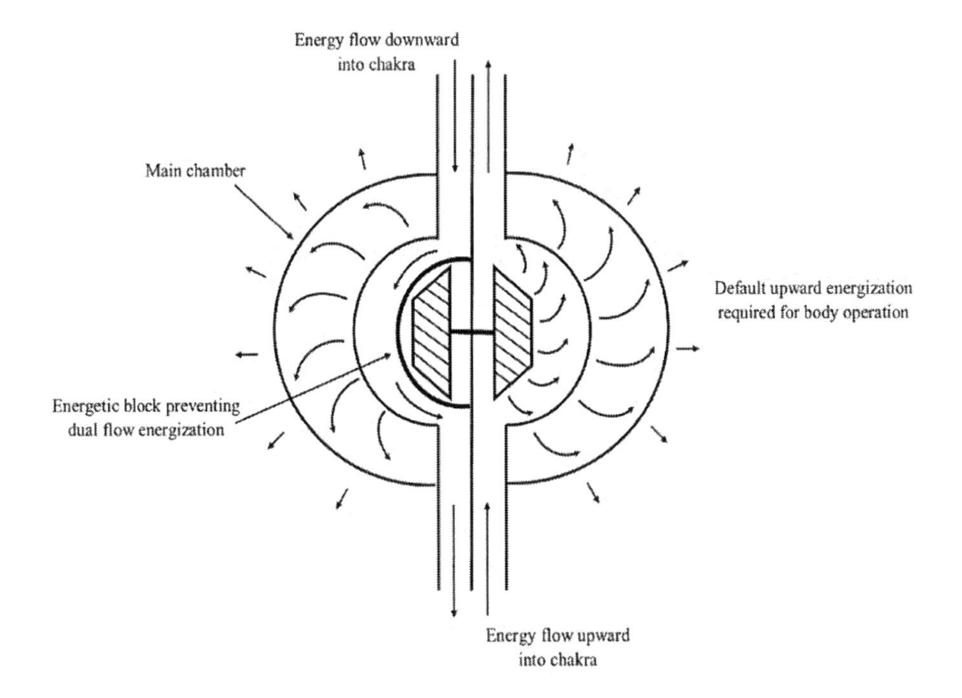

Figure 64 - Chakra Seals 1

The image above is a side view of the chakra vortex shown in Figure 61. Upward default energy is shown energizing the primary vortex impeller. The energy from the primary impeller moves into the main chamber of the chakra and flows outward in a single direction. An energetic block has been placed over the secondary impeller preventing activation even though dual flow has been established. The energy flows past the secondary impeller and moves through the network to the next chakra.

Figure 64 shows a cut-away view of the energetic structure of the dual energy vortex within each chakra. Continuing with our pump analogy, imagine the center of each chakra contains a dual flow vortex impeller with the rotation of each dependent upon the flow it receives.

All chakras receive energy from the upward flow as they energize the material form. This meets the minimal requirements of the body network and holds it to the basic energetic template. The upward energy powers the primary vortex impeller which spins it out in a single direction into the main chamber. Imbalances can accumulate on the impeller, or on the lens of the main chamber.

An imbalance in the vortex impeller will cause the energy radiating from it to spin outward in an imbalanced manner as more energy radiates in one direction while another area receives less. Imbalances on the impeller originate through two modalities. One is the absorption of negativity through the conscious array that is then transmitted into the chakra network and become lodged there rather than flowing into the physical body. The other source is through repetitive negative focus of the conscious mind. Smudges on the lens of the chakra's main chamber occur from past traumas to physical bodies that have not been properly identified and released.

These are the main types of blockages within the upward chakra network that allow the body to stray from its template as the minimum energy required to maintain it is impeded. Energetic seals are not placed within the upward default pathways of the chakras. Any blockage within the default pathway is a byproduct of absorption, focus, or trauma. Purposely created energetic seals exist within the downward secondary chakra network and prevent downward energy from energizing the secondary vortex impeller as it bypasses the sealed chakra and continues downward to the next. The secondary vortex of the seven main chakras can be sealed in this manner and the reasons they have been sealed are as unique as the consciousnesses they exist within. One other seal can be placed, used primarily by strong willed ascended consciousnesses playing in lower density constructs, the cap seal.

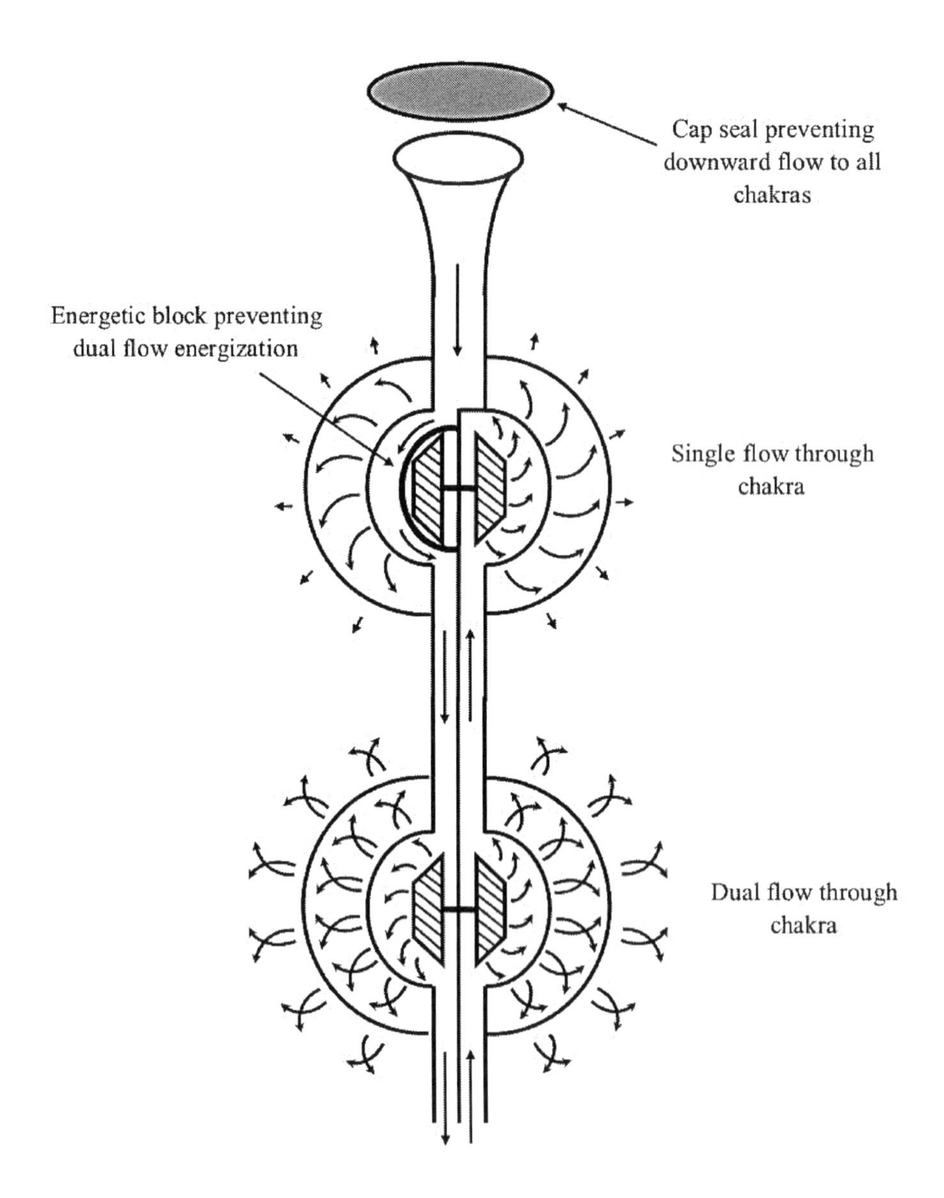

Figure 65 - Chakra Seals 2

The image above shows the crown chakra, the third eye chakra, and two scenarios. Above the crown chakra is the representation of the cap seal. Placing the cap seal over the entry to downward flow prevents dual energization of the chakra network. The cap seal prevents the neural network from receiving energy above sub-octave 3:5. This prevents the operative consciousness from accessing abilities beyond the standard five senses. In scenario two the cap seal is not present, but an energetic block has been placed over the downward vortex impeller of the crown chakra. The crown remains energized by single flow as the energy bypasses it and moves downward to energize the third eye chakra. The efficiency and balance causes energy to flow out in all directions of the third eye chakra at more than twice the rate of single flow energization.

Figure 65 shows the crown chakra with its opening to downward energy and the third eye chakra. Two scenarios are portrayed in the image. The most limiting block to the system would be the cap seal over the downward opening. The cap seal is shown above the opening for clarity, but in practice would seal the opening as the name implies. In scenario one, the cap seal completely blocks downward flow from entering the system. All chakras are prevented from dual flow activation preventing extra sensory abilities. For scenario two, assume the cap seal is not present and dual flow has been achieved. The energy is shown moving down into the crown chakra, but the seal prevents activation of the impeller. While this is an unlikely scenario, allow it for this discussion. Bypassing the crown chakra, it proceeds to the third eye where it is utilized to energize dual flow within the chakra. As the image attempts to convey, the energy entering the body from a balanced and fully energized chakra is more than double that of a sealed or imbalanced chakra and swirls out in all directions.

Blockages within the chakra system -regardless of origin- are temporary. They have been created by manipulating the cohesion and spin rate of the energetic particulate of consciousness. The spin state of an energetic particle is influenced and realigned when impacted by an external energy of greater magnitude. Stated plainly, this means that blocks can be removed by consciousness that has attained the balance and energetic capacity to identify and dissolve them. This can be accomplished by an external consciousness oriented to the purpose of healing and service, but the clearing will have a deeper impact upon the forward trajectory if the consciousness being blocked aligns itself to the task of release and continues the journey after the healing.

Chapter Thirty

The Planetary Chakra System

Consciousness begins its journey of individualization within a planetary consciousness that has created an energetically neutral location for its incubation. As previously discussed, this neutral zone -or zero point- has been created by sequestering excess energy in material creations. The basic component of consciousness beginning the journey toward individualization and the foundation of material structures are the same, energetic particulate donated from planetary consciousness. What separates one from the other is the intention of their creation and what ultimately holds the intention. Planetary spheres created as incubators are considered the body of a planetary consciousness. The particulate comprising the planetary body is not available to begin the process of individualization as it serves as inanimate material. Inanimate material is bound and held in discreet packets through energetic focus as it performs its service to the collective.

If the planet is a physical manifestation of intention within a planetary consciousness, it follows that its solidification is the result of focus through an energetic network. These pathways function much like the chakra network and the neural system within the human body. The planetary surface chakras have acquired many names as have the lines of energy that flow between them. These intersecting points connected by an energetic grid are responsible for solidifying all timeline constructs in play on a planet. To get an understanding of what these lines and intersecting points energize we need only look at the atomic structure of our material world. The best designs are simplistic and repeatable where complexity comes from layers of repeating and intersecting patterns.

The Dodecahedron and the Icosahedron Grid Network

The dodecahedron and the icosahedron are two of the five Platonic solids. A Platonic solid is a three-dimensional solid comprised of plane (flat two-dimensional) surfaces that contain equal length sides and equal angles. All corners of the solid (vertexes) must contain the same number of sides.

For a three-dimensional shape, the additive angles of each side at each vertex must equal less than 360 degrees. The 360-degree limitation coupled with the requirement of the same number of sides of equal length gives us the triangle, the square, and the pentagon to work with as we design three-dimensional platonic solids. Other polygons may have equal sides and angles, but they cannot be assembled where the additive angles at the vertex do not exceed 360 degrees. With a sum of 360 degrees at the vertex, the object becomes flat and loses its three-dimensional profile. These limitations allow for only five assemblies that have been termed, platonic solids. They were named after the Greek philosopher Plato, who aptly theorized that they formed the foundation of material composition.

The five Platonic solids are as follows; three triangles meeting at a vertex to create a tetrahedron. Four triangles meeting at a vertex to create an octahedron. Five triangles meeting at a vertex to create an icosahedron. Three squares meeting at a vertex to create a cube, and three pentagons meeting at a vertex to create a dodecahedron. Building from the foundation of these Platonic solids comes more complex Archimedean solids, Petrie polygons and increasingly complex planar facets that comprise the material world. With an understanding of what a platonic solid is, we find within them the dodecahedron and the icosahedron composed of identical sides that contain equilateral angles. These characteristics create a balanced, strong, and stable grid network.

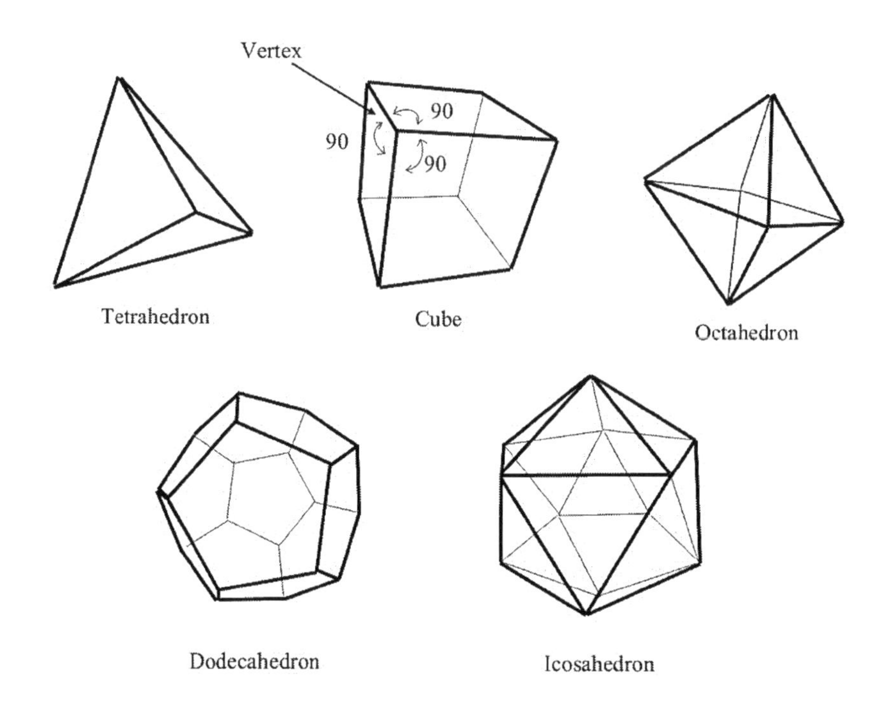

Figure 66 - Platonic Solids

The five platonic solids are shown above. A platonic solid is a three-dimensional form created by planes with equal angles (polygons). The additive value of angles at the vertex must equal less than 360 degrees for the shape to maintain a three-dimensional profile. Only the five combinations above meet these requirements. The three Triangles in the tetrahedron (3 x 60° = 180°) Four triangles in the octahedron (4 x 60° = 240°). Five triangles in the Icosahedron (5 x 60° = 300°). Three squares (3 x 90° = 270°), and three pentagons (3 x 108° = 324°). These shapes contain order, balance, and strength. They are the foundations of matter upon which increasingly complex combinations are built.

The planetary chakra network of the Earth is connected by an energetic network that combines the stabilities found within the dodecahedron and the icosahedron. There are two energetic grids required to solidify the material environment. The outer grid exists at the outer reaches of the planetary atmosphere and is relatable to the chakra energetic network used to empower the neural network within embodied consciousness. It is energized by the planetary consciousness and manifests the gaseous environment if one is required by the lifeforms.

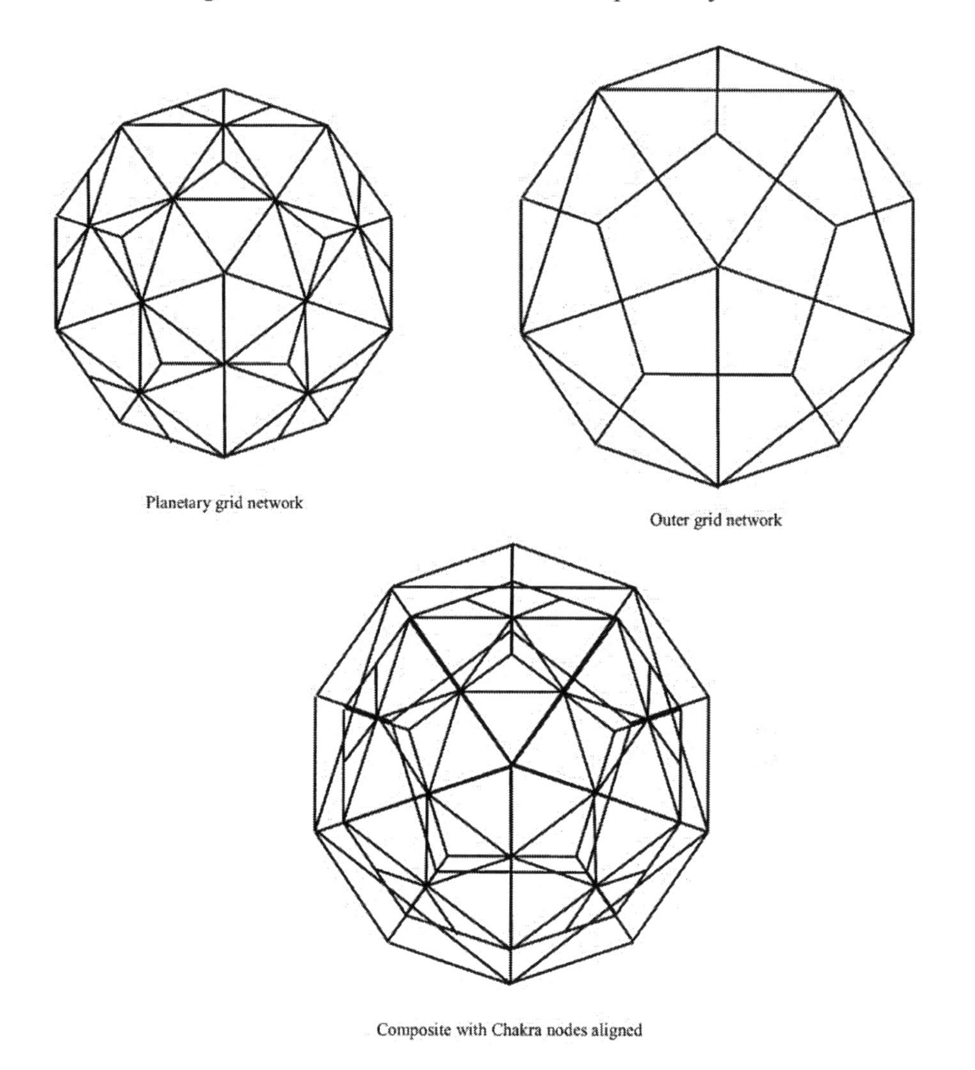

Figure 67 - Planetary Chakras

The chakra and energy grids of the planet are shown above. The planetary grid network exists at the physical surface and stabilizes the matter within the various timeline constructs. The outer grid exists beyond the upper reaches of the atmosphere and aligns with the main points of the planetary network. The relationship between the planetary and outer grid is the same as the chakra energetic within consciousness to that of the physical neural network of the human body. Energy will be the strongest at the main intersecting points where both grids meet. The energetic intensity at these locations can be felt by those who have achieved dual flow within their systems.

The planetary grid exists at the material surface and is the planetary version of the neural network within the physical form. It receives its energy from the outer grid through the main vortex (vertex) points where both grids align. These locations then transmit that energy through the energetic connections that create the planetary grid. The vortex points and the energetic lines connecting them create planar grids like the sides of a platonic solid. Within these grids the energetic connections energetically resonate at the oscillating frequency required to solidify matter within the various timeline constructs. More than one hundred individual timelines are currently in play on this planet. Each timeline observes their view of the planet to be the only one in existence, with each material timeline solidified from the resonant variations of energy transmitted through the grid network.

To prevent paradox concerns, an important concept must be addressed related to timeline constructs solidified within planetary grids. When conscious energy ceases to energize a material form , that form becomes an inanimate structure. For biological structures on earth, decay results over time as organisms begin the process of dissolution. A physical vehicle of consciousness does not immediately dematerialize upon removal of the consciousness that created and empowered it. This is also true of material planetary structures that are moved beyond their energetic grid. Interstellar space travel is possible and expected as part of the maturation process. The structures embodied lifeforms create to contain and move them through their respective galaxies do so because once solidified, stable matter retains its form until impacted by an external force. That external force may come from the planetary grid network as a result of a timeline divergence, from intentional manipulation by embodied lifeforms, or from proximity to an overpowering energetic source such as a system star or black hole interface.

The Power of Planetary Grid Points

The grid points upon the planetary surface are connectors that receive large amounts of energy required to power their portions of the grid network. There are multiple timelines currently being solidified and the grid points are receiving the energy to maintain all of them. Consciousness beyond sub-octave 3:6 will be able to feel the energy flowing through these points when they are in proximity to them. How that energy is interpreted will depend upon the orientation and awareness of the consciousness. Because these locations are energetic focal points between all the timelines in play, they also contain special abilities. Material constructs are separated as the resonant frequencies within matter is shifted higher. This effectively stacks one material envelope upon the other while maintaining the required physical separation. From the perspective of a grid point, all timelines can be seen due to the energetic function they are performing. A consciousness at sub-octave 3:6 or above who is energetically aware can look outward from within the energy of a grid point vortex and see, and/or feel, multiple timelines that they have resonant experience within. This is a function of co-resonance within their particulate resulting from an energetic alignment to that timeline from a previous physical incarnation. Whether consciousness observes a historical or future timeline in relation to their current incarnational experience will depend upon where they have been and where they are going.

Planetary grid points perform the same function as major meridians within the physical neural network and as such are aided by energetic acupuncture. Many ascended consciousnesses that have come to assist the ascension of this planet find themselves drawn to the various grid vortexes. The grid is the neural network of the planetary body and as such is susceptible to accumulation of negative energy blockages at its meridians. This planet has been immersed in the polarity envelope for an extended period of timespace. As a result, many of the planetary chakras were saturated with negative energy. While the operative consciousnesses of these embodied light workers have differing reasons why they go to these grid points, the main objective is the same; to bring their energy to these points and help clear the blockages.

The Multiverse Perspective

Within the rotational sphere of prime creator, our material universe exists within a single consciousness. Within this universal consciousness, galactic consciousnesses exist that design generalized pathways of ascension. System consciousnesses follow that general design as they contain and govern the material spheres. These three energetic reductions in consciousness, Universal, Galactic, and System, are singular entities energizing singular creations. Planetary consciousnesses exist at the sixth density octave. As previously stated, sixth density is the entrance to locked synchronization within the oscillating bandwidth of universal consciousness. At sixth density and above, immersion within, and usage of universal energy requires a singular focus. There are currently eighteen universal consciousnesses existing within the rotational sphere of prime creator. A nineteenth is in the process of formation. These are literal multiple universes. They do not overlap, their creations are unique unto themselves, and each one contains a distinct and segregated oscillating bandwidth.

Any concept of an overlapping multiverse must begin at the planetary consciousness level and the pathways of ascension they create within the lower densities. The planetary consciousness is operating within the sixth density harmonic and reducing that energy to create the lower density timeline constructs that consciousness incarnate and ascend within upon the planet. As discussed, multiple material timeline constructs exist on every planet designated for ascension. These collective constructs are created and merged as the ascension pathways dictate, limited only by the required balance within the galactic sector. If you could observe all the timelines in play on a planet from a distance, they would appear as shimmering golden envelopes stacked one upon the other. In each, a collective of consciousnesses goes about their affairs unaware the other exists. If you then moved your viewing perspective to the center of universal rotation -termed god source in the first book- you would see all the shimmering constructs on all the planets in all the galaxies. From this perspective it would appear as if multiple universes were stacked one upon the other, each superimposing their creations upon the same planets. However, if you looked closer at the overlapping planetary constructs you would see the energetic availability within each envelope, and the energy each consciousness embodied within them is producing as they strive upward in energetic capacity.

Perspective of the Universe from within a Timeline

The material and energetic creations within universes are orderly creations. Before universal consciousness begins to create material ascension pathways, the energetic gradients available to create within have already been established. The subsequent oscillating bandwidths in which ascending timelines are solidified is a universal constant that all galaxies and planets adhere to. Because of this uniformity, a spacecraft leaving one timeline will see the universe from their current oscillating bandwidth. Whatever materially exists on another planet at that bandwidth is what will be observed when inspected. A single planet may contain several space faring timelines with various interstellar capabilities. The satellites and craft from one timeline will not be observed by another unless the craft has been specifically designed to alter its resonant octaves -and that of its occupants- and slip between timelines.

This is the true nature of creation within the universe and prime creator. Now that you have acquired this knowledge, you can observe it yourself. All that is required is the balance and desire to do so.

Part 3

Meditations and Modalities

Chapter Thirty One

The Conscious act of Meditation and Quiet Mindfulness

In the first book we discussed the concept of quiet mindfulness and provided the entry exercises that assisted in silencing the chatter of the operative ego consciousness. The terms meditation and quiet mindfulness are similar in the fact that both require silent introspection, but dissimilar in objective when defined correctly. The barrier between the operative ego consciousness and the totality of your experience is termed the veil of forgetfulness. It is this barrier that you cross as you engage in contemplative exercises. If you went to a street corner and began asking people if they engage in meditation four categories would emerge:

- Those with no intention of trying that new age thing.
- Those who tried once or twice but did not feel anything and stopped.
- Those who know what it is, feel something when they try, but do not have time.
- Those who practice regularly and are enriched by the process.

As you ponder these four categories, let's overlay the energetics of consciousness onto them. Returning to the octaves within the upward spiral we find the energetic capacity of consciousness below sub-octave 3:5 insufficient and unable to extend beyond the barrier of the operative ego consciousness. This is a design function of the veil of forgetfulness and it exists to keep consciousness engaged in the lessons of life needed to acquire opposing perspectives. The veil acts like training wheels on a bicycle as it keeps you separated from larger understandings during your path toward balance within the polarized envelope. When consciousness reaches sub-octave 3:6, their array has obtained enough rotational balance to begin generating the energetic halo beyond the barrier. It is here they feel the connectivity of something larger than themselves and the pull toward collectivity begins. It is this pull that awakens consciousness and initiates the search for higher understandings. This is also the juncture where contemplative exercises become a powerful tool that can accelerate the process. The amount of assistance and acceleration contemplative exercise provides will depend upon the energetic capacity and the determination of consciousness engaging in them. Focused intention brings to bear the power within a conscious array and is the single most effective tool to accelerate ascension within the upward spiral. It is focused intention during contemplative exercises that can be used to amplify the energy of your consciousness within the veil and move beyond it. To help visualize this ability, consider this simple equation.

$$(Dc + Ec) >< Fc*(Dv + Ev)$$

The equation above represents the energetic composite of the totality of consciousness outside the veil to the combined energy and focus of the operative consciousness within the veil.

Where:

Dc represents the total density of consciousness being sequestered from the awareness of the operative consciousness by the energetic veil.

Ec represents the total energetic capacity of the sequestered portion. Dv represents the density of the operative consciousness existing within the veil.

Ev is the energetic capacity of that density within the veil, and

Fc is the energy of intention that is focused toward crossing the veil.

In all cases, the energy within the totality of consciousness will be orders of magnitude higher than the portion contained within the veil. However, this equation illuminates the power that focused intention brings into your contemplative exercises. Intentional focus is shown above as an energetic multiplier and is the magnifying glass that collects and concentrates your energy toward a specific purpose. If that purpose is to pierce the veil, it will do so.

The Difference between Meditation and Quiet Mindfulness

The discussion of focused intention exposes the nuances between meditation and quiet mindfulness as forms of inner contemplation. In the strictest sense, meditation is the act of surrender and immersion into the vastness of universal consciousness. This is accomplished through the intentional act of thoughtless thought. This statement appears to be a contradiction, but it is not when you consider that conscious awareness is created through particulate in motion. Along the journey from first density inception to fully actualized consciousness, the particulate that creates awareness is in a constant state of motion and expansion. Consciousness does not rest, ever. When you are awake within your body you are actively driving your consciousness through intentional focus. When you decide to sit in a quiet space and focus on nothing, you are literally opening the window of your consciousness so that the sounds of the universe can enter. This is a focused, conscious intention to seek something beyond the known self by idling all other thought. From an ascended viewing perspective, engaging in this type of meditation creates a light within the consciousness that shines outward. This is known as the calling, and in a free will universe this is the signal that assistance is being requested and can be provided. The assistance you receive from your calling will depend upon your chosen pathway toward increasing balance and density within the upward spiral and the intention within the calling.

If the definition of meditation is intentional thoughtlessness, quiet mindfulness would then be the destination beyond it. Having mastered the ability to achieve thoughtlessness, you then begin to focus the energy of your consciousness toward a goal. The exercises in the first book included the first steps toward intentional thoughtlessness and included focused intentions that prepared you for more advanced intentions. We have explained in detail how the movement of the particulate within consciousness generates coherent oscillating waves. In addition to creating your individual bandwidth of awareness within the cosmos, the energetic waves also represent the energy of intention that you possess. As consciousness moves into octave 4:0, the waveform complexity it contains has begun the process of collective synchronization. This development allows those who are engaged in the process of synchronization the ability to assume control of their collective timeline construct. The timeline that this text exists within is transiting into the energetic octave of fourth density. The energy of the fourth density envelope is available now for those who are actively seeking it. The effectiveness of the energetic manipulation exercises that follow require a balanced connection between the rotational sphere, the chakra energy system, and the neural energy system of the body. As shown in the energetic balance equation, the results you manifest will be proportional to the focus you apply to the process. In any undertaking, proficiency comes through effort and determination.

Stillness vs Movement During Contemplative States

For thousands of years the Chinese have used Tai Chi and Qi Gong movements in association with a contemplative state to remove tension and increase the flow of energy through the body. Tension and stress within the body are manifestations of energetic imbalances within the physical neural network. Imbalances can be caused by physical stressors that the body and operative mind are responding to, or from imbalances within the rotations of consciousness. Imbalances within consciousness are transported through the chakra energy system, causing imbalances within the chakras or neural network that block energy transport and manifest as tension and stress on the systems of the body.

When you sit in a traditional meditative position and remain immobile as you focus upon a goal, you are using your consciousness to affect a response. If you are attempting to connect with the universe, idling the body and disconnecting from it is appropriate. However, if you are focusing on moving energy through your consciousness into your body, your body should move in rhythm with your intentions. The body you inhabit is a manifestation of your consciousness. It exists within your spherical geometry and is powered by the energetic oscillations that occur there. The neural network receives this energy, empowers the body with it and discharges any excess through the hands and feet. As consciousness gains an understanding of this pathway, the body can be charged to excess and will temporarily hold this charge. The energy can then be purposely focused and discharged through the hands to perform various healings. The first task toward this goal is to remove any imbalances and expand energy transfer through the system so that the entire network can be felt. During the exercises presented, you should envision energy moving through the chakra and neural networks, flowing in unison as your body becomes an extension of consciousness in motion.

Mantras: The Power of Audible Vibrational Intention

The use of sound to heal and focus is well documented throughout history. External sound healing comes in many forms that include singing bowls, tuned metal forms, and chants in acoustically designed reverberation chambers to name a few. These physical immersions in external sound frequencies assist in clearing and alignment of the neural energy networks and if powerful enough, the chakras. The modality employed involves resonant vibrational pressure waves that impact the neural network of the body. This occurs both through the auditory input from hearing the sounds and through the physical interaction of the pressure waves with the neural network. The combination causes a sympathetic response that moves through the neural network dissolving blockages using resonant action. If the frequencies are correctly tuned to their designated task, even the most skeptical consciousness will admit to feeling something.

Another more personal form of sound healing is through mantras. A mantra is a spoken word or phrase that carries a vibration associated with the sounds being formed, and an intention associated with its use. Mantras effect a similar, but more powerful response than external sound healing. This occurs as the spoken words create physical vibrational intentions that reverberate through the body. The physical effects of the resonant waves are amplified as the sounds created within the target body are accompanied by the focused intention of that consciousness. Mantras serve a powerful dual role during still intention and active focused intention exercises. Before you begin the exercises, it would be wise to practice the mantras they contain. The mantra will be the portion you are asked to recite and will be bounded by quotations. Your vocal cords are specifically tuned for optimal resonance within your physicality. Sit quietly and slowly speak the mantras as you focus on how the sounds reverberate through your body. Raise and lower the pitch as you speak. Speak in monotone or add inflections. Continue to experiment until you find a combination that you can feel resonating through your chest cavity into your arms and legs. If you have never attempted this before it may take some practice until you feel the resonance in your arms and legs, but when you do feel it, you will know. Mantras that resonate in this manner with focused intention behind them are powerful tools. As you continue to work with the mantras in these exercises, the mechanics behind them will come into focus. Before long, you may find yourself creating mantras of your own that serve specific purposes.

Reduce the Static and Assume Control

As the energy within your consciousness grows, focused intention makes the veil permeable and the true nature of who and what you are will begin to shine through the cracks. You must incorporate the revelations you receive and balance yourself in the new awareness. This is a continual process where new information comes after the assimilation and balancing of previous information. As you grasp your energetic nature and your position in the universe, continued growth from this juncture requires additional focus and effort. You can no longer stumble toward ascension in the darkness.

The exercises that follow assume that you have been untethered from artificial electronic wave generators: Cell phones, smart watches, Wi-Fi hubs, Bluetooth wireless devices, etc. These devices create energetic waves that insert a level of instability that reduces the efficiency of intentional focus upon creational energy. This is the same concept as attempting to manually tune a shortwave radio into a specific station. If there is only one station broadcasting, it will be easier to locate because there is silence on either side of the frequency it is generating. Conversely, if the airwaves are cluttered with competing stations, it will require more effort to find the one you are looking for amongst the static.

The requirement is not to find a location devoid of artificial electronic waves, but to stay outside of energetic proximity of the devices. Ten to twenty feet (three to six meters) from the devices will be sufficient to reduce their impact to an acceptable level.

The exercises are divided into two categories, still intentions and focused movement. We begin with still intentions as they are required to balance your consciousness and bring you to the highest oscillating capacitance. With your etheric battery fully charged, we then balance the energy networks and move that energy into the physical body where it can be used. While it may seem counter intuitive to reconnect and move the body during a meditative state, the opposite is true as you connect to the body and use it as an energetic battery and transmitter.

Chapter Thirty Two

Still Intentions

The technical information provided in part one described the interactions of oscillating particulate that creates conscious awareness. The depth of discussion was required to bring an understanding of the processes involved in creating individualized awareness. With this technical understanding, focused intention can be appropriately applied to modify the interactions as movement into higher states of awareness becomes a free will choice. As you look within your consciousness during the stillness exercises, use all that you have learned to visualize the processes in as much detail as possible.

Immediate manifestation in the higher density octaves is normal and results from focused intention free of distraction. Doubt and fear are created at lower oscillating wavelengths and must be purged if you are to embrace the higher energies. As you begin to feel the changes within you from the following exercises you must remain focused and confident as you move forward. You should perform each exercise a minimum of three times before proceeding to the next one. After you have practiced all the still intentions, move on to the focused moving intentions. Practice the movements until they become fluid and flowing. For optimum effect, you should set time aside each week to move through the entire still and focused sequence. This sets a baseline within your energy systems as the repetition performs periodic maintenance. Begin each sequence with the mind quieting meditations from the first book or whatever you would normally perform to reach a meditative state. When you meditate regularly, dropping into thoughtless thought becomes effortless. If it is not effortless yet, continue to practice and ease will come with the repetition as the destination and what it feels like when you arrive becomes familiar.

Once you have achieved thoughtless thought and are ready, reactivate your focus and begin the still intentions. Start with one and get familiar with it. Then incorporate another one as you move from one intention to the other, eventually flowing through all of them. When you have memorized the still intentions, begin to incorporate the focused moving intentions. Do this by standing when you finish the sequence of still intentions and begin the focused intentions without leaving the meditative state. As you progress through the entire sequence, set the intention to feel the balance and resulting power building within your consciousness and body.

Visualizing Dual Flow

Balancing your rotations and downward flow was briefly touched upon in the first book in the exercise to clear the sphere of consciousness. With the expanded understandings of particulate interactions provided in this text comes the ability to further conceptualize and control the process. Dual flow within the toroidal column of consciousness begins as the energetic needs of consciousness requires increased particulate interaction. This occurs without focused intention in the same manner as digestion occurs within the human body. Although digestion and utilization of the resulting energy within the body is an autonomic function, its efficiency can be increased through proper diet, the use of supplements, and exercise. The same is true of the efficiency and energetic exchange rate that occurs within consciousness. This mindfulness exercise allows you to assume control and increase efficiency. As you perform the clearings, try to feel the balance and acceleration they provide.

Your true awareness is a result of harmonic oscillations within a sphere. While in a body, your perspective of awareness is locked into a fixed orientation composed of visual receptors and a neural network. This leads to the feeling that your awareness exists somewhere behind your eyes. Because of the physical connection between awareness and sight, you instinctively focus your attention by moving your head and using your eyes. This fixed orientation does not exist within consciousness and your perception of vision can move around the sphere at will. The limitations of embodiment must be released as you discard any preconceived ideas of where your visual perspective should be as you focus on your rotating array during the meditation and mindfulness exercises. You can be in it, above it, below it, and anywhere in between.

With this understanding you can both feel and observe the rotations creating your awareness. There are millions of rotational particulate pathways required to create individualized self-awareness within consciousness. This text has simplified those pathways to eleven so the concepts that create them could be understood. As you envision the rotations in this exercise, the actual number is unimportant. What is important is that you understand the basic composition and the gradients of perceived light the energy within the particles emit.

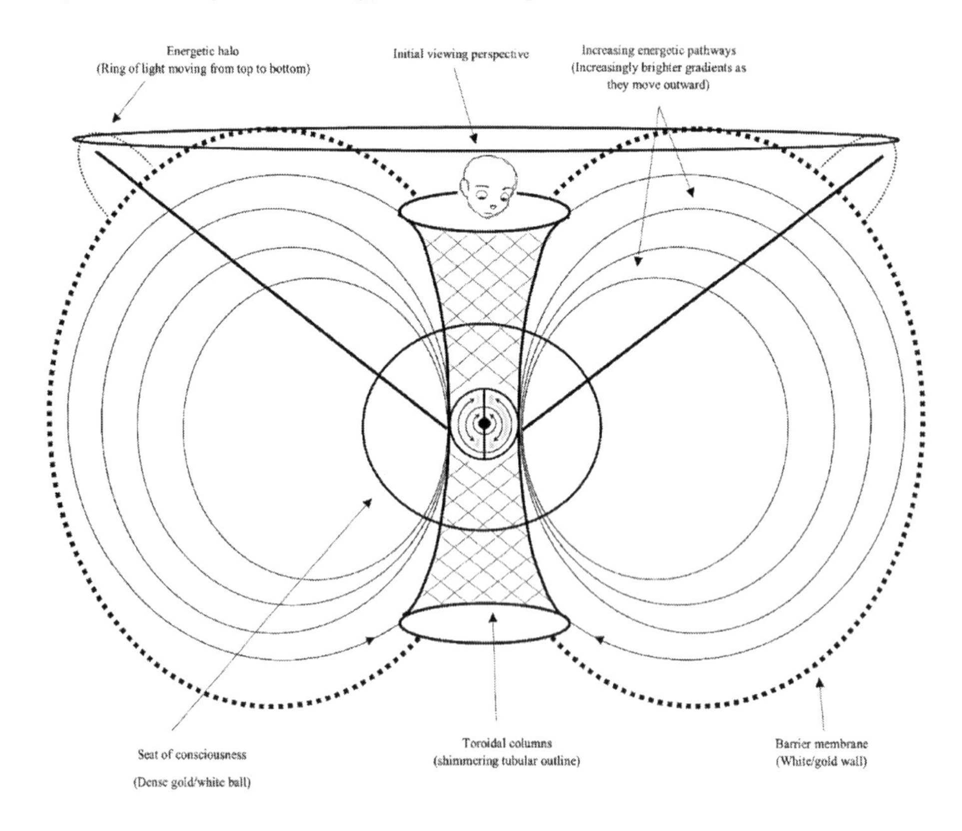

Figure 68 - Energy Gradients

The image above is the view of consciousness during stillness exercise 1. Looking down from your crown chakra you should observe a shimmering tube with a dense ball of gold/white energy at its center. Extending from the ball will be a visible energetic field that becomes brighter as it nears the barrier. The barrier membrane will be a shimmering white/ gold that looks like light being refracted from a multi-faceted diamond. The energetic halo is a ring of light that begins at the top of the column and moves around the outside of the barrier terminating at the bottom of the column.

Figure 68 shows the initial viewing perspective of consciousness when entering the still intentions. In a meditative state you perceive images through the interpretation of your consciousness and not with material optics. Because of this, some variation to what colors you observe may occur. However, the energy levels within rotating photonic particulate produce distinct emissions that can be observed and interpreted. The more energy a particle contains, the higher its perceived oscillating spectrum will be when viewed through the abilities of consciousness. Deeper and darker energy hues indicate low or negative energetic rotations. Use the figure above as the template for what you are attempting to achieve, a higher energetic capacitance, and increasingly balanced rotations.

Stillness Exercise 1

Sit comfortably in whatever normal meditative position you use for meditation. However, a position that you can easily stand up into with some room to move is preferred. As you master the stillness exercises, they will be followed directly by the focused moving exercises. For optimum results, you should have mastered the ability to reach the meditative state of thoughtless thought without difficulty. If you have not, do your best to clear your mind of thought before proceeding or review using the exercises in the first book. When you first begin this exercise, the perspective should be from the crown chakra looking down as shown in Figure 68. After you have obtained visualization from that perspective, shift the vantage point as required.

Silence the active mind using the technique that you find most effective. When you are comfortable in the infinite expanse of nothingness, begin to focus on your true nature. Visualize a golden sphere materializing around your awareness. It begins as a faint glow that slowly becomes brighter. The golden sphere is your totality of consciousness containing the encoded particulate of everything you have ever experienced. There is no time limit to this viewing perspective, watch the sphere increase in radiance as long as you like. When the sphere is sufficiently bright and you are ready, look downward. The column of your array should be visible. Along the periphery of the column, observe the particles increasing in brightness as they travel upward in a swirling pattern. At the center of the column is a compact ball of energetic particulate generating your awareness. Looking through the ball, the column extends to the lower edge of your golden sphere.

When you are ready, shift your focus from your particulate and observe the flow of creational energy entering the bottom of the column. The creational particulate creates trails as it accelerates into the column that look like golden tinsel. Shift your view to the top of the column and observe the same golden tinsel trails entering and moving toward the ball at the center. Focus for a moment on the tinsel strands. They should be flowing into the column opening in straight lines or gentle arcs. You should not see any strands that appear wavy or bunched. With a view of the flow in both directions, envision two energetic hands that begin to move through the golden tinsel from the center of the column outward as if straightening tangled hair. As you do this recite the following, "I am releasing all blockages, intentional or accidental that are preventing my accelerated energetic expansion."

Continue to move your energetic hands through the column as you recite the mantra five times or until you see straight, golden streams of energy flowing toward the center from either side.

When you are ready, move your focus to the center of the column and the ball of energetic particulate. See the opposing swirling motion at the center as the creational energy changes from gold to grey and is pushed out. Continue to observe the exchange of energy as you focus on the feeling of empowerment it provides. When you begin to feel the flow, move closer to the swirling exchange. Feel the effortless exchange as the counter rotating swirls of creational particulate transfers its energy to your consciousness. Maintain focus upon the swirling flow as you set the intention to increase the efficiency of transfer. Visualize the swirling flow accelerating as it moves faster through the column. You can feel the energy coursing through you, energizing and expanding you into the next octave.

Maintain this intention as long as you like. When you are finished, either move directly to exercise 2 or exit in gratitude giving thanks as you slowly shift your focus from the higher awareness and reorient yourself with the body using the methods from the first book, or whatever works best for you.

Balancing the Rotations of Consciousness

This balancing exercise is meant to directly follow the dual flow exercise. Perform the dual flow procedure and mantra as many times as feels appropriate. The feeling that you have completed an exercise comes from the portion of your consciousness you are manipulating. Become sensitive to the changes that occur as you perform the intentions. The first exercise included a minimum requirement of five intentions but that is an arbitrary starting point. As you work with these exercises, one person may feel complete after two cycles of the intentions while another may require twenty. In all cases, listen to your internal direction as you may be clear in one area and blocked in another. Your consciousness will provide the feedback required to focus your attentions where they are needed.

In the exercise that follows you will be using your new knowledge of the rotational composition of consciousness. You will be watching the particulate moving through its increasing rotations as you check and smooth any imbalances. You will eventually be able to visualize the process as you acclimate to the sensory inputs of consciousness. You are learning to see and hear using a different process that does not contain the limitations of the physical senses. It may take some time to learn how to use your new senses to see, hear, and feel in the energetic realm. With continued practice you will be able to use this exercise to focus upon specific pathways and tap into the information the particulate contains. The image below shows the visualization of the energetic halo portion of the exercise.

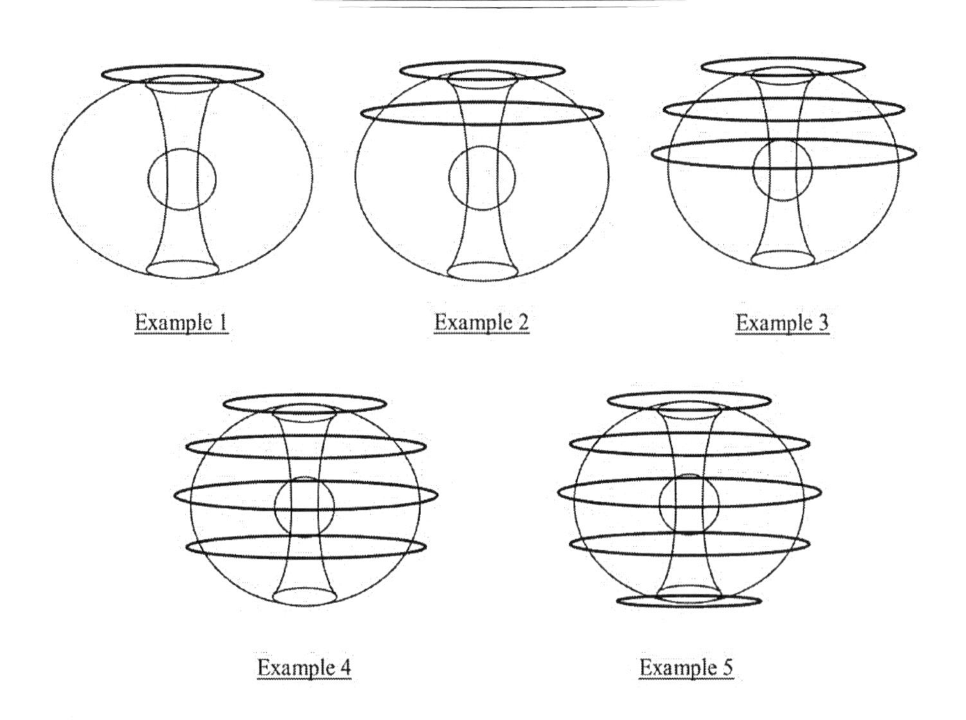

Figure 69 - Multiple Halo

The images above show a representation of how the energetic halo will appear during Stillness Exercise 2. The speed of a single halo moving around the sphere will continue to increase until it appears stationary at the top of the column as shown in Example 1. As the speed of oscillating equilibrium continues to increase, the first ring will move down, and a second will appear as shown in Example 2. Examples 3 and 4 show additional rings being added as the process continues. Five halos are shown in Example 5 that will continue to move downward. The lowest ring will disappear at the bottom of the column as another reappears at the top. Continued work with the stillness exercise will make the rings increase in speed around the sphere.

As the harmonic alignment of particulate within rotational pathways increases, the resulting halo emanations follow. The initial result of increasing alignment is an acceleration of the halo around the sphere. The acceleration will increase until the halo once again appears stationary at the top. However, when it begins to move again a second halo will appear behind it, then a third behind that one and so on until multiple halos move around the sphere as shown in Examples 1 through

5 above. The objective in the following exercise is to envision multiple halos moving around the outside of the sphere. This is a mid-fourth density configuration whose intensity will fade between performances of this exercise. The fade is a result of the current energies within this timeline that continue to impact your barrier (for now). However, during the time that you are operating with a multiple halo configuration, very few embodied consciousnesses will be able to negatively impact your energy.

Stillness Exercise 2

When you finish Stillness Exercise 1, move your viewing perspective to the center of the seat of consciousness. This is the focal point of your unique awareness and your energetic core. As you look out from this vantage point feel the energy surging around you, that energy is your true form. Visualize the rotations occurring as the particles gain energy and move upward along their pathways. Your consciousness has an oscillating tempo that can be felt and heard using the senses of consciousness. Listen closely as the rhythmic vibrations that accompany the particles shifting upward create a humming strobe effect. Feel the rhythm and listen as you visualize the rotational pathways from Figure 21. The rotational pathways beyond the center mass are appendages of your consciousness. When you can see the rotations, shift your viewing perspective to expand and encompass the entirety of the sphere. Stretching your awareness in this manner feels like a pulling or falling in all directions at once. Continue to expand your awareness until the sensation stops. When it does, envision the entirety of your rotations, moving with the rhythmic tempo you felt at the center. When you are comfortable in this perspective and observing the rotations in time with the rhythm recite the following, "I am synchronizing with the universal harmonic. I release and realign anything that is not within its resonance."

As you say this, observe the energetic halo extending beyond your barrier. With each recitation it grows brighter and moves faster around the sphere. Says the words deliberately and with focus. Take a breath between each sentence as you watch the energetic halo complete a cycle around the sphere. Images may begin to flood your awareness and are a sign of success. Allow them to come and go without responding or losing focus on the task at hand. What you see will depend upon where in the oscillating spectrum your energy is connecting. Continue to recite the mantra as you watch the halo move faster and faster around the sphere until it appears stationary at the top. As the rotations continue to increase in balance and speed, the stationary halo will move down as a second one appears behind it. This process will continue until multiple halos are moving down the outside of the sphere. When you see this, stop reciting the mantra and listen once again for the rhythmic hum. The halos will be moving in time to the vibrational rhythm of your consciousness. It is a wonderful feeling to be home again. Stay here as long as you like. When you are finished, either move directly to exercise 3 or exit in gratitude giving thanks as you slowly shift your focus from the higher awareness as you reorient yourself with the body using the methods from the first book, or whatever work for you.

Clearing and Balancing Chakra Flow

The first stillness exercise tuned the channel that transports energy to your consciousness. The second exercise aligned the emanations of your consciousness to oscillate within the tempo of the universal spectrum. The depth of information provided in part one allows a visualization that gives these simple tuning intentions their effectiveness. The deeper the memorization, the more effective the exercises will become. The increase in energetic efficiency and capacitance of consciousness that results from these exercises must have a clear pathway into the body if it is to be utilized. The final exercise in the stillness sequence will clear the energetic pathway into the body.

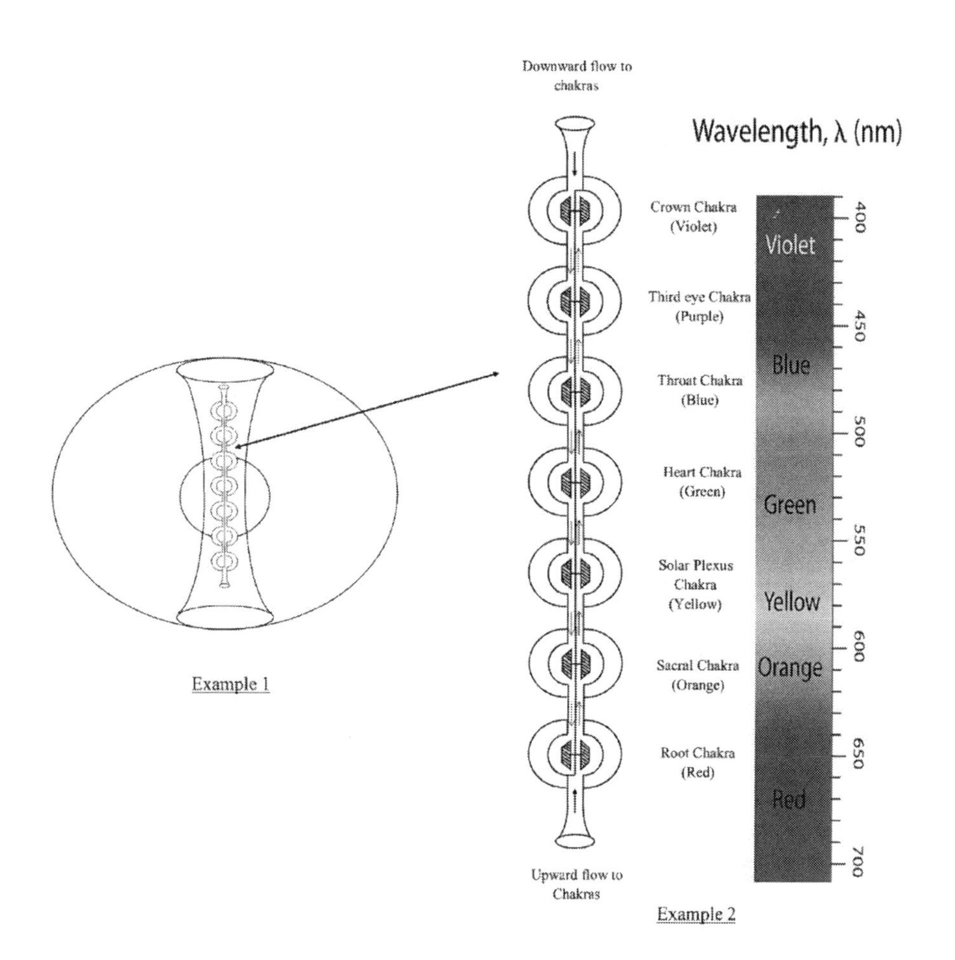

Figure 70 - Chakra Flow

Example 1 above shows the location of the chakra energy network within the toroidal column of the consciousness sphere. Maintaining the relationships between the energetic pathways focuses intention and increases effectiveness of clearing and realignment. During visualization of the chakra network in Stillness Exercise 3, it is important to maintain a reference to the toroidal column. As you are asked to focus individually upon the chakras, maintain perspective of where they are located in the network and how the energy flows when unimpeded. Example 2 above shows the relationship between the chakras and dual flow activation. Energy from consciousness enters the chakra network from the top and bottom and flows into the neural network through the dual impellers. As shown above, the only exit path for energy entering the network is through the chakras into the body. The chakra colors are a result of the energy levels they are exposed to in the toroidal column.

Figure 70 shows the chakra energy network with dual flow activated. The chakra network exists at the wall of the toroidal column with half of it embedded in the rotations of consciousness and the other half within the flow of creational particulate. The embedded half contains a portion of both impellers and passively energizes unblocked chakras through energetic absorption. The bottom funnel is embedded in the toroidal wall and receives energy as conscious particulate travels upward along their pathways. When the heart chakra energizes, the gateway to downward flow opens and fully energizes the secondary impellers. The secondary impellers receive energy from the top funnel also embedded in the toroidal wall. The secondary pathway is energized from the downward flow of creational energy into the chakra network. When the exercise asks you to visualize the chakra network remember where it is located and how it is embedded in the toroidal column. The respective colors of the chakras are listed in Example 2. The colors of the chakras are causally related to the level of energy they exist at within the toroidal column. The photonic nature of consciousness correlates to the visible light spectrum as shown in Example 2. This means that as you increase energy within the chakras their color radiance moves upward within the visible light spectrum. Therefore, as the chakras energize through dual flow, the colors they emit should be toward the upper energy limit of their color, not the lower. This is an especially important consideration with the lower three chakras. This means that the root chakra should be a light red bordering on orange, the sacral chakra light orange toward yellow, and so on.

The exercise below contains two variations. The initial intentions are to be performed as you begin to work with these exercises. When you feel a continued crown chakra and third eye activation, the graduated intentions should be performed.

Stillness Exercise 3

When you finish Stillness Exercise 2, maintain the perspective of the entirety of your sphere. Observe the toroidal column at the center and allow the chakra energy network to come into focus. The seven chakras are there, as is the energy network that connects them together. As they materialize before you, their brightness shines in all directions. Focus on the heart chakra, feeling the energy flowing through it into your body. It should be radiating a bright green glow that lightens toward blue. Visualize the dual impellers spinning at full speed as you recite the following, "I am initiating dual flow and releasing any blockages, intentional or accidental preventing full activation."

Repeat the mantra at least three times as you feel the resulting energization within your physical heart space. The radiating warmth is the same feeling as being in love. The radiance is being created through the love of self, demonstrated through these exercises as you acknowledge the truth of what you are. Visualize the energy from your heart chakra flowing in both directions as it energizes the other chakras. As you do this, the color within each one begins to radiate outward. Focus on the root chakra and visualize dual flow within it as the red color it emits lightens toward orange. Say the mantra again as you watch the light grow brighter and feel the energy surging into your physical network. When you are satisfied with the response of the root chakra, move to the sacral chakra and repeat the process. The sacral chakra should radiate an orange glow that lightens toward yellow as you recite the mantra. Repeat the process with solar plexus chakra as the yellow hue moves toward green. When you are satisfied with the work you have done with the lower chakras, continue with the initial or graduated intentions below.

Initial Intentions

Visualize all of the energy from the lower chakras creating a swelling within the heart chakra. See the heart chakra as a balloon with the opening pointed upward toward the throat chakra. As the chakra swells it shines with increasing radiance, a beautiful greenish blue permeating the entirety of your consciousness sphere. Continue to observe the swelling until you feel that the heart chakra is about to burst like an overfilled balloon. When it can hold no more, the opening of the balloon releases and energy rushes upward along the chakra network toward the throat chakra. Observe the remaining three chakras as the energy rushes through one to the other. Visualize the simultaneous increasing radiance of the throat, third, eye and crown chakras that the energy is creating as you repeat the mantra for these chakras. "I am initiating dual flow and releasing any blockages, intentional or accidental preventing full activation." Concentrate on the dual impellers rotating within the chakras and feel the energy flooding your body. The entire chakra network is immersed in dual flow, shining brightly, and in its perfected state. Hold the image of the chakra network in perfect alignment as long as you like as you feel the energy.

When you are satisfied with the work you have done, either move directly to Moving Exercise 1 or exit in gratitude giving thanks as you slowly shift your focus from the higher awareness as you reorient yourself with the body using the methods from the first book, or whatever work for you.

Graduated Intentions

Visualize the heart chakra and focus on the dual flow moving through it. Recite the following, "I understand and release any emotional imbalances, inflicted or received, in this lifetime or any other."

As you repeat the mantra, watch as the green color it emits lightens toward blue and increases in radiance. If images appear as you are performing the realignment, allow them. These will be the highly charged experiences that need to be balanced. The objective is to greet the images in neutrality without emotional input. Highly charged experiences will require more time to realign and release. Remember, there is no judgement -good or bad- associated with experiences in the higher octaves, there is only experience. Since you are moving into the higher octaves, you too must release judgement. Repeat the mantra as long as you like or until the images cease. When you are satisfied, move to the throat chakra.

Visualize the throat chakra and focus on the dual flow moving through it. Recite the following, "I release anything that has prevented me from hearing or speaking my truth, in this lifetime or any other."

As you repeat the mantra, watch as the blue color becomes deeper and more radiant. Again, if any images appear allow them. What you see will be associated with the journey your consciousness has taken to get where you are now. For many on earth, this journey contains some less than desirable experiences. Whatever images appear must be met with understanding and not anger or fear. As previously stated, you must release all judgement. Repeat the mantra as long as you like or until the images cease. When you are satisfied, move to the third eye chakra.

Visualize the third eye chakra and focus on the dual flow moving through it. Recite the following, " I am activating my second sight and empathic abilities to help myself and others find the path that leads to truth, love, and unity."

As you say these words, feel the power they contain reverberating through the entirety of your consciousness. Re-envision the energetic halos from Stillness Exercise 2 and watch as the energy of the words increases the diameter of the rings. This is the power of unity within the universal harmonic, the energetic love that exists within it, and the truth of what you are that cannot be denied once it is felt. As you watch the halos move around the sphere, the radiance of the third eye chakra becomes a bright purple that extends into the halos. If any images appear as you perform this, allow them. What you see will depend upon your organic ascension pathway and the resulting baseline frequency. Images of physical aliens or holographic light bodies should not be interpreted as anything other than an indication of who you may have been or who might be assisting you now. When you are satisfied, move to the crown chakra.

As you visualize the crown chakra, reorient your view to within it. Once there, look down and observe your physical body in its current state of meditation. As you look down you can see the chakra network extending from the crown chakra into the center of your body. The energy and colors of the various chakras are radiating outward in all directions creating a beautiful vibrant color palette that is fully energizing your body. Maintain the perspective of your awareness just above your physical head and begin to slowly tap each finger on your hand to its thumb. As you tap your fingers, focus on the fact that your awareness is not behind your eyes, it is above your head. You are now operating from your crown chakra. When you can maintain this perspective while moving your fingers, begin to slowly move your arms in a flowing manner outward with palms up.

When you are ready, from the seated position stand up with your feet shoulder width apart and move directly to Moving Exercise 1 or exit in gratitude giving thanks as you slowly open your eyes.

Chapter Thirty Three

Moving Intentions

Balancing and Aligning your Energy Network

The first book contained an exercise that manually expanded photonic density by energizing the chakra / body system and then pushed that energy outward into consciousness using focused intention. The ability to charge a system to excess and then direct that energy - into the physical or into the realm of consciousness - is an important concept. Either is possible as the conduits flow in both directions. "Energy flows where focus goes."

The following exercises move energy through the chakra system and into the body to be used. You will visualize the energy and use intention to move it. You are the captain of your human vessel and it will respond to your commands. Pushing your limits during physical exercise expands the ability of your body as it responds to the increased demands being placed upon it. Athletes prepare in advance by storing calories and carbohydrates to fuel the body during periods of extended physical exertion. Teaching your body to store conscious energy to perform strenuous energetic tasks requires a similar method of training. Under the veil, the body systems are automatically energized without conscious intervention. As consciousness enters fourth density, this autonomous function can be managed and tuned through intentional focus. If you have never used your energy systems for anything other than daily existence, they will be weak as you begin the exercises. However, the feedback that something is changing will come quickly and increased capacity will follow.

Manipulating material creation using the energy of consciousness begins with an understanding of how the energy is stored and how it is used to manifest action. Using intentional focus, excess energy can be collected and directed toward a specific purpose. It is up to you to decide what that purpose is. However, this text has gone to great lengths to align the reader within the universal harmonic. Energy acquired through this connection exists to embrace and unify. It cannot be used to impose your will or elevate yourself above others. Universal truth is free and is meant to be shared with all who seek it. Step into these exercises humbly from a place of purity and love for all and you will be embraced by that which you seek.

All moving exercises should begin with soft flowing movements as you visualize the energy moving with intention. As you become proficient in these practices you will begin to feel an energization occurring within your body as the energy flows through its network. The initial result will be a tenseness within the muscular structure that causes an isometric resistance. This is an indication that the energy in the body is moving beyond what it previously considered normal. When you feel resistance, you must focus on allowing the energy to move within and through you so that the movements once again become soft and flowing.

Your hands are energetic implements. As with any tool, an understanding of their operation is required for proper use. Opening them in an expanded cupped manner (as if reaching for a basketball) focuses most of the energy through the palms with residual going through the fingers. This formation creates a containment field with your hands that acts as an energetic net. In the exercises presented, this configuration is used to shape and form the energy radiating from the hands. In healing, the expanded cup is used to encapsulate portions of a patient's body and focus energetic rejuvenation. Making your hands straight like a knife (Judo chop) shifts the energy to radiate out of the fingertips and around the outside. In the moving exercises provided, this configuration is used to cut, push, and clear your energy systems. In healing, the knife hand is used as its name implies, to cut and clear energetic imbalances from patients before the expanded cup is used to cradle and heal the location. When you are asked to place your hands in these shapes, see the energy radiating accordingly. During the exercises do not allow your hands to touch each other. These exercises are opening the energy channels within your hands for external work. Touching your hands together with the energy channels open will create an internal circuit between them that closes the external capabilities of single hand techniques. The internal circuit is used during still intentions and specific dual hand formation focusing techniques.

The first exercise focuses upon pulling energy from consciousness into the physical system and using it to clear and balance the energy networks powering your body.

Moving Exercise 1

If you are entering this exercise from Stillness Exercise 3, you will already be in the standing rest position. If not, close your eyes and stand with your feet shoulder width apart, your arms at your side, and your hands open with palms facing your legs. This is the standing rest position. From the standing rest position, open your hands into the expanded cupped position. With both hands expanded, move them together in front of your heart until the palms are almost touching but do not let them touch each other. Inhale deeply and slowly as you envision the dual energy flowing equally from your chakras into the body network as you move your hands apart slightly. As you exhale, push the energy from your body network through your arms and out of your hands as you move them closer. As you do this, visualize the energy creating a swirling ball between your cupped hands that you are compressing as the energy makes the palms warmer. You are charging your hands with energy. Repeat this as many times as you like, moving the energy through your hands and visualizing the increasing brightness.

Initial Charging Technique

When you are satisfied with the energy you have created in your hands, take a deep breath as you shift to knife hands. Rotate your hands so that the fingers of your left hand point upward while the fingers of your right hand point downward. Move your left hand up and your right hand down along the centerline of your body as you recite the following, "I am clearing all blockages, intentional or accidental from my physical and energetic networks,"

You should move slow enough that your hands are fully extended, one just above your forehead and the other just below your groin, as you finish the mantra. With your hands still extended and fingers pointing in the same directions, inhale deeply as you reverse the movement and return your hands to the starting position in front of your heart center.

As you are moving your hands away from the heart center reciting the mantra, visualize the words pushing any imbalances out of your body into the chakra network as the golden energy from your hands pushes them out leaving a smooth and energized network behind them. When you inhale and reverse the movement, you should visualize fresh energy being pushed from the chakra network into the heart center. As you inhale, feel that fresh wonderful energy moving through the chakra system into your body as the energy surges within you.

With your hands once again in front of your heart center, reverse your hands so the fingers on the right hand now face upward and the fingers on the left hand face downward. As you rotate your hands, visualize the ball of energy being created between them again as the energy coming from each hand swirls and rotates. Repeat the mantra as you move your left hand down and your right hand up along the centerline of the energy network. Your fingers should stay pointing up or down as appropriate. Move slow enough that your hands are fully extended as you finish the mantra. With your hands still extended and fingers pointing up and down, inhale deeply as you reverse the movement and return your hands to the starting position in front of your heart center.

Repeat the process, rotating your hands at the heart center to reorient your fingertips and push the energy at least five times or as many as feels comfortable.

As you perform these movements, visualize a golden glow forming along the path your hands travel. The golden light is your energy in perfect balance being absorbed into your body, energizing it to a higher level with each movement. When you are finished, return your hands to the expanded cup position in front of your heart and proceed to Moving Exercise 2, or place your hands together in a praying formation to seal your channels. Exit in gratitude as you lower your hands, giving thanks as you slowly open your eyes.

You should perform this exercise once a week to clear any imbalances you may have picked up. Once you become familiar with the exercise you can perform it in just a few minutes when you feel the need for balance and an energy boost during your day.

Feel and Flow (Clearing a Space)

Having cleared your energy network of any blockages and charged your battery, you are ready to start working with the energy. If you have been active within the awakened community prior to engaging with this text, you have probably encountered the phrase, "Clearing and cleansing a space." This is a common practice healers and energy workers perform before they open their energetic networks in an unfamiliar setting. There is nothing magical or mystical about this process. The only requirement is knowledge of how your energy systems operate and your desire to practice and become adept at storing, moving, and using that energy. If you intend to clear a space, you should start with Moving Exercise 1 to increase your energy before using it to clear with this exercise. The amount of energy your physical network contains depends upon the focus you have placed upon balancing the chakra system and intentionally charging it. Using the vital energy within your system for external work without first charging it is not a recommended practice as a baseline is required to maintain your body's perfected blueprint.

The following exercise will help you visualize and feel the flow of energy that your intentional focus is creating. As you become familiar with the default movements, you may feel the desire to insert additional movements that flow with the intentions. You should stay with the originals until they are second nature. When they become effortless, allow whatever movements feel appropriate. In all cases, the movements should flow seamlessly from one to the other. As you get comfortable with the arm movements you may begin to step forward with the foot of the side that is moving. This adds energetic capacity to the movement, but also adds complexity. Fluid, flowing intention filled movements are far more effective than multiple movements that reduce focus on the energy.

This exercise can be performed anywhere with the intention behind it modified to suit the circumstance. Perform it regularly in your home to keep it clean, to clear a space you intend to do work in, or on a planetary vortex to assist in clearing it. In each case, the basic mantra provided will be effective. With practice you will be able to feel the energy and target its effectiveness in the various settings. If desired, modify the associated mantra to your location as you feel guided.

This exercise adds another hand formation, the closed cup. As the name implies, you are cupping your individual hands as you would to scoop and hold water without dripping. Again, your hands should never touch during these exercises.

Moving Exercise 2

If you are entering this exercise from Moving Exercise 1, you will already be standing with your hands in the expanded cup position in front of your heart. If not, close your eyes and assume the standing rest position. When you are centered and ready, move your hands to the expanded cup position in front of your heart.

Take a deep breath and feel the energy surging into your body as you move your hands apart slightly. As you exhale move your hands closer together, once again visualizing the ball of energy being created and compacted between your hands. Repeat this two more times and hold your breath for a moment on the third inhale. Feel the energy welling up within you like a balloon about to burst. Move your hands to the closed cup position and place the left over the right with fingers pointing to either side of your body. Do not allow your hands to touch. As you exhale, move your right cupped hand outward away from your body in an arc with a slow and flowing motion. Envision your right hand with a pool of energy in it that resembles golden glitter. As you sweep your hand outward around your body in a circular motion, rotate your palm so that it is facing the ground as your arm reaches its outstretched limit in line with your ear. As you sweep and turn your hand, the glitter gently wafts outward filling the space of wherever you are. Return your right hand to the starting position under your left hand by bending at the elbow and scooping back into position. As you are performing the motions recite the following, either out loud or as a silent intention, "I bathe this space with the energy of love and creation as I share freely and in service to all."

With your right hand under your left, inhale and rotate your hands as if you were holding an energy ball in them so that the right is now over the left. With your left hand cupping the energy, exhale as it sweeps outward repeating the motion you performed with your right hand. Repeat this process at least five times with each arm as you recite the mantra silently or aloud.

If you feel as if your energy is low during the process, stop when both hands are in front of your heart and return them to the expanded cup position. Inhale deeply and slowly as you envision the dual energy flowing equally from your chakras into the body network as you move your hands apart slightly. As you exhale, push the energy from your body network through your arms and out of your hands as you move them closer. As you do this, visualize the energy creating a swirling ball between your cupped hands that you are compressing into your hands as the energy makes the palms warmer. Do not let your hands touch.

When you are finished clearing and energizing, return your hands to the expanded cup position in front of your heart and proceed to Moving Exercise 3, or place your hands together in a praying formation to seal your channels. Exit in gratitude as you lower your hands, giving thanks as you slowly open your eyes.

Focusing and Pushing Energy

Charging your network to capacity provides the ability to use that stored energy to push the energy outward to perform specific tasks as was done with the previous feel and flow exercise. Like leaving the headlights on in your car without it running, you will slowly drain your energetic battery performing these exercises if you do not recharge it. This is especially true as you begin to narrow your focus and perform more complicated tasks. If you feel that your energy levels are low at any point during the exercise, perform the recharge portion. The recharge portion is different in this exercise as more energy is required to focus and push. The same is true for healing patients, as large amounts of energy are required to realign external systems. You should become acutely aware of your energy levels and intentions, especially if you feel called to heal others. The focus for healing should be on emitting energy to realign and dissipate. As with other energy systems, your hands have the ability to absorb as well as transmit. You must set the intention to inhibit inward flow during healing.

As the heading implies, you should be pushing energy into an object you are focused upon. You must aim your energy the same as you would aim a weapon at a target to increase your odds of successfully impacting it. It docs not matter if the objective is in physical proximity or at a distance, visualize your objective and the energy will flow there.

This exercise adds another hand formation, the open palm. It is similar in appearance to the knife hand but differs in use and intention. You create the open palm in the same manner as you would use your hand to push a door open or ask a car to stop if you were in front of it. Unlike the knife hand, the fingers do not need to be together and touching during open palm. The open palm is used in association with the movement of extending the arm to focus and push energy in a specific direction. If used in conjunction with a light impact and proper intention during healing, the resulting energetic exchange can be profound for the recipient.

Moving Exercise 3

If you are entering this exercise from Moving Exercise 2, you will already be standing with your hands in the expanded cup position in front of your heart. If not, close your eyes and assume the standing rest position. When you are centered and ready, move your hands to the expanded cup position in front of your heart.

Graduated Charging Technique

Inhale deeply and slowly as you envision the dual energy flowing equally from your chakras into the body network as you move your hands apart slightly. As you exhale, push the energy from your body network through your arms and out of your hands as you move them closer. As you do this, visualize the energy creating a swirling ball between your cupped hands that you are compressing as the energy makes the palms warmer. When you are satisfied with the energy you have created in your hands, take a deep breath as you shift to knife hands. Rotate your hands so that the fingers of your right hand point downward while the fingers of your left hand point upward. Move your right hand down and your left hand up along the centerline of your body while maintaining knife hands. As you do this visualize the energy from your fingertips pushing any blockages out of your chakra network. When your hands are extended, just above your head and just below your groin, move them into the closed cup configuration and rotate them so that they will scoop and compress energy as you return them to in front of your heart. Move your hands back toward your heart while visualizing them scooping energy from the chakra energy network into the heart chakra. Rotate your hands around so that the right is over the left while you compress the ball of energy and feel it moving through the heart chakra into your body. Resume the knife hand configuration with the fingers of your left hand pointing downward and the right pointing upward. Repeat the process as you move your left hand down and your right hand up, then cupping and returning to the heart center. Repeat this process until you are satisfied with the charging of your system. When you are satisfied, return to the expanded rest position and continue with the two handed push.

Two Handed Push

In the expanded rest position, begin to push energy into the space between your hands. Do this by expanding your hands as you inhale and pushing them together as you exhale. Repeat this process until you feel you have sufficiently charged your hands. Inhale one more time without moving your hands apart. In one fluid motion, move both hands into the open palm configuration as you rotate them outward, exhaling as you push their energy out by fully extending the arms. When the push is complete, rotate your fingers downward to disconnect and return your hands to the expanded cup position in front of your heart. Repeat the push as many times as you like, recharging between pushes as your energy level dictates. Do not let your hands touch during this process.

Alternate One Handed Push

Perform the charging sequence as you would for the two handed push. The one handed push is similar to the two handed push in charging and intention. The difference is that you are tightly focusing the energy into a single location. This is an important consideration during healing or if you are charging a small inanimate object. The one handed push is also used during forceful intentions to prevent infringements. When pushing with one hand, rotate the stationary hand in the same direction as the hand that is pushing. For healing or charging, the stationary hand should align behind the extended hand. Return to the expanded cup position as described in the two handed push. Recharge your hands and repeat the process with either hand as many times as needed.

When you are finished with the focused push, return your hands to the expanded cup position in front of your heart. If you have just finished all six intentions in series, place your hands in the closed cup configuration and extend your arms, palms upward in front of you and then outward in a semi-circle until your arms are outstretched on either side. Hold this position for a moment as you take a single breath and consciously imagine the energy of the universe swirling around you. Inhale once again as you move your extended arms upward until they form a Y above your body. Exhale as you bring both hands down along your energy channel, fingers facing each other until your arms are extended below your root chakra. Let your arms swing out past your body as you set the intention to close your energy systems.

End of meditation sequence.

Chapter Thirty Four

Supplemental Exercises

Meditations for the Planetary Vortex Points

Planetary vortex points are the meridians within the planetary neural network. The polarization this planet has experienced is embedded within these meridians and the lines that connect them. Focused intentions to help share energy and healing with the earth perform the same function as the intentions to clear individual blockages. The difference is the energetic capacitance of these locations and the energy required to clear them. Vortex points or connecting grids that have had fierce battles fought over them will be deeply saturated. Pushing your energy into these areas while in proximity assists in their cleansing. The locations of the planetary grid and vortex points is widely available elsewhere and should be researched. If you find yourself at one of these locations, you can modify Moving Exercise 2 or 3 to share your energy. In Moving Exercise 2, modify the mantra to suit your intention to assist in clearing the grid as you sweep your hands outward. In Moving Exercise 3, when you push your energy with both hands, push downward toward your feet rather than outward. As previously stated, the exercises and mantras are starting points that help you feel the energy and become comfortable with the abilities you can manifest in the octave of fourth density. Do not bind your power with preconceived limitations of what can and cannot be performed with mantras and the energy of your intention. When you have mastered the exercises in this text, allow yourself to be guided into new uses for your energy. Follow where your individuality leads you.

Forcefully Pushing Energy

Pushing with forceful intention changes the dynamic of the energy and the way it impacts its target. Thus far, the intentions behind the acquisition and usage of creational energy have been associated with soft flowing motions and thoughts of peace, unity, and love. Forceful intentions incorporate quick snapping motions combined with sharp focused blasts of energy. Forceful positive intentions are primarily used to stop, overpower, and realign that which would otherwise infringe upon your chosen path. While positive energy cannot be used to infringe upon another, it stands ready to prevent infringements for those who know how to wield it. Forcefully pushing energy can be accomplished through still or moving intentions.

Forceful Movement

In the expanded rest position, begin to push energy into the space between your hands. Do this by expanding your hands as you inhale and pushing them together as you exhale. Repeat this process until you feel you have sufficiently charged your hands. Inhale one more time without moving your hands apart. In one fluid motion, move your hands into the open palm configuration as you rotate them to face away and exhale forcefully as you push both hands outward. When your arms are almost extended, snap them outward to full extension and retract slightly as you visualize the energy snapping from the palms of your hands. This can be performed with one or two hands.

Forceful Still Intention

When using positive energy, forceful still intentions are used to stop unwanted energy infringements. As you become sensitive to your energy levels you will know when something is affecting it. A positive co-resonance between energetic halos should be met with an inner recognition and a feeling of energization. A negative infringement will feel oppressive, stifling, and constricting. Individual response to a negative drain will vary and is therefore difficult to describe. However, the difference in energetics between a positive connection and a negative one is as contrasting as the emotions of love and hate.

The feeling of being drained can occur in proximity to incarnated or etheric consciousness. It will be easy to identify and focus upon an actual person that you think is pulling you down. Targeting becomes more difficult when you cannot see where the drain is coming from. The first book included a shielding exercise that can be used to harden your barrier membrane. The concept behind that shielding exercise was the temporary balancing of rotations within the E-11 pathway. This closes the energetic gaps those imbalances create. The effectiveness of that exercise diminishes as consciousness resolves their major imbalances and enters fourth density. Recall from Figure 21 that your barrier membrane will be weakest at the bottom of your toroidal column. If you have progressed to the point of being able to see energy, focus your attention there and you may be surprised by what you find.

Identified Source

When you can identify the source of the infringement, focus your energetic intention upon it. This can be done visually by looking at it, or by holding the image in your consciousness. Repeat aloud or silently a short mantra that affirms your rejection. It can be as simple as "No", "I do not allow", "I Reject", or whatever you feel emphasizes and underlines your declination of the connection. As you say your mantra, envision the words leaving your consciousness as energy blasts that pop with force from you. An easy visualization of the blasts are rings that follow one behind the other and repeatedly impact the source. Continue until you feel the connection has been severed. If you perform this technique and you still feel the drain, you should remove yourself from proximity and recharge.

Unknown Source

There are several sources that can cause unidentified energetic drains. When you cannot identify where the drain is coming from, the only thing that is important is making it stop. If you feel that your energy is being impacted and you cannot identify a source, you must generalize your refusal. The method is similar to an identified source except that you are going to focus on your barrier membrane. As you say your mantra, visualize it creating blast bubbles that expand in all directions. You are transmitting your rejection of the connection in a sharp and forceful manner. Continue until you feel the connection has been severed or move to a different location.

PARTING THOUGHTS

The information presented in this second offering has attempted to provide an understanding of the operation of consciousness, the loving intention of your creation, and your maturing relationship with an energetic universe. Third density constructs provide consciousness a safe energetic envelope to explore and grow within. In polarized envelopes, third density is the orienting density where consciousness chooses to move toward collectivity or to be the obstacle to it. Throughout history are records of people with what appeared to be magical abilities to manipulate their surroundings. While unique with respect to others at the time, their abilities were not magical or a gift from a deity. They were the result of intense focus and application. When you shift your focus from being a body within a material construct to understanding that the form and the construct are creations of consciousness, the controls begin to materialize. It is here that your journey shifts, as the energy and knowledge you possess requires that you move from participant to co-creator. The acquisition of the information in this text places you firmly in fourth density and has been designed to support a continued transition into the fifth density octave.

Earlier, the physical brain was likened to a temporary information storage device and your conscious array the hard drive of your computer. This becomes an important distinction as your material form ages and ultimately ceases operation. The temporary storage device of the brain may have sectors that become corrupted, but the information has already been backed up to the hard drive and is not lost. If you have focused your intention on assimilating the information provided here, it exists in the hard drive of your conscious array. When your incarnation ends and your awareness returns to your true self, you will know exactly what you are and how to operate the vehicle you find yourself in. The still meditations presented provide a fifth density perspective of existence within consciousness. As you continue to work with these exercises, modify them as you feel guided and explore your true nature. As you continue to become familiar with the landscape of your true consciousness, the fear and disorientation associated with the death of the body will fade.

At the time of publication, this text exists in a diverging construct with an upward positive trajectory. As you practice expanding your energetic halo, you must use it to elevate your fellow consciousnesses in the manner that you find appropriate. The easiest way is to consciously radiate love and gratitude when you are in proximity to others and this should be done at every opportunity. Some will be called to use their hands and energy to heal. Others will want to share their evolving perspectives. In all cases it is important to remain humble and acknowledge that you are merely another awakened participant within the universal dance. No one is better, smarter, more powerful, or tapped into some special knowledge reserved for them. We, the consciousnesses comprising the universe -and the universe itself- all exist within the upward ascending spiral. The only difference between consciousnesses within the spiral is that some began their journey earlier than others. Those of us who have climbed more stairs are obligated to illuminate the pathway for those who follow.

Printed in Poland
by Amazon Fulfillment
Poland Sp. z o.o., Wrocław
04 September 2023

c5c7d910-53b2-4e74-b494-71f188a4ea44R01